Lecture Notes in Computer Science 15597

Founding Editors

Gerhard Goos
Juris Hartmanis

Editorial Board Members

Elisa Bertino, *Purdue University, West Lafayette, IN, USA*
Wen Gao, *Peking University, Beijing, China*
Bernhard Steffen, *TU Dortmund University, Dortmund, Germany*
Moti Yung, *Columbia University, New York, NY, USA*

The series Lecture Notes in Computer Science (LNCS), including its subseries Lecture Notes in Artificial Intelligence (LNAI) and Lecture Notes in Bioinformatics (LNBI), has established itself as a medium for the publication of new developments in computer science and information technology research, teaching, and education.

LNCS enjoys close cooperation with the computer science R & D community, the series counts many renowned academics among its volume editors and paper authors, and collaborates with prestigious societies. Its mission is to serve this international community by providing an invaluable service, mainly focused on the publication of conference and workshop proceedings and postproceedings. LNCS commenced publication in 1973.

Bin Sheng · Hao Chen · Tien Yin Wong ·
Carol Y. Cheung · Bo Qian
Editors

Ultra-Widefield Fundus Imaging for Diabetic Retinopathy

First MICCAI Challenge, UWF4DR 2024
Held in Conjunction with MICCAI 2024
Marrakesh, Morocco, October 10, 2024
Proceedings

Editors
Bin Sheng
Shanghai Jiao Tong University
Shanghai, China

Tien Yin Wong
Tsinghua University
Beijing, China

Bo Qian
Nanjing University of Aeronautics
and Astronautics
Nanjing, China

Hao Chen
The Hong Kong University of Science
and Technology
Hong Kong, China

Carol Y. Cheung
The Chinese University of Hong Kong
Hong Kong, China

ISSN 0302-9743   ISSN 1611-3349 (electronic)
Lecture Notes in Computer Science
ISBN 978-3-031-89387-2   ISBN 978-3-031-89388-9 (eBook)
https://doi.org/10.1007/978-3-031-89388-9

© The Editor(s) (if applicable) and The Author(s), under exclusive license
to Springer Nature Switzerland AG 2025

This work is subject to copyright. All rights are solely and exclusively licensed by the Publisher, whether the whole or part of the material is concerned, specifically the rights of translation, reprinting, reuse of illustrations, recitation, broadcasting, reproduction on microfilms or in any other physical way, and transmission or information storage and retrieval, electronic adaptation, computer software, or by similar or dissimilar methodology now known or hereafter developed.
The use of general descriptive names, registered names, trademarks, service marks, etc. in this publication does not imply, even in the absence of a specific statement, that such names are exempt from the relevant protective laws and regulations and therefore free for general use.
The publisher, the authors and the editors are safe to assume that the advice and information in this book are believed to be true and accurate at the date of publication. Neither the publisher nor the authors or the editors give a warranty, expressed or implied, with respect to the material contained herein or for any errors or omissions that may have been made. The publisher remains neutral with regard to jurisdictional claims in published maps and institutional affiliations.

This Springer imprint is published by the registered company Springer Nature Switzerland AG
The registered company address is: Gewerbestrasse 11, 6330 Cham, Switzerland

If disposing of this product, please recycle the paper.

Preface

Diabetic retinopathy (DR) is a common complication of diabetes and one of the leading causes of preventable blindness among working-age adults. With the global prevalence of DR expected to rise significantly in the coming decades, early detection and timely intervention are essential for effective disease management. Ultra-widefield (UWF) fundus imaging, which provides an ultra-wide 200-degree view of the retina, has emerged as a valuable tool for DR management. Compared to traditional color fundus photography (CFP), UWF fundus imaging allows for better visualization of peripheral retinal lesions, which are associated with more severe disease progression. However, the manual grading of UWF fundus images remains labor-intensive and time-consuming, highlighting the need for automated image analysis. Artificial intelligence (AI) has demonstrated significant potential in enhancing DR management efficiency and diagnostic consistency, but its success relies on the availability of large-scale, well-annotated datasets to ensure reliable model training and validation. Developing robust AI models for DR diagnosis using UWF fundus imaging will not only improve screening accessibility and clinical workflow efficiency but also contribute to better patient outcomes through earlier and more accurate detection of disease progression.

To advance state-of-the-art automatic DR analysis using UWF fundus images, we organized the Ultra-Widefield Fundus Imaging for Diabetic Retinopathy Challenge (UWF4DR 2024), which was a part of the 27th International Conference on Medical Image Computing and Computer Assisted Intervention (MICCAI 2024). The challenge consisted of three clinically relevant subtasks: image quality assessment for ultra-widefield fundus (Task 1), identification of referable diabetic retinopathy (Task 2), and identification of diabetic macular edema (Task 3). For Task 1, the dataset consists of 434 training images, 61 validation images, and 99 testing images. For Task 2, the dataset consists of 201 training images, 50 validation images, and 129 testing images. For Task 3, the dataset consists of 167 training images, 45 validation images, and 111 testing images.

The submission and evaluation process for the challenge was conducted on the Codalab platform (codalab.lisn.upsaclay.fr), where all automated assessments took place. Participants gained access to the dataset upon registering on the platform and signing a consent form agreeing to the challenge rules. Additionally, the official challenge website provided essential information, including rules, announcements, timelines, and real-time rankings. At the conclusion of the challenge, each team was required to submit a detailed paper outlining their methodology and results. These submissions covered key aspects such as data preprocessing, augmentation techniques, model architecture, optimization strategies, and post-processing methods. Teams participating in multiple tasks had the flexibility to submit either separate papers for each task or a single comprehensive paper detailing their approaches across different tasks. Ultimately, we received 17 papers from the participating teams, each presenting a diverse array of methodologies. Specifically, 8 papers detailed the approaches for Task 1, 10 for Task 2, and 9 for Task 3.

These teams were considered for the final official ranking and were invited to showcase their work at a half-day satellite event at MICCAI 2024, providing a platform to share their insights with the broader research community.

This proceeding features 17 papers, each presenting a diverse array of state-of-the-art deep learning approaches developed for the various tasks in the UWF4DR challenge. All submissions underwent a single-blind peer review process, with each paper reviewed by at least three reviewers. The review process focused on assessing the novelty, clarity, formatting, and overall quality of the work.

We would like to express our sincere gratitude to all participants of UWF4DR, the challenge committee members, reviewers, and MICCAI organizers. Their efforts and invaluable contributions were instrumental in the successful organization of this challenge.

February 2025

Bin Sheng
Hao Chen
Tien Yin Wong
Carol Y. Cheung
Bo Qian

Organization

Program Committee Chairs

Bin Sheng	Shanghai Jiao Tong University, China
Carol Y. Cheung	The Chinese University of Hong Kong, Hong Kong, China
Tien Yin Wong	Tsinghua University, China

Program Committee

Hao Chen	The Hong Kong University of Science and Technology, Hong Kong, China
Bo Qian	Nanjing University of Aeronautics and Astronautics, China
Yixiao Jin	Tsinghua University, China
Xiaoyan Hu	The Chinese University of Hong Kong, Hong Kong, China
Xiangning Wang	Shanghai Sixth People's Hospital, China
Junlin Hou	The Hong Kong University of Science and Technology, Hong Kong, China
Dawei Yang	The Chinese University of Hong Kong, Hong Kong, China
Zhouyu Guan	Shanghai Sixth People's Hospital, China
An Ran Ran	The Chinese University of Hong Kong, Hong Kong, China
Tingyao Li	Shanghai Jiao Tong University, China
Timothy Lai	The Chinese University of Hong Kong, Hong Kong, China
Carmen Chan	The Chinese University of Hong Kong, Hong Kong, China
Simon Szeto	The Chinese University of Hong Kong, Hong Kong, China
Mary Ho	The Chinese University of Hong Kong, Hong Kong, China

Contents

Image Quality Assessment with Model Fusion for Ultra-widefield Fundus 1
   Bo Yang, Yangyang Yan, Di Liu, Qicheng Li, and Yue Zhang

AI Algorithm for Ultra-widefield Fundus Imaging for Diabetic
Retinopathy - RDR, DME 10
   Bo Yang, Yue Zhang, Di Liu, Qicheng Li, and Yangyang Yan

Lightweight and Accurate: ShuffleNet for Diabetic Retinopathy
and EfficientNet for Diabetic Macular Edema Diagnosis 18
   *Berthold Scheuringer, Moritz Haderer, Martin Marinschek,
   Oleksandra Menzatiuk, and Vera Pils*

Efficient Deep Learning Models for Ultra-widefield Fundus Imaging
for Diabetic Retinopathy 36
   Abdul Qayyum, Moona Mazher, and Steven A. Niederer

Bag of Tricks for Ultra-widefield Fundus Image Quality Assessment 47
   Junfeng Sun, Xinliang Wang, and Yunchao Gu

Bag of Tricks for Diabetic Retinopathy and Diabetic Macular Edema
Classification in Ultra-widefield Imaging 55
   Hyeonmin Kim, Yunnie Cho, Ohhyun Kwon, and Dongha Lee

Deep Self-supervised Learning for Ultra-widefield Fundus Image Quality
Assessment 63
   *Ammar M. Okran, Saif Khalid Musluh, Saddam Abdulwahcb,
   Domenec Puig, and Hatem A. Rashwan*

Reliable DL-Based Referable Diabetic Retinopathy and Diabetic Macular
Edema Detection Using Ultra-widefield Fundus Images 75
   *Saif Khalid Musluh, Ammar M. Okran, Saddam Abdulwahab,
   Hatem A. Rashwan, and Domenec Puig*

Deep Learning-Based Detection of Referable Diabetic Retinopathy
and Macular Edema Using Ultra-widefield Fundus Imaging 88
   *Philippe Zhang, Pierre-Henri Conze, Mathieu Lamard,
   Béatrice Cochener, Gwenolé Quellec, and Mostafa El Habib Daho*

A Comprehensive Approach to Diabetic Retinopathy Classification:
Combining ResNet34 with Enhanced Preprocessing for Ultra-widefield
Fundus Imaging 101
   Yeon Su Park and Ji Hye Won

An Ultra-efficient Method for Real-Time Ultra-widefield Fundus Image
Quality Assessment 110
   Justin Engelmann and Lucas Gago

Ultra-fast Detection of Referable Diabetic Retinopathy and Macular
Edema in Ultra-widefield Fundus Imaging Using a Unified Risk Score 118
   Justin Engelmann and Lucas Gago

Efficient Deep Learning Approaches for Processing Ultra-widefield
Retinal Imaging 125
   Siwon Kim, Wooyung Yun, Jeongbin Oh, and Soomok Lee

EfficientNet-B1 Based Diabetic Retinopathy Detection
from Ultra-widefield Fundus Images 135
   Monalisa Bakshi and Chandra Sekhar Seelamantula

Many-MobileNet: Multi-model Augmentation for Robust Retinal Disease
Classification 144
   Hao Wang, Wenhui Zhu, Xuanzhao Dong, Yanxi Chen, Xin Li,
   Peijie Qiu, Xiwen Chen, Vamsi Krishna Vasa, Yujian Xiong,
   Oana M. Dumitrascu, Abolfazl Razi, and Yalin Wang

DME-MobileNet: Fine-Tuning nnMobileNet for Diabetic Macular Edema
Classification 155
   Xuanzhao Dong, Yalin Wang, Yanxi Chen, Xin Li, Hao Wang, Peijie Qiu,
   Xiwen Chen, Abolfazl Razi, Yujian Xiong, Oana M. Dumitrascu,
   and Wenhui Zhu

Automatic Identification Method for Diabetic Macular Edema
in Ultra-widefield Fundus Images 165
   Heyou Chang, Zhikang Ge, Jian Zhang, Heng Zhang, and Hao Zheng

Author Index 175

Image Quality Assessment with Model Fusion for Ultra-widefield Fundus

Bo Yang[1,2(✉)], Yangyang Yan[1], Di Liu[1], Qicheng Li[3], and Yue Zhang[4,5]

[1] AIFUTURE Lab, Shenzhou Digital Building, No. 16 Suzhou Street, Haidian District, Beijing 100085, China
yeungbo@gmail.com
[2] Wonderful Things Lab, No. 1 Xingfu Street, Huairou Science City, Huairou District, Beijing 101407, China
[3] College of Computer Science, Nankai University, No. 38 Tongyan Road, Haihe Education Park, Jinnan District, Tianjin, China
[4] Department of Ophthalmology, Beijing Hospital, National Center of Gerontology, Institute of Geriatric Medicine, Chinese Academy of Medical Sciences, Beijing, China
[5] Graduate School of Peking Union Medical College, Beijing, China

Abstract. The study addresses the challenge of image quality assessment in ultra-widefield fundus imaging (UWF) for diabetic retinopathy (DR) diagnosis. With the rise of UWF, which offers a broader field of view and higher resolution than traditional methods, the need for accurate image quality assessment is paramount. The research focuses on the limitations of UWF image quality assessment, which is still in its infancy compared to color fundus photography (CFP). The study utilizes a dataset of 434 UWF images, categorized as "gradable" and "ungradable" quality, to develop and validate a deep learning model. The model incorporates data augmentation and pseudo-labeling to improve generalization and robustness. By integrating various lightweight models, the study achieves a significant boost in performance, reducing inference time while securing a first-place ranking in a competition. This research underscores the importance of UWF in DR diagnosis and the necessity for robust image quality assessment to ensure accurate lesion identification and early intervention. As the top team, we have open-sourced our code on GitHub at https://github.com/yeungbo/MICCAI-UWF4DR-2024.

Keywords: Image Quality Assessment · Ultra-Widefield Fundus Imaging · Diabetic Retinopathy · Artificial Intelligence

1 Introduction

Diabetic retinopathy (DR) is a prevalent complication associated with diabetes mellitus and stands as a leading cause of visual impairment among adults. The global prevalence was estimated at approximately 103 million adul,ts in the year 2020. Projections indicate an increase to 130 million by 2030 and a further rise to 161 million by 2045. DR is classified into five distinct classes according to the International Clinical Diabetic Retinopathy (ICDR) severity scale:

no significant retinopathy, mild non-proliferative diabetic retinopathy (NPDR), moderate NPDR, severe NPDR, and proliferative diabetic retinopathy(PDR). Referable DR, which encompasses moderate NPDR and all more severe forms, includes diabetic macular edema (DME) as a defining characteristic feature [1, 2].

The diagnosis of DR primarily relies on ophthalmoscopy and various fundus imaging techniques. To prevent vision loss, timely screening, referral, and early treatment are widely accepted as consensus. Standard color fundus photography (CFP) is currently the gold standard for DR detection, but the 7-standard fields fundus montage developed by the Early Treatment Diabetic Retinopathy Study (ETDRs) covers only 75° of the fundus, approximately 30% of the total retinal area, and may miss some peripheral lesions, including neovascularization. [3] The advent of ultra-widefield fundus imaging (UWF) has effectively addressed the blind spots of traditional fundus imaging, with a single acquisition angle reaching 200° and an acquired image covering approximately 80% of the total retinal area. Compared to CFP, UWF offers broader field of view, non-dilation, and high resolution. By observing lesions hidden in the peripheral retina (PPL), PPL is present in 30%–40% of DR patients and indicates a more severe DR in 11% of cases. The application of UWF is beneficial for early diagnosis of DR and timely intervention, demonstrating promising prospects in DR treatment [4].

In recent years, the automatic diagnosis of retinal diseases has garnered significant research and clinical interest, aiming to alleviate the burden on ophthalmologists and enable large-scale, regular screening of diabetic patients through fundus imaging. Currently, DR detection in CFP images using artificial intelligence has become increasingly mature. However, the assessment of CFP image quality is a critical step before image analysis. The main factors for fundus image quality assessment include the identification of image artifacts, clarity, and field of view clarity. Objective and accurate image quality assessment is crucial to ensure that the images used for classification have sufficient quality, particularly in the early stages of diseases with subtle lesion features. Many algorithms have been developed to effectively assess the quality of CFP images, but the assessment of UWF image quality is still immature. Research on the effective analysis of UWF fundus images using computer-aided systems is limited. [5–9] Therefore, although UWF has a higher image quality than CFP and reduces the rate of ungradable images, there still needs to be a good image quality guarantee for the accuracy of lesion identification.

To promote the technical level of ultra-widefield images in DR analysis, we participated in the Ultra-Widefield Fundus Imaging Diabetic Retinopathy Challenge. The challenge aims to incentivize researchers to develop different task algorithms for DR analysis, including UWF fundus image quality assessment.

2 Data Preparing

2.1 Dataset

We began by studying the competition dataset: the official dataset provided 434 ultra-widefield fundus images, divided into two categories: "gradable image"

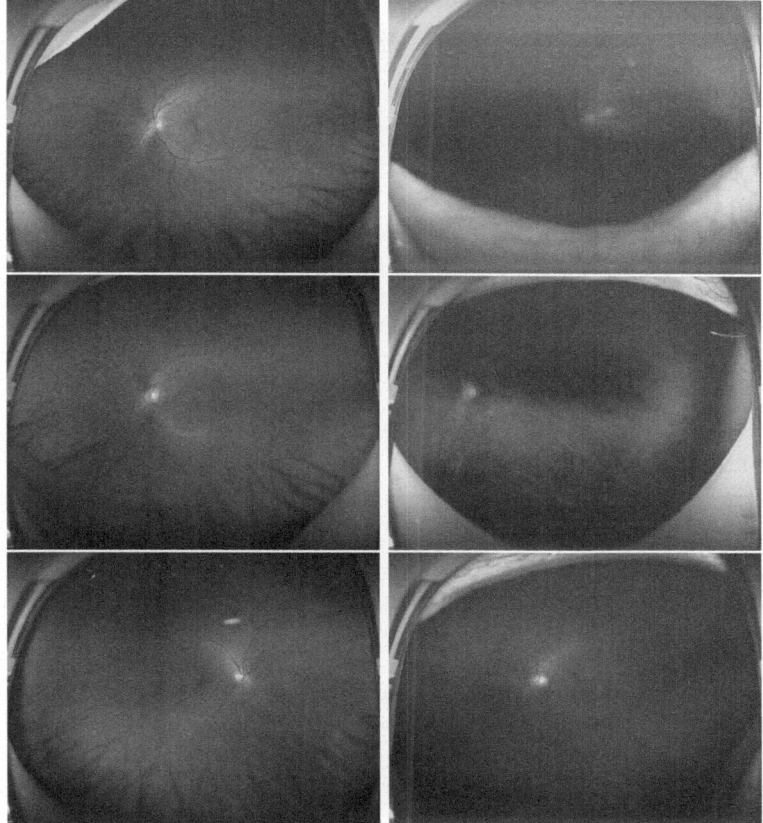

Fig. 1. Examples of UWF fundus images for "gradable image" (on left side) and "ungradable image" (on right side).

with 229 images and "ungradable image" with 205 images, as shown in Fig. 1. Subsequently, we divided the dataset into training and validation sets at an 8:2 ratio, and also set aside a 5-fold cross-validation dataset for later evaluation of the algorithm model's performance.

To enrich the training set and enhance the model's performance and generalization ability, we implemented a series of data augmentation operations aimed at improving the model's robustness and adaptability: Random cropping, Resizing, Random flipping, Random rotation and Image normalization.

2.2 Pseudo-label Generation for Data Augmentation

To further enrich the training dataset, we utilized 256 ultra-widefield fundus images and their 5-class diabetic retinopathy (DR) labels provided by the Deep-Diabetic-Retinopathy-Image-Dataset (DeepDRiD) project. We employed the five

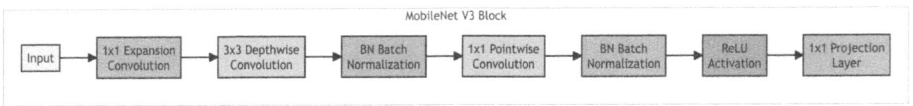

Fig. 2. MobileNet V3 Block Architecture.

trained models to perform inference on these 256 images, thereby obtaining prediction probability values from each model for every image. Based on a set threshold of 0.1, we filtered out 18 images where all five probability values were below this threshold, defining these images as the "ungradable" class data. These images were used to supplement the training set, enhancing the model's ability to recognize ungradable images.

3 Methodology

3.1 Base Model Construction and Evaluation

Initially, we selected MobileNetV3Small model [10] as the base network architecture, the MobileNetV3Small network architecture consists of the following components: first, a standard convolutional layer that halves the input size and reduces the number of channels to 16. It then passes through 11 bottleneck structures with different convolutional parameter configurations, resulting in a feature map size reduced to 1/32 of the original and a channel count of 96. Subsequently, a 1×1 standard convolutional layer increases the number of channels to 576, followed by a 7×7 pooling layer that reduces the feature map size to 1/224 of the original. Finally, two linear layers serve as the classification head, with the first linear layer having 1024 neurons and the second having the number of classification units.

The most core structure of MobileNetV3Small model is found in the bottleneck module, as shown in the Fig. 2. below. It first utilizes a 1×1 convolution for dimensionality expansion, followed by a 3×3 depthwise separable convolution. An attention module, SE, is then added, which adjusts the weights of each channel. Finally, a 1×1 convolution is applied to maintain the dimensionality consistency with the current input, achieving the residual sum of both.

3.2 SqueezeNet1.1 Model

Moreover, we selected another lightweight network model SqueezeNet1.1 [11] as the base network architecture, the SqueezeNet1.1 network architecture is composed of the following components: initially, a convolutional layer halves the input size and reduces the number of channels to 64. It is then followed by a pooling layer with a stride of 2, which further halves the input size. Next, it passes through two Fire modules and one pooling layer, resulting in a feature map size reduced to 1/8 of the original and a channel count of 128. This process is repeated with two additional Fire modules and one pooling layer, further

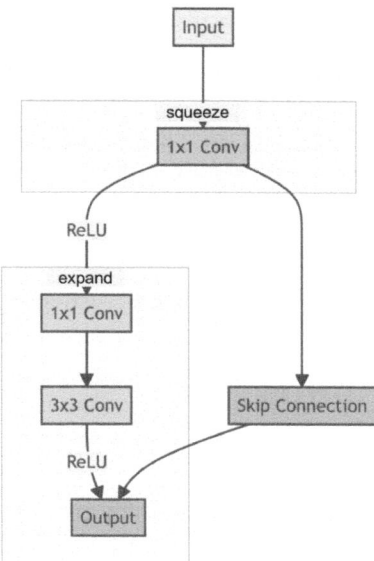

Fig. 3. Fire Module of SqueezeNet.

reducing the feature map size to 1/16 of the original and the channel count to 256. Subsequently, it goes through four Fire modules, maintaining the feature map size at 1/8 of the original and the channel count at 512. The final classification head consists of two parts: a convolutional layer and an AdaptiveAvgPool layer. The convolutional layer uses 1×1 convolution kernels, with the number of kernels corresponding to the number of classification units, set to 1 in this experiment. The AdaptiveAvgPool layer is used to adapt to different input sizes, ensuring that the final feature map size is 1×1.

The most core structure in SqueezeNet1.1 is the Fire module, as shown in the Fig. 3. The squeeze layer uses only 1×1 convolution kernels, with the number of kernels being N. The expand layer uses two sizes of convolution kernels, with N1 kernels of 1×1 size and N3 kernels of 3×3 size. During operation, N1 is set to N, and N3 is set to N, allowing the squeeze layer to limit the number of input channels, thereby effectively reducing the number of parameters.

During the model training phase, we utilized the Adam optimizer with an initial learning rate of 0.0001. To prevent overfitting and improve the model' s performance on the validation set, we implemented a learning rate decay strategy: when the AUC (Area Under the Curve) on the validation set does not show significant improvement over a continuous 5 epochs (training cycles), the learning rate is reduced to 0.1 times of the original value. Additionally, we set the batch_size to 16 and conducted training for 100 epochs on the 5-fold cross-validation dataset. This method yielded 5 independent model weights, which were submitted to the competition' s official website for evaluation. The evaluation results of each model are shown in Table 1, and these results will be used for subsequent model selection and optimization.

Additionally, two MobileNetV3Small models were trained using datasets with image sizes of 224×224 and 112×112, respectively, while a SqueezeNet model was constructed using the 224×224 dataset. The evaluation results of each model on the official validation set are presented in Table 1.

Table 1. Single Model Performance Evaluation.

Model Type (Image Size)	AUROC	AUPRC	Sensitivity	Specificity	CPU_Time
MobileNetV3Small - 224x224	0.8863	0.9409	0.7838	0.9167	0.0219
MobileNetV3Small - 112x112	0.8784	0.9312	0.6757	0.9583	0.011
SqueezeNet - 224x224	0.8581	0.9074	0.9189	0.75	0.0194

According to the content of the Table 1, it displays the performance comparison of three different models across various metrics. AUROC (Area Under the Receiver Operating Characteristic Curve) is a commonly used metric to evaluate the performance of binary classification models. It represents the area under the curve of the receiver operating characteristic plotted at different classification thresholds. The closer the value of AUROC is to 1, the better the model' s classification ability. AUPRC (Area Under the Precision-Recall Curve) is another metric used to evaluate the performance of binary classification models. It represents the area under the precision-recall curve plotted at different classification thresholds. The closer the value of AUPRC is to 1, the more accurate the model' s predictions. Sensitivity is the ability of the model to correctly predict positive samples, which is the proportion of true positives correctly predicted among the true positives. Specificity is the ability of the model to correctly predict negative samples, which is the proportion of true negatives correctly predicted among the true negatives. CPU time represents the time used by the model during the computation process.

Based on the data in the table, we can see that different models have some differences in these metrics. For example, the "MobileNetV3Small - 224×224" model performs the best in terms of specificity, while the "SqueezeNet 224×224" model performs the best in terms of sensitivity. Additionally, for different image sizes, the CPU time of MobileNetV3Small also varies.

4 Model Fusion

However, compared to the models of our competitors, the AUROC of our three models is not satisfactory, indicating that there is room for improvement in the classification ability of our models. In order to enhance the AUROC, we need to ponder on how to improve our models without significantly increasing CPU time. This is a topic worthy of in-depth consideration and research.

To address this issue, we explored the implementation of model fusion strategies. Model fusion is a technique that combines the predictions of multiple models to obtain more accurate and stable results. By leveraging the complementary nature of different models' predictions, we can maximize overall performance.

During the process of model fusion, we considered the following strategies:

Voting: This strategy involves aggregating the predictions of multiple models and selecting the class with the highest number of votes as the final prediction. Voting is suitable when the errors made by different models are relatively independent of each other.

Weighted Average: In this approach, the predictions of multiple models are combined using weighted averaging. The weights can be determined based on the performance or confidence of the models on the training set. Weighted averaging is applicable when different models have advantages in different metrics.

Stacking: Stacking involves using an additional model, known as a meta-model, to combine the predictions of multiple base models. The meta-model is trained to predict the final outcome, utilizing the hierarchical relationships between the models. This method can further improve performance.

However, these strategies did not yield significant improvements for AUROC performance in our specific scenario. Therefore, we employed an innovative fusion strategy called sorting fusion. Firstly, the outputs of each model are sorted, and then a threshold, denoted as a1 and a2, is used for decision-making. When the outputs of all models are greater than a1, the fused model outputs the maximum value among the model outputs. When the outputs of all models are less than a2, the fused model outputs the minimum value among the model outputs. For other cases, the fused model outputs the median value. In practical applications, the threshold values and decision criteria can be customized based on specific circumstances.

By applying this strategy, we successfully fused three lightweight models and improved the AUROC performance of our model by approximately 0.055 during the validation (preliminary) stage. Ultimately, throughout the validation phase, test phase, and the final stage of the competition, we consistently secured the first place on the results leaderboard, as demonstrated in Table 2.

Table 2. Model Fusion Performance Evaluation.

Phase (Image Size)	AUROC	AUPRC	Sensitivity	Specificity	CPU_Time
Validation Phase (ranking)	0.9409 (1)	0.9607 (1)	0.9189 (3)	0.9167 (2)	0.0725 (5)
Test Phase (ranking)	0.9716 (1)	0.9821 (1)	0.9322 (2)	0.9500 (2)	0.0464 (2)

5 Conclusion

Through the aforementioned methods, this study not only enhanced the generalization performance and robustness of the model by employing data augmentation and pseudo-label generation techniques, but also optimized the model structure. Additionally, by integrating diverse lightweight models, the study achieved a significant improvement in model performance while concurrently reducing inference time, ultimately securing the first-place ranking in the competition evaluation.

Acknowledgments. We would like to extend our sincere gratitude to the experts who provided invaluable medical expertise and technical support throughout our research work. Their knowledge and guidance played a crucial role in shaping the direction and improving the quality of our study.

References

1. Teo, Z.L., Tham, Y.C., Yu, M., Chee, M.L., Rim, T.H., Cheung, N., et al.: Global prevalence of diabetic retinopathy and projection of burden through 2045: systematic review and meta-analysis. Ophthalmology **128**(11), 1580–91 (2021)
2. Blonde, L., Umpierrez, G.E., Reddy, S.S., McGill, J.B., Berga, S.L., Bush, M., et al.: American association of clinical endocrinology clinical practice guideline: developing a diabetes mellitus comprehensive care plan-2022 update. Endocr. Pract. **28**(10), 923–1049 (2022)
3. Das, T., Takkar, B., Sivaprasad, S., Thanksphon, T., Taylor, H., Wiedemann, P., et al.: Recently updated global diabetic retinopathy screening guidelines: commonalities, differences, and future possibilities. Eye (Lond.) **35**(10), 2685–98 (2021)
4. Vujosevic, S., Aldington, S.J., Silva, P., Hernández, C., Scanlon, P., Peto, T., et al.: Screening for diabetic retinopathy: new perspectives and challenges. Lancet Diab. Endocrinol. **8**(4), 337–47 (2020)
5. Abramovich, O., Pizem, H., Van Eijgen, J., Oren, I., Melamed, J., Stalmans, I., et al.: FundusQ-net: a regression quality assessment deep learning algorithm for fundus images quality grading. Comput. Methods Programs Biomed. **239**, 107522 (2023)
6. Li, Z., Jiang, J., Zhou, H., Zheng, Q., Liu, X., Chen, K., et al.: Development of a deep learning-based image eligibility verification system for detecting and filtering out ineligible fundus images: a multicentre study. Int. J. Med. Inform. **147**, 104363 (2021)
7. Liu, L., Wu, X., Lin, D., Zhao, L., Li, M., Yun, D., et al.: DeepFundus: a flow-cytometry-like image quality classifier for boosting the whole life cycle of medical artificial intelligence. Cell Rep Med. **4**(2), 100912 (2023)
8. Liu, R., Wang, X., Wu, Q., Dai, L., Fang, X., Yan, T., et al.: DeepDRiD: diabetic retinopathy-grading and image quality estimation challenge. Patterns (N Y). **3**(6), 100512 (2022)

9. Mansour, O.Y., Ramadan, I., Abdo, A., Hamdi, M., Eldeeb, H., Marouf, H., et al.: Deciding thrombolysis in AIS based on automated versus on whatsApp interpreted ASPECTS, a reliability and cost-effectiveness analysis in developing system of care. Front. Neurol. **11**, 333 (2020)
10. Howard, A., et al.: Searching for mobilenetv3. In: Proceedings of the IEEE/CVF International Conference on Computer Vision **1314**, 1324 (2019)
11. Iandola, F.N.: SqueezeNet: alexNet-level accuracy with 50x fewer parameters and< 0.5 MB model size. arXiv preprint arXiv:1602.07360 (2016)

AI Algorithm for Ultra-widefield Fundus Imaging for Diabetic Retinopathy - RDR, DME

Bo Yang[1,2(✉)], Yue Zhang[3,4], Di Liu[1], Qicheng Li[5], and Yangyang Yan[1]

[1] AIFUTURE Lab, Shenzhou Digital Building,
No. 16 Suzhou Street, Haidian District, Beijing 100085, China
yeungbo@gmail.com
[2] Wonderful Things Lab, No. 1 Xingfu Street,
Huairou Science City, Huairou District, Beijing 101407, China
[3] Department of Ophthalmology, Beijing Hospital, National Center of Gerontology, Institute of Geriatric Medicine, Chinese Academy of Medical Sciences, Beijing, China
[4] Graduate School of Peking Union Medical College, Beijing, China
[5] College of Computer Science, Nankai University, No. 38 Tongyan Road, Haihe Education Park, Jinnan District, Tianjin, China

Abstract. Diabetic retinopathy (DR) is a leading global cause of vision impairment. The International Clinical Diabetic Retinopathy (ICDR) system has been proposed to standardize the grading of DR severity . Ultra-widefield (UWF) imaging, which offers a 200-degree view, enhances the detection of peripheral pathology often overlooked by standard imaging methods. Recent studies have demonstrated the effectiveness of deep learning algorithms in analyzing UWF images for automated DR detection, thereby improving sensitivity, specificity, and risk stratification. These advancements underscore the potential of combining UWF imaging with deep learning to enhance DR detection and management, providing a more comprehensive view of disease progression and reducing the rates of ungradable images for more reliable diagnostics. This synthesis highlights the importance of integrating advanced imaging techniques with AI for early and accurate DR detection, which is crucial for preventing vision loss in diabetic patients. To address this, we participated in the Ultra-Widefield Diabetic Retinopathy Challenge, developing algorithms for DR severity and DME classification based on UWF images. We employed EfficientNet-B7, known for its efficiency and generalization capabilities, and enhanced its performance through data augmentation and pseudo-label generation. These techniques expanded training datasets, improved model robustness, and leveraged unlabeled data, resulting in significant performance gains. Training on a 5-fold cross-validation dataset, our optimal model achieved an AUC increase of 0.66%-2%. Our findings underscore the potential of UWF imaging and machine learning to enhance DR management, paving the way for automated systems that streamline DR assessment and timely interventions, ultimately preventing vision loss in diabetic patients.

Keywords: Diabetic Retinopathy · Ultra-Widefield Retinal Imaging · Data Augmentation · Pseudo-Label Generation

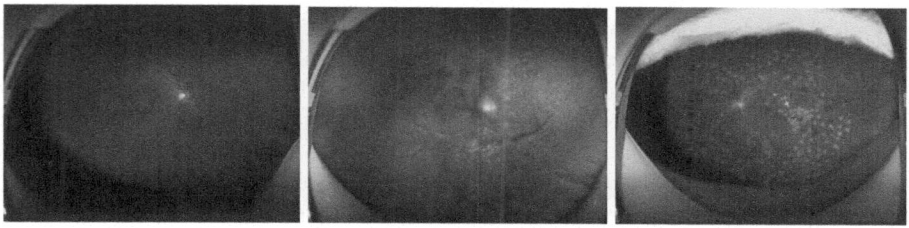

Fig. 1. Examples of UWF fundus images for (a) Normal (b) RDR and (c) DME.

1 Introduction

Diabetic retinopathy (DR) remains a leading cause of vision impairment among working-age adults globally. Recent estimates suggest that approximately 103 million adults worldwide had DR in 2020, with projections indicating this number could increase to 161 million by 2045 [1]. The International Clinical Diabetic Retinopathy (ICDR) classification system was proposed by Wilkinson et al. in 2003 [2] to provide a globally standardized grading scale for the clinical severity of diabetic retinopathy. The ICDR classification system is based on findings from the Early Treatment Diabetic Retinopathy Study (ETDRS) and the Wisconsin Epidemiologic Study of Diabetic Retinopathy (WESDR), providing an important reference standard for the management of diabetic retinopathy worldwide. Early detection and timely treatment are crucial for preventing vision loss. Ultra-widefield (UWF) retinal imaging has emerged as an advanced technique for DR screening and analysis. As shown in Fig. 1, UWF imaging provides a panoramic view of up to 200° of the retina in a single capture, compared to the 30–50° field of view of conventional fundus cameras. This expanded field of view allows visualization of peripheral retinal pathology that may be missed by standard imaging.

Recent studies have demonstrated the effectiveness of deep learning algorithms in analyzing UWF images for automated DR detection: Oh et al. [3] developed a deep learning system for DR detection using UWF fundus images. Their algorithm, based on a ResNet-34 architecture, achieved an AUC of 0.915 when classifying DR severity using images extracted from UWF photographs. Importantly, they found that using the Early Treatment Diabetic Retinopathy Study (ETDRS) 7-standard field image extracted from UWF images outperformed analysis of just the central retina. Zhao et al. [4] created a deep learning algorithm to detect neovascular leakage on UWF fluorescein angiography (UWF-FA) images. Their ensemble model, combining ResNet152v2, EfficientNetB6, and Inception-ResNetV2 architectures, achieved an AUC of 0.96 for detecting neovascular leakage. This is significant as neovascularization indicates progression to proliferative DR, requiring prompt intervention. Nagasawa et al. [5] developed a deep learning system to detect treatment-naïve proliferative DR using non-FA UWF images. Their algorithm achieved high sensitivity (94.7%) and specificity (97.2%) in distinguishing proliferative DR from non-proliferative stages.

Silva et al. [6] demonstrated that peripheral lesions identified on UWF imaging are associated with an increased risk of DR progression over time. This highlights the importance of wide-field imaging in risk stratification.

These studies underscore several key advantages of combining UWF imaging with deep learning for DR detection. Firstly, it improved detection of peripheral pathology, which may be missed by conventional imaging. Secondly, the combination of UWF with deep learning algorithms increases the sensitivity and specificity in identifying referable DR and proliferative DR, leading to more accurate diagnoses. Additionally, this approach enables automated risk stratification by considering both central and peripheral retinal findings, offering a holistic view of disease progression. Lastly, it reduces the rate of ungradable images when compared to traditional fundus photography, thus ensuring more reliable diagnostic outcomes.

Despite the advancements, several challenges hinder the broad adoption of UWF imaging and deep learning in diabetic retinopathy (DR) detection. Key issues include the need for standardized datasets to validate technology across diverse populations, the integration of multi-modal imaging data for a comprehensive DR assessment, and the clinical validation of AI-assisted systems. Addressing these challenges is crucial for the practical and effective implementation of these technologies, ensuring accurate DR detection and prevention of vision loss in diabetic patients.

By leveraging the advancements in image analysis and machine learning techniques, we strive to enhance the efficiency and accuracy of diagnosing and monitoring DR using UWF retinal images. The outcomes of this work will contribute to the development of automated systems that have the potential to streamline the assessment of DR and enable timely interventions, ultimately preventing vision loss in diabetic patients. As the top three teams, we have open-sourced our code on GitHub at https://github.com/yeungbo/MICCAI-UWF4DR-2024. In the following sections, we will present the methodologies and results of our algorithmic approaches for DR severity classification and DME classification using UWF retinal images. We will discuss the challenges encountered and the potential implications of our findings in the field of diabetic retinopathy management.

2 Data Preparing

Initially, we conducted an investigation into the competition dataset:

1. for RDR task, the official dataset provided a total of 201 ultra-widefield fundus images, which were categorized into two classes: "Referable Diabetic Retinopathy" (RDR) with 112 images and "Non-Referable Diabetic Retinopathy" (non RDR) with 89 images.
2. for DME task, the official dataset comprised 167 ultra-widefield fundus images, which were divided into two categories: "Diabetic Macular Edema" (DME) with 77 images and "No Diabetic Macular Edema" (NDE) with 90 images.

Subsequently, the dataset was divided into training and validation sets at an 8:2 ratio, and a 5-fold cross-validation dataset was also set aside for the subsequent evaluation of the algorithmic model's performance.

To enrich the training set and enhance the model's performance and generalization ability, we implemented a series of data augmentation operations aimed at improving the model's robustness and adaptability:

Random cropping: The images were randomly cropped with scaling parameters set to scale=(0.90,1.1) and ratio=(0.9,1.1) to increase the diversity of the images.

Resizing: The cropped images were resized to 448×448 pixels to ensure consistency in the input image dimensions.

Random flipping: The images were randomly horizontally and vertically flipped to simulate potential image rotations in real-world applications.

Random rotation: The images were randomly rotated within an angle limit of 30° to enhance the model's adaptability to angle variations in images.

Image normalization: The processed image data were normalized to a mean (mean) of [0.485, 0.456, 0.406] and a standard deviation (std) of [0.229, 0.224, 0.225] to optimize the model training process.

For the validation set, the data augmentation process was slightly different, employing the following three augmentation algorithms:

Resizing: The images were resized to 512×512 pixels to prepare for subsequent central cropping.

Central cropping: The resized images were centrally cropped to obtain 448×448 pixel images.

Image normalization: As with the training set, the images were normalized to mean=[0.485, 0.456, 0.406] and std=[0.229, 0.224, 0.225].

3 Methodology

We selected EfficientNet-B7 [7] as the base network architecture, renowned for its efficient performance and good generalization ability. To accelerate the training process and enhance model performance, we modified the classification head by adjusting the number of output neurons to 1, to accommodate the binary classification task of UWF fundus image quality assessment.

The EfficientNet-B7 network structure, as shown in Fig. 2, primarily consists of the following components: First is the Stem module, which is mainly composed of convolutional layers, including 64 3×3 convolutional kernels with a stride of 2, which halves the size of the feature map after passing through this layer. It is followed by BatchNormalization and Swish activation functions. Then, there are 7 MBConv modules, which are the core building blocks of EfficientNet, as shown in the figure below. The MBConv module is a depthwise separable convolution with expanded layers, where the expansion convolution uses a 1×1

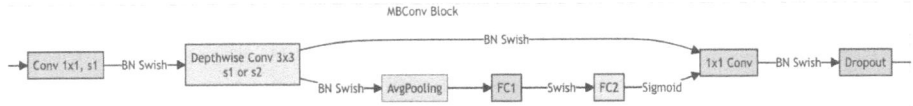

Fig. 2. Schematic Representation of the MBConv Block within the EfficientNet-B7 Architecture.

convolution to expand the dimension of the feature map, the depthwise convolution employs 3×3 or 5×5 convolutional kernels, the projection convolution reduces the dimension of the feature map back to the initial dimension, and the SE module is used to adjust the weights of the feature map channels. The final classification head is composed of convolutional layers, a GlobalAvgPool layer, and fully connected layers. Here, the convolutional layer uses 1×1 convolution kernels to reduce dimensions, pooling layers are used to unify the size of the feature map to 1×1, and the number of neurons in the fully connected layer corresponds to the number of classes.

To accelerate model training and enhance its performance, this study employed pre-trained weights from EfficientNet-B7 on the ImageNet-1K dataset as the initial weights. This approach allows the model to converge quickly on less training data while retaining the knowledge learned by the pre-trained model on a wide range of visual features.

During the model training phase, we utilized the Adam optimizer with an initial learning rate of 0.0001. To prevent overfitting and improve the model's performance on the validation set, we implemented a learning rate decay strategy: when the AUC (Area Under the Curve) on the validation set does not show significant improvement over a continuous 5 epochs (training cycles), the learning rate is reduced to 0.1 times of the original value. Additionally, we set the batch_size to 16 and conducted training for 100 epochs on the 5-fold cross-validation dataset. This method yielded 5 independent model weights, which were submitted to the competition's official website for evaluation. The evaluation results of each model are shown in Table 1, and these results will be used for subsequent model selection and optimization.

Table 1. Baseline Model Performance Evaluation.

Task	Cross1	Cross2	Cross3	Cross4	Cross5
RDR	0.9852	0.9754	0.9852	**0.9901**	0.9737
DME	**0.9762**	0.9722	0.9702	0.9484	0.9543

From Table 1, it can be observed that the best model obtained from the competition organizer's provided data, using conventional data augmentation algorithms, was achieved top 10 performance in validation phase on leaderboard.

However, compared to the models of our competitors, the AUROC of our three models is not satisfactory. This signal suggests that we need to find a better solution to enhance generalization performance.

4 Data Augmentation and Pseudo-Label Generation

Data augmentation is a technique used to expand training datasets by applying various transformations to generate new samples. It helps to mitigate overfitting, improve generalization, and address imbalanced datasets. By exposing models to a wider range of variations and conditions, data augmentation enhances their robustness and adaptability to real-world scenarios.

Pseudo-label generation [8] is a semi-supervised learning technique that assigns pseudo-labels to unlabeled data based on model predictions. This approach enables the utilization of a larger amount of unlabeled data, improving generalization and reducing the reliance on labeled data. Pseudo-label generation also facilitates iterative model refinement, where the quality of pseudo-labels and model performance improve iteratively.

Together, data augmentation and pseudo-label generation offer significant benefits in machine learning. Data augmentation expands datasets, enhances model robustness, and helps address class imbalance. Pseudo-label generation leverages unlabeled data, improves model generalization, and allows for iterative model refinement. These techniques contribute to improved training, performance, and practical applicability in various machine learning applications.

To further enrich the training dataset, we utilized 256 ultra-widefield fundus images and their 5-class diabetic retinopathy (DR) labels provided by the Deep-Diabetic-Retinopathy-Image-Dataset (DeepDRiD) project. [9] For RDR task, A threshold of 0.13 was set, and images with all 5 probability values below this threshold were filtered out, yielding a total of 22 images to supplement the "Non-Referable Diabetic Retinopathy" (non RDR) class. Building upon the official competition dataset, an additional 22 images were added, bringing the total training set to 223 images. This included 111 images for the "Referable Diabetic Retinopathy" (RDR) class and 112 images for the non RDR class. The same dataset division, data processing and augmentation, as well as network structure and pre-trained weights were repeated. The model was then trained on the latest 5-fold cross-validation dataset.

For DME task, similarly, the five baseline models trained on the DME task were used to perform inference on the 256 ultra-widefield images. This resulted in 5 prediction probability values for each image. A threshold of 0.9 was set,

Table 2. Data Augmented by Pseudo-labeling Techniques for Enhancing Training Datasets

Data Source	NRD	DME
DeepDRiD	22	21

and images where all 5 probability values exceeded this threshold were selected, yielding a total of 21 images to supplement the "Diabetic Macular Edema" (DME) class.

Table 2 illustrates the distribution of pseudo-labeled data across two diagnostic categories: Non-Proliferative Diabetic Retinopathy (NPDR) and Diabetic Macular Edema (DME). To enhance training, the dataset has been augmented with synthetic data. Sourced from the DeepDRiD dataset, the table shows that there are 22 instances labeled as non RDR and 21 instances labeled as DME.

These images were used to supplement the training set, enhancing the model's ability to recognize RDR and DME pattens. After the data augumentation with pseudo-label generation, we retrained the RDR and DME models, and the weights of each model were submitted to the competition's official website for evaluation, with the results shown in Table 3.

Table 3. Enhanced Model Performance Evaluation.

Task	AUROC	AUPRC	Sensitivity	Specificity	CPU_Time
RDR	**0.9967**	0.9977	1.0	0.9524	0.2253
DME	**0.9940**	0.9951	0.9167	1.0	0.2665

As depicted in Table 3, the overall performance of the trained models has been significantly enhanced through the incorporation of data augmented by secondary methods and pseudo-labeling techniques. The optimal model's AUC has been increased by approximately 0.66%~2%. Ultimately, we secured the first place in the validation phase and attained third place in the final test phase of the competition.

5 Conclusion

The Ultra-Widefield Diabetic Retinopathy Challenge aimed to enhance the technological level of UWF imaging in DR analysis. Our participation involved developing algorithms for DR severity and DME classification using UWF retinal images. To enrich the training dataset, we utilized 256 images from the DeepDRiD project, filtering and selecting images based on specific thresholds to supplement the "Non-Referable Diabetic Retinopathy" and "Diabetic Macular Edema" classes. The models were trained on a 5-fold cross-validation dataset, and their performance was significantly improved, with the AUC of the optimal model increasing by approximately 0.66%~2% due to the supplementation of data through secondary augmentation and pseudo-labeling. This approach demonstrates the potential of UWF imaging and machine learning in improving DR management and preventing vision loss in diabetic patients.

Acknowledgments. We would like to extend our sincere gratitude to the experts who provided invaluable medical expertise and technical support throughout our research work. Their knowledge and guidance played a crucial role in shaping the direction and improving the quality of our study.

References

1. Teo, Z.L., Tham, Y.-C., Yu, M., Chee, M.L., Rim, T.H., Cheung, N., et al.: Global prevalence of diabetic retinopathy and projection of burden through 2045: systematic review and meta-analysis. Ophthalmology **128**, 1580–1591 (2021). https://doi.org/10.1016/j.ophtha.2021.04.027
2. Wilkinson, C.P., et al.: Proposed international clinical diabetic retinopathy and diabetic macular edema disease severity scales. Ophthalmology **110**(9), 1677–82 (2003)
3. Oh, K.R., Kang, H.M., Leem, D., et al.: Early detection of diabetic retinopathy based on deep learning and ultra-wide-field fundus images. Sci. Rep. **11**(1), 1897 (2021)
4. Zhao, P.Y., Bommakanti, N., Yu, G., et al.: Deep learning for automated detection of neovascular leakage on ultra-widefield fluorescein angiography in diabetic retinopathy. Sci. Rep. **13**(1), 9165 (2023)
5. Nagasawa, T., et al.: Accuracy of ultrawide-field fundus ophthalmoscopy-assisted deep learning for detecting treatment-naïve proliferative diabetic retinopathy. Int. Ophthalmol. **39**(10), 2153–2159 (2019). https://doi.org/10.1007/s10792-019-01074-z
6. Silva, P.S., Cavallerano, J.D., Haddad, N., et al.: Peripheral lesions identified on ultrawide field imaging predict increased risk of diabetic retinopathy progression over 4 years. Ophthalmology **122**(5), 949–956 (2015)
7. Tan, M.: Efficientnet: rethinking model scaling for convolutional neural networks. arXiv preprint arXiv:1905.11946 (2019)
8. Lee, D.H.: Pseudo-label: the simple and efficient semi-supervised learning method for deep neural networks. In: Workshop on Challenges in Representation Learning, vol. 3, No. 2, p. 896. ICML Jun 16 (2013)
9. Liu, R., et al.: Deepdrid: diabetic retinopathy—grading and image quality estimation challenge. Patterns. **3**(6) (2022)

Lightweight and Accurate: ShuffleNet for Diabetic Retinopathy and EfficientNet for Diabetic Macular Edema Diagnosis

Berthold Scheuringer[1], Moritz Haderer[1], Martin Marinschek[1], Oleksandra Menzatiuk[1,2], and Vera Pils[1,3,4]

[1] Johannes Kepler University, Linz 4040, Austria
miccai.challenge.jku@gmail.com
[2] Silicon Austria Labs, Linz 4040, Austria
[3] BOKU Core Facility Bioinformatics, BOKU University, Vienna 1180, Austria
[4] Institute of Statistics, Department of Landscape, Spatial and Infrastructure Sciences, BOKU University, Vienna 1180, Austria

Abstract. Diabetic Retinopathy (DR) is a leading cause of preventable blindness, affecting over 100 million adults globally, with prevalence expected to rise significantly by 2045. Early detection of DR and diabetic macular edema (DME) is crucial for timely treatment . This study addresses the challenges of DR diagnosis using ultra-widefield (UWF) fundus images, which provide a 200-degree retinal view. We participated in the MICCAI 2024 UWF4DR challenge, tackling three tasks: image quality assessment, DR detection, and DME identification, using Auto-Morph, ShuffleNet, and EfficientNetB0 models, respectively. Our approach secured competitive leaderboard rankings, highlighting the potential of deep learning models for scalable, automated DR diagnosis in clinical settings.

Keywords: Diabetic Retinopathy · Ultra-Widefield Fundus Imaging · Diabetic Macular Edema · Deep Learning

1 Introduction

As of 2020, an estimated 103 million adults were affected by Diabetic Retinopathy (DR), and this number is projected to rise to 161 million by 2045 [1]. DR is a major complication of diabetes mellitus and is one of the leading causes of preventable blindness among working-aged individuals worldwide [2].

Early signs of DR [3] include microaneurysms, which manifest as small, sharply defined red dots on the retina due to abnormal leakage from retinal blood vessels. When these vessels swell and rupture, they are hemorrhages. Continued leakage from these capillaries leads to the formation of exudates, which are fluid deposits rich in protein and cellular material, often seen as yellow spots near the outer retinal layers, a condition known as diabetic macular edema (DME).

Manual diagnosis of DR is time-consuming and resource-intensive. However, computer-aided diagnosis can greatly reduce both time and costs. In recent years, machine learning and deep learning have proven to be highly effective tools in this domain [4–6]. Traditionally, the gold standard for DR classification has been standard color fundus photography, which provides a 30 to 50-degree field of view encompassing the macula and optic nerve. However, ultra-widefield (UWF) fundus imaging, which offers a broader 200-degree view of the retina, has emerged as an advantageous alternative.

Despite various methods proposed for detecting DR in retinal fundus images, the task remains challenging [3]. Key difficulties stem from the spherical shape of the eye, leading to uneven lighting—brighter in the center and darker at the periphery—as well as low image contrast and the small size of lesions such as microaneurysms. Further, normal retinal structures share visual similarities with pathological features like exudates and hemorrhages or DR-related features can sometimes be distorted by image pre-processing techniques, making detection even more complex.

2 Details on the MICCAI UWF4DR 2024 Challenge

The ultra-widefield fundus images for diabetic retinopathy (UWF4DR) challenge is associated with the International Conference on Medical Image Computing and Computer-Assisted Intervention (MICCAI)[1]. In this challenge, the objective was to classify ultra-widefield (UWF) fundus images and consisted of three tasks. Task 1 involved determining image quality, distinguishing between poor quality (label 0) and good quality (label 1). Task 2 required classifying images based on the presence of DR (label 1) or absence (label 0). Task 3 focused on identifying the presence (label 1) or absence of DME (label 0).

Participants were provided with a training dataset, which was utilized for model development. Additionally, a separate validation dataset was used for performance evaluation and a public leaderboard score. The validation data remained unknown to the participants throughout the competition (Table 1). In the end, the participants could run their proposed model on the test set with a hidden leaderboard. Despite our limited GPU resources, our models achieved 5th, 7th, and 6th place on the public leaderboard, respectively.

Table 1. Different Tasks in the MICCAI Challenge.

Task	Name	Training Set	Validation Set
1	Image quality assessment for ultra-widefield fundus	434	61
2	Identification of referable diabetic retinopathy	201	50
3	Identification of diabetic macular edema	167	45

---

[1] https://codalab.lisn.upsaclay.fr/competitions/18605.

To evaluate the performance of the models comprehensively, the Area Under the Curve (AUC) and the average inference time per image was used as evaluation metrics. The ranking score is calculated as:

$$\text{Ranking Score} = \text{AUC} - 5\% \times \text{Time (seconds)}$$

Although the inference time provided by Codalab (challenge platform) serves as a reference, it may fluctuate. Therefore to ensure fairness, an average out of 100 iterations is calculated. A higher ranking score indicates better performance. Auxiliary metrics such as AUPRC, sensitivity, and specificity will be used as tie-breakers if needed.

3 Dataset

The UWF fundus images were provided as colored JPG files with a resolution of 800 × 1016 pixels. The dataset for task 1 consisted of 434 UWF fundus images. To enhance the dataset, we incorporated additional public data from the Deep-DRID dataset [7]. Label 5 in the Deep-DRID dataset indicated bad quality and we relabeled them as 0. DR is indicated as having different severity levels, which uses a scale of 0 to 4 and was changed to label 1. An example of both datasets can be found in the Appendix (Supplemental Fig. 11).

The dataset used for task 2 consisted of UWF4DR and Deep-DRID. Images labeled with 0 indicated no presence of DR, while those labeled with 1 indicated the presence of DR. As we had a binary task, we also had to change the Deep-DRID labels. Zero was kept 0 for no DR, and 1–4 was changed into 1, for DR. Example images for both labels can be seen in Fig. 1.

For task 3, we utilized a dataset consisting of 167 UWF fundus images as provided: 77 images with DME (labeled as 1), and 90 images without DME (labeled as 0) (see Appendix Supplemental Fig. 12). Table 2 presents the distribution of image labels for every task in both datasets.

Table 2. Label Distribution Across UWF4DR and Deep-DRID Datasets.

Task	Label	UWF4DR	Deep-DRID	Total
Task 1	0	205	4	**209**
	1	229	198	**427**
	Total	**434**	**202**	**636**
Task 2	0	89	60	**149**
	1	112	138	**250**
	Total	**201**	**198**	**399**
Task 3	0	90	–	**90**
	1	77	–	**77**
	Total	**167**	–	**167**

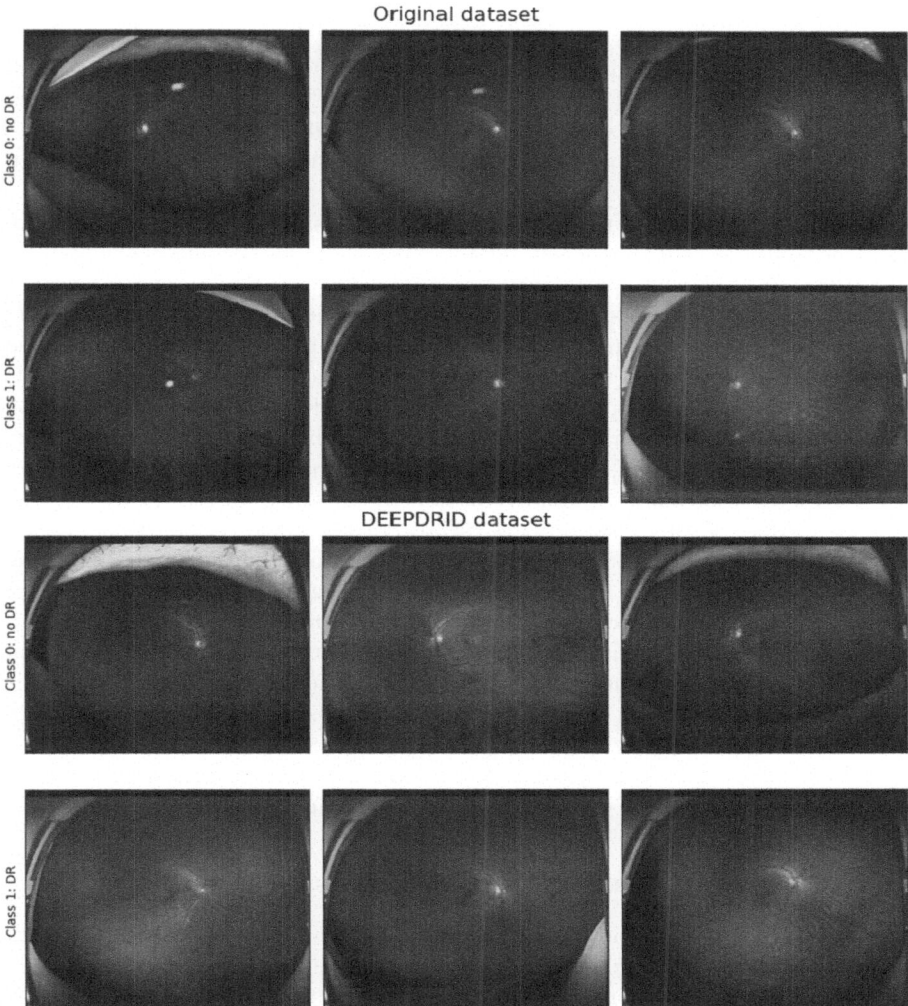

Fig. 1. UWF fundus images (task 2). Patients that have DR versus not. Additionally, we also included images from Deep-DRID.

4 Method

We used different data augmentations for preprocessing and a different model for each task as different models seem to be superior at each task. We used an Automorph model for defining the quality of image, ShuffleNet for identifying DR and an EfficientNet for DME.

4.1 Preprocessing

Our data augmentation methods spanned from general computer vision techniques to more specialized medical imaging approaches. For the quality assessment, we resized the images to 800x800 using zero padding to preserve the aspect ratio. Additionally, we applied random horizontal and vertical flips to augment the data.

To focus the model on relevant retinal structures for detecting DR, we used GIMP to apply an elliptical mask, setting areas of the image outside the pupil - specifically those showing parts of the imaging device - to 0. This step effectively eliminates unnecessary background information. Each image is masked before entering the augmentation pipeline. For data augmentation, we first applied a residual Gaussian blur with 0.5 probability, which adds each image to its own blurred version. Next, Contrast Limited Adaptive Histogram Equalization (CLAHE) was used to enhance local contrast - again with probability 0.5. Furthermore, each image had a 50% chance of undergoing a horizontal flip and a one-third chance of being randomly rotated by an angle uniformly distributed between $-10°$ and $+10°$, introducing variation to enhance model robustness.

A series of pre-processing steps were applied to help the model focus on features relevant to DME. Initially, we applied histogram equalization to half of the images, followed by geometric transformations (random horizontal flips).

All images were normalized using the ImageNet mean and standard deviation. These steps aimed to enhance the model's ability to identify DR and DME while minimizing false positives due to artifacts or noise. It should be mentioned, that we had limited hardware resources and therefore focused on constructing a pipeline consisting of several hardware-resource efficient neural architectures, which we could train with our limited number of available GPUs.

4.2 Automorph Model: Image Quality Assessment

We utilized the AutoMorph model [8] for the image quality assessment. AutoMorph is based on the EfficientNetB4 architecture [9] and features a fully connected head for feature extraction and a final output layer that produces a single scalar value. AutoMorph, a publicly available model, is designed for automated analysis of retinal vascular morphology on fundus images, aiding research in both ophthalmic and systemic diseases. AutoMorph was pretrained on two large image quality grading datasets: EyePACS-Q [10] (28,792 fundus images) and DDR-test [11] (13,673 fundus images), which allowed us to leverage the model's robust feature extraction capabilities for our image quality assessment task. The method pipeline for the task 1 can be seen in Fig. 2.

4.3 ShuffleNet for Diabetic Retinopathy

We implemented the ShuffleNet architecture [12], a computation-efficient convolutional neural network (CNN) that leverages group convolutions, channel

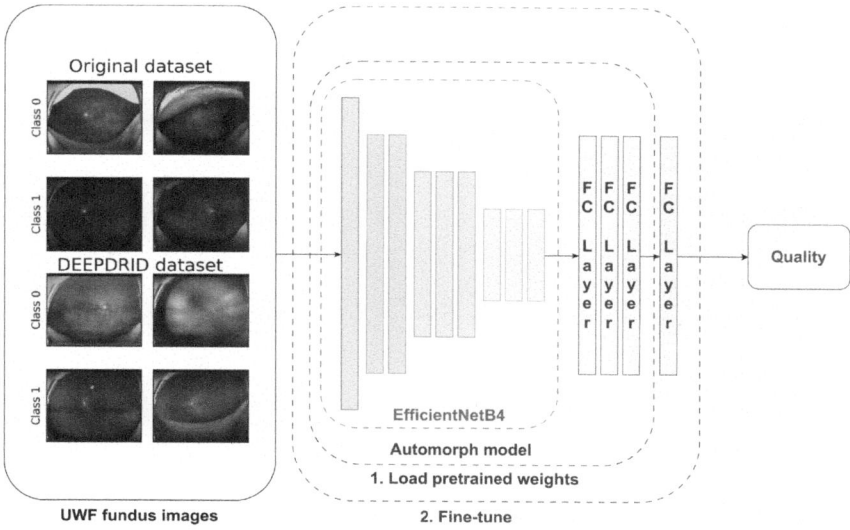

Fig. 2. The framework of our proposed method for image quality assessment.

shuffling, and depthwise separable convolutions to reduce the number of parameters and computational cost while maintaining performance. After loading the pretrained model, we fine-tuned it on our dataset, modifying the final fully connected layer to output a single scalar value corresponding to the binary classification task. The ShuffleNet model was initialized with weights pretrained on the ImageNet dataset. Pretraining on ImageNet allows the model to leverage robust feature extraction capabilities developed from a large and diverse dataset (Fig. 3).

4.4 EfficientNetB0 for Diabetic Macular Edema

We proposed the use of EfficientNetB0 [9], pre-trained on ImageNet [13]. EfficientNet combines the concept of compound scaling, mobile inverted bottleneck convolutional layers, and squeeze-and-excitation modules to enhance both accuracy and efficiency, specifically reducing CPU time measured on the leaderboard. The final output of the model is a binary classification indicating the presence or absence of DME. We employed transfer learning by initializing the model with weights pre-trained on the ImageNet dataset. This pre-training provided a strong foundation for feature extraction, improving the model's ability to recognize relevant patterns. The method pipeline for task 3 can be seen in Fig. 4.

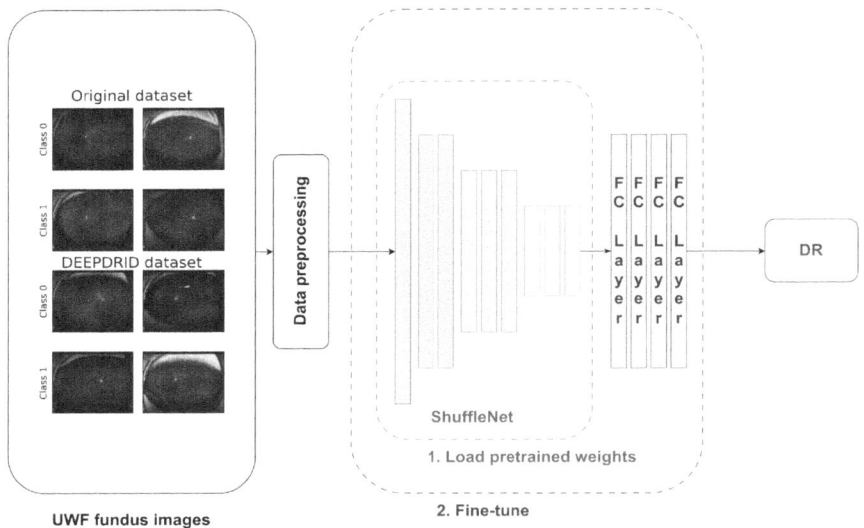

Fig. 3. The framework of our proposed method for DR identification.

5 Results

After training (for training details see Appendix A.1), model predictions were evaluated on the public leaderboard during the validation phase, which served as a test scenario to evaluate our methods and ensure that our code submission was in the correct format. The best models in the validation phase were then evaluated in the test phase with a hidden leaderboard, to assess generalization to unseen data.

Our model performed well in assessing the quality in our validation set and the public leaderboard with a score of 0.9326 (Table 3). The successful classification of image quality is essential for filtering out suboptimal images and ensuring that only the best-quality data is used for DR and DME analysis. What stands out, is a lot of images were determined as good quality but were in fact bad quality (false positive) (Table 4), which is also obvious with the specificity or true negative rate.

Early detection of DR can prevent progression to more severe stages and complications such as DME. When evaluating our model on the leaderboard, we achieved strong results in detecting DR, with a classification score of 0.9770 during the validation phase and 0.9842 in the test phase (Table 3). In the training phase, this had the lowest false positive and false negative amount of images. These results highlight the robustness of our model suggesting that the model generalizes well to unseen data.

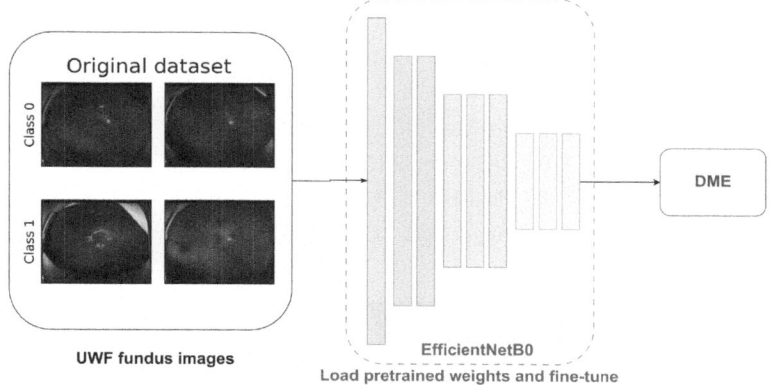

Fig. 4. The framework of our proposed method for DME classification.

As DME can lead to significant vision impairment if left untreated, its accurate diagnosis is essential in managing DR. Our method demonstrated strong performance in detecting DME, as evidenced by the consistent results across the validation and leaderboard datasets with 0.9643 and 0.9820, respectively (Table 3). As with DR we have more false negative images, which is worrisome because the disease might not be detected in a clinical setting.

These findings confirm the effectiveness of our approach in identifying both DR and its complications, offering a reliable tool for automated diagnosis (Fig. 6).

Table 3. Performance metrics of the best submission on our validation sets as well as on the public leaderboard

Metric	Task 1			Task 2			Task 3		
	Training	Leaderboard		Training	Leaderboard		Training	Leaderboard	
		Validation Phase	Test Phase		Validation Phase	Test Phase		Validation Phase	Test Phase
AUROC	0.9898	0.9326	0.9326	1.0000	0.9770	0.9842	1.0000	0.9643	0.9820
AUPRC	0.9949	0.9546	0.9546	1.0000	0.9881	0.9814	1.0000	0.9687	0.9800
Sensitivity	0.9767	0.9322	0.9322	1.0000	0.9310	0.9483	1.0000	0.8750	0.9000
Specificity	0.9762	0.8000	0.8000	1.0000	1.0000	0.9577	1.0000	0.9524	1.0000
CPU Time	-	0.5590	0.4853	-	0.1146	0.0778	-	0.3159	0.3630
Total	-	0.9326	0.9326	-	0.9770	0.9842	-	0.9643	0.9820

Table 4. Confusion Matrix

Task	Training			Validation		
	1	2	3	1	2	3
True Positive	42	23	16	37	29	22
True Negative	39	15	18	13	22	11
False Positive	2	3	0	12	1	1
False Negative	4	0	0	4	3	5

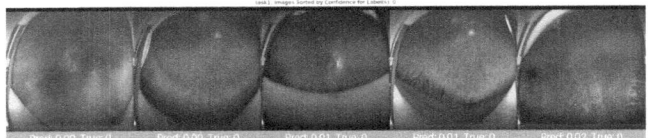

Fig. 5. Prototypes for poor quality (Validation Phase). Images that are blurred, over- or underexposed or where the person was blinking were classified correctly by our model.

6 Discussion

Catching DR in its earlier stages allows for treatment that can slow or halt progression before it reaches a more severe state, reducing the risk of complications such as DME or proliferative diabetic retinopathy.

We first focused on image quality assessment, which is essential to ensure that the images used in diagnosis are clear and usable. One of the most common issues leading to poor-quality images is blinking during image capture, resulting in images obscured by the eyelid or eyelashes. Additionally, other factors like blurring, under- or overexposure, and the presence of artifacts can severely affect image quality. These issues can compromise the model's ability to make accurate predictions and highlight the importance of filtering out suboptimal images before analysis (Fig. 5).

In the confusion matrix (Table 4), there were more false positives than false negatives identified for the training set. When we look at the images, which were falsely classified as poor quality (false negatives), we could see green holes/spots, which could be artifacts, or laser photocoagulation after intervention (Fig. 7). Whereas, looking at misclassified as good quality (false positive), the culprit is harder to find. The Automorph model probably could not identify large black segments in the lower part of the picture as negative.

During our training, we observed that for poor-quality images, the model, using the Grad-CAM [14] visualization technique (Fig. 8), focused primarily around the periphery of the macula in cases where the eyes were only partially closed due to blinking. Despite the challenges, the model correctly labeled these images as class 0. Notably, there was a prominent line in the lower region of the image where the model placed significant importance, which appeared to resem-

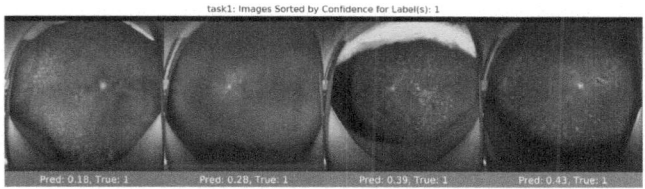

Fig. 6. Criticism for Quality Control (Training Phase): Some images exhibit artifacts that were incorrectly classified as poor quality, even though they should have been identified as good quality. This misclassification represents a false negative.

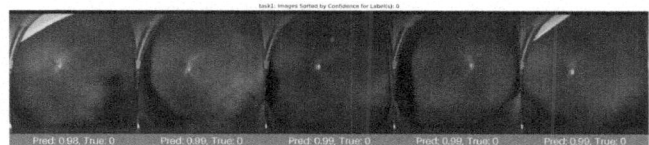

Fig. 7. Criticism for Quality Control (Validation Phase): Instances of false positives, where images of poor quality were mistakenly classified as good quality.

ble lens-related artifacts. It is possible that these artifacts, along with blinking, served as clear indicators for the Automorph model to classify the images as poor quality during training. However, these were not the case for the validation phase (people blinking, dirty lens), and the model consistently classified such images as positive.

Next, we focused on identifying DR. The Grad-CAM images (Fig. 9, and Supplemental Fig. 13) showed that the model was attending to the correct regions of the macula during its decision-making process. Small, localized areas of attention were consistent with known pathological features such as microaneurysms and hemorrhages. These findings suggest that the model successfully learned to detect these early signs of DR, which is crucial for accurate screening.

In the confusion matrix (Table 4), we observed a higher number of false positives compared to false negatives during training. From a medical perspective, this is a favorable outcome. In screening applications, it is generally better for a model to overestimate the presence of disease (false positives) rather than underestimate it (false negatives). Missing a case of DR (a false negative) could lead to delayed diagnosis and treatment, increasing the risk of visual impairment. False positives, while requiring further examination, are less harmful, as they ensure that no cases of DR are missed, providing an extra layer of caution in clinical practice. The validation phase showed a shift toward more false negatives. This change is concerning because, in clinical practice, false negatives pose a greater risk. The change in error patterns between the training and validation phases might suggest potential overfitting. In the training phase, the model may have been more conservative (leading to more false positives), but the validation

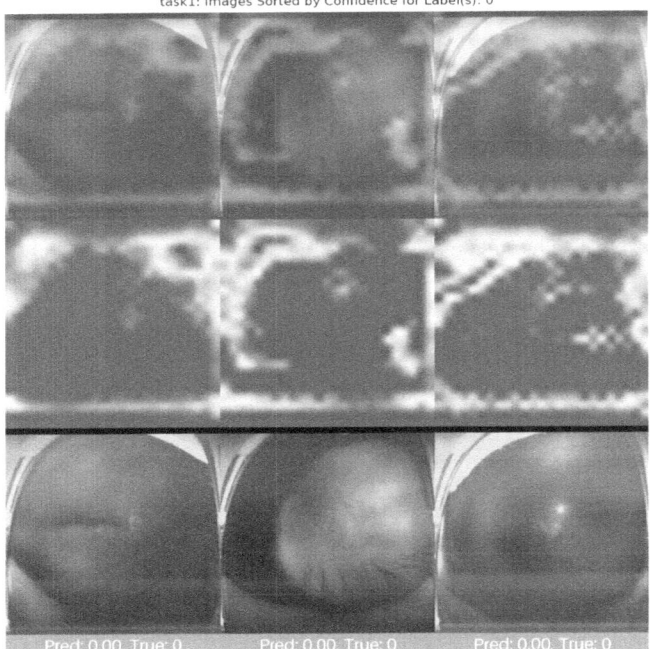

Fig. 8. Training Phase: Grad-CAM of poor quality images: overlay, grad-CAM, and original image (from top to bottom).

phase shows an increase in false negatives, which indicates the model might not generalize well to new, unseen data.

Lastly, classifying DME showed a different pattern of attention in the Grad-CAM visualizations. Here, the model focused on flat areas where exudates, which are lipid or protein deposits, tend to accumulate. The model's ability to concentrate on these regions indicates that it could effectively identify DME based on key retinal features (Fig. 10 and Supplemental Fig. 14).

One challenge we encountered during the training process was early overfitting of the model. To address this, we employed several strategies tailored to the dataset. These included using cross-validation, applying various data augmentation techniques, and incorporating the Deep-DRID dataset for both image quality and identification of DR to increase data diversity. We also experimented with different learning rate schedulers, such as ReduceOnPlateau, CosineAnnealingLR, and StepLR, as well as multiple loss functions, including BCELoss with class weights, FocalLoss, and SmoothL1 Loss.

Additionally, we utilized pre-trained models, such as those trained on ImageNet or Automorph, and explored reducing the model complexity to prevent overfitting. The results presented in this paper represent the best outcomes from this extensive screening process. One avenue we have yet to explore is ensemble

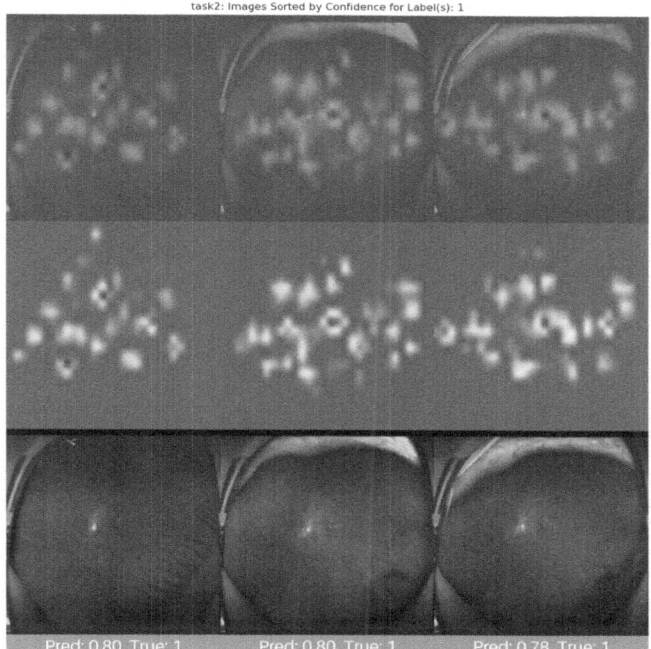

Fig. 9. Validation Phase: Grad-CAM of DR assessment: overlay, grad-CAM, and original image (from top to bottom).

learning, which could further improve model robustness and performance. This remains an important direction for future work. Further validation on larger datasets and in diverse clinical settings remains also necessary to confirm the generalizability of our approach.

In conclusion, our results highlight the importance of ensuring high-quality images for accurate diagnosis, while the Grad-CAM visualizations provide insights into the model's decision-making process across different tasks. The balance between false positives and false negatives in medical models is crucial, and our model's tendency to generate more false positives aligns with the overarching goal of minimizing missed diagnoses in DR screening. While our current model demonstrates effectiveness in detecting changes in DR, there is significant potential for enhancement. The challenges we encountered and the alternative approaches we explored provide valuable insights for future research directions in this critical area of ophthalmological image analysis.

7 Link to Public Code Repository

The implementation of our method, along with the pre-trained models and evaluation scripts, is available at the following public repository:

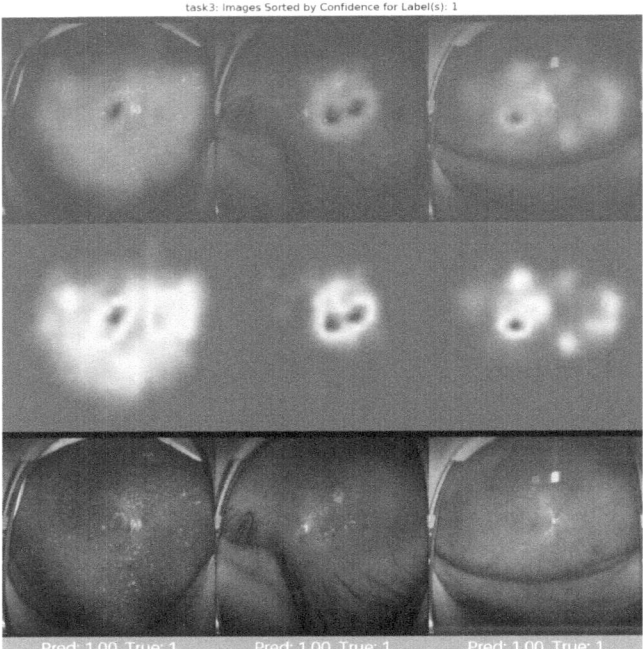

Fig. 10. Validation Phase: Grad-CAM of DME assessment: overlay, grad-CAM, and original image (from top to bottom).

https://github.com/moritsih/AILS-MICCAI-UWF4DR-Challenge.git

Acknowledgments. This research was supported by the Institute for Machine Learning of the Johannes Kepler University Linz. We are specifically grateful to Andreas Mayr and Niklas Schmidinger for their continued feedback and support and to Christian Huber for his valuable feedback and insightful suggestions.

Disclosure of Interests. The authors declare no competing interests.

A Appendix

A.1 Training Details

We randomly split the dataset of the training phase into an 80:20 ratio for training and validation. The model accuracy and generalization capabilities were tested on an independent but identical distributed validation dataset, those results were then evaluated on a public test server. The best models from the validation phase could be submitted in the test phase, where they were evaluated on a hidden leaderboard.

To avoid overfitting, we selected the model state that yielded the lowest loss on the validation split. For image quality assessment, training was initialized with a learning rate of 1×10^{-4}. The model was trained for 40 epochs with a batch size of 4, achieving the best validation loss at epoch 9. A learning rate scheduler was employed to reduce the learning rate by a factor of 0.5 if no improvement in validation loss was observed for five consecutive epochs, helping to prevent overfitting by fine-tuning the model during periods of stagnation.

For assessment of DR, the loss function combined Binary Cross-Entropy (BCE) loss and Smooth L1 loss, with equal weights of 0.5 for each. The initial learning rate was set to 1×10^{-3}, with a reduction factor of 0.5 when the validation loss plateaued. However, the model continued to improve, so the learning rate did not reduce. The training was carried out with a batch size of 32 for 25 epochs. To address class imbalance, we applied an oversampling strategy to equalize the classes in the dataset. The best validation loss was achieved at epoch 24, with most images being classified correctly.

For identifying DME, our best submission utilized EfficientNetB0. The model was trained for 20 epochs with a batch size of 8, achieving optimal performance at epoch 12. A learning rate scheduler adjusted the learning rate when validation loss stopped improving, reducing it from 1×10^{-4} to 5×10^{-5} as training progressed. We employed BCEWithLogitsLoss, which combines a Sigmoid layer with BCELoss, as the loss function. The AdamW [15] optimizer was used.

A.2 Supplemental Materials

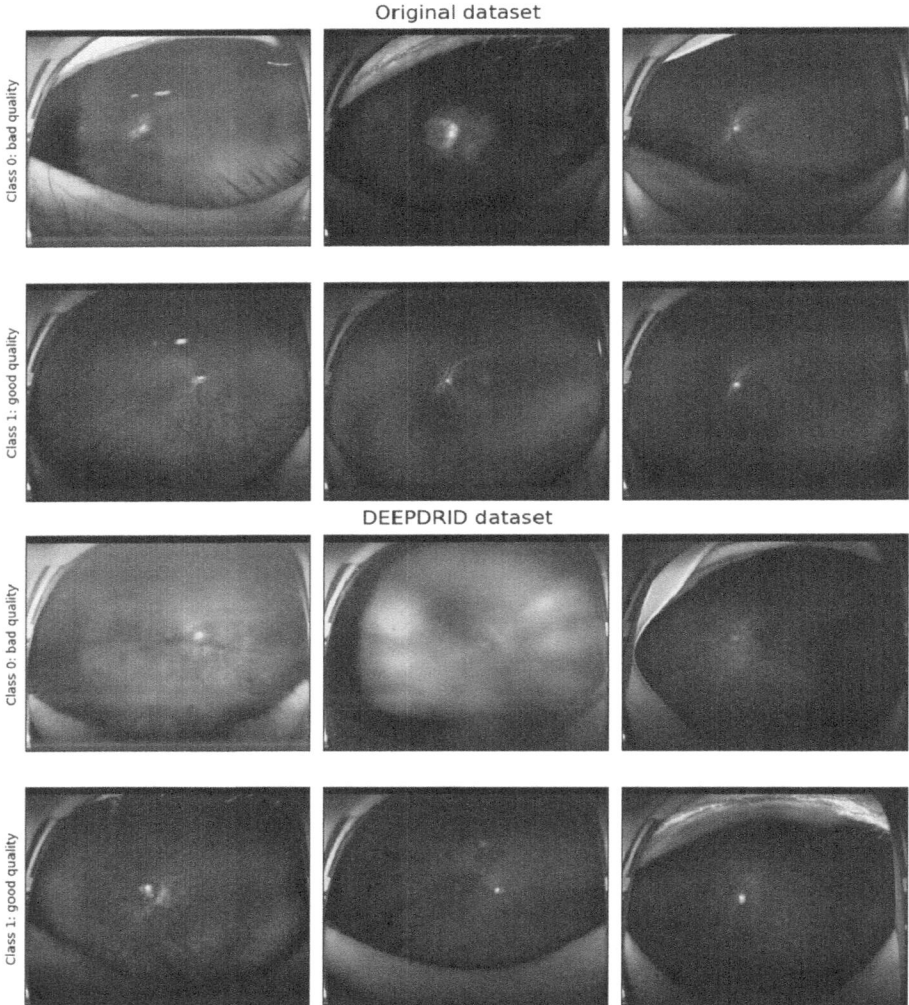

Fig. 11. UWF fundus image from Task 1.

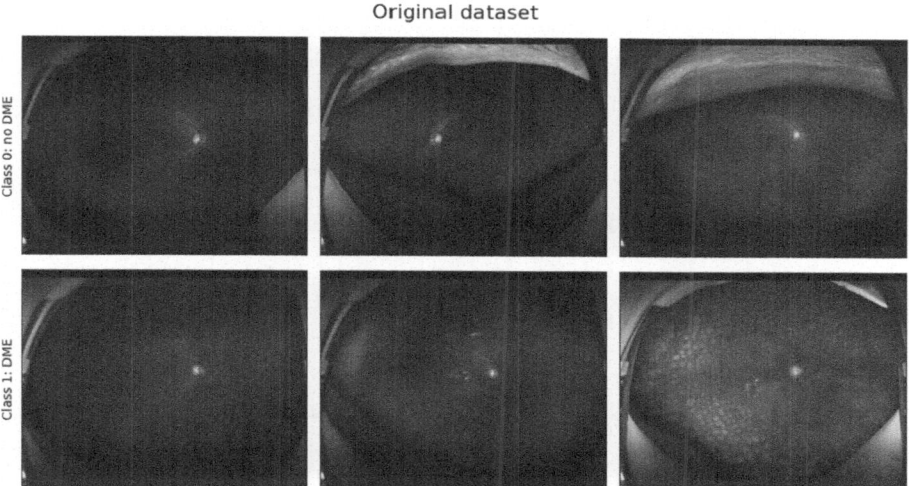

Fig. 12. UWF fundus image from Task 3.

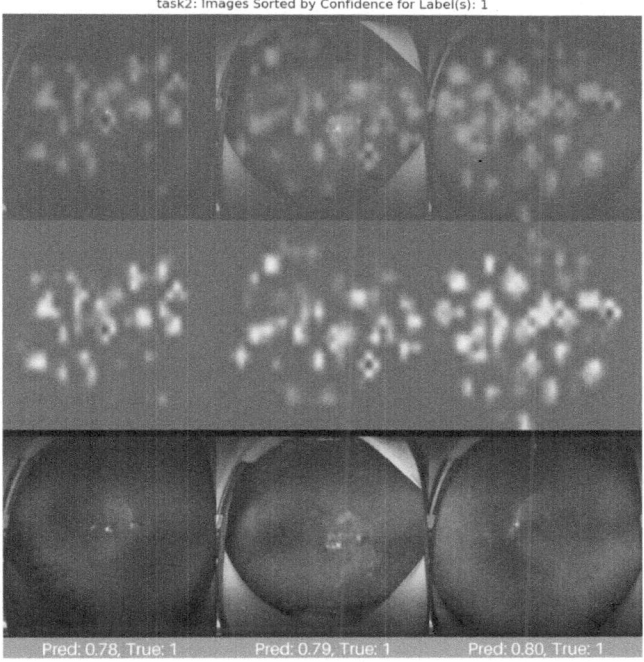

Fig. 13. Training Phase: Grad-CAM of Task 2 - DR (labeled 1): overlay, grad-CAM, and original image (from top to bottom).

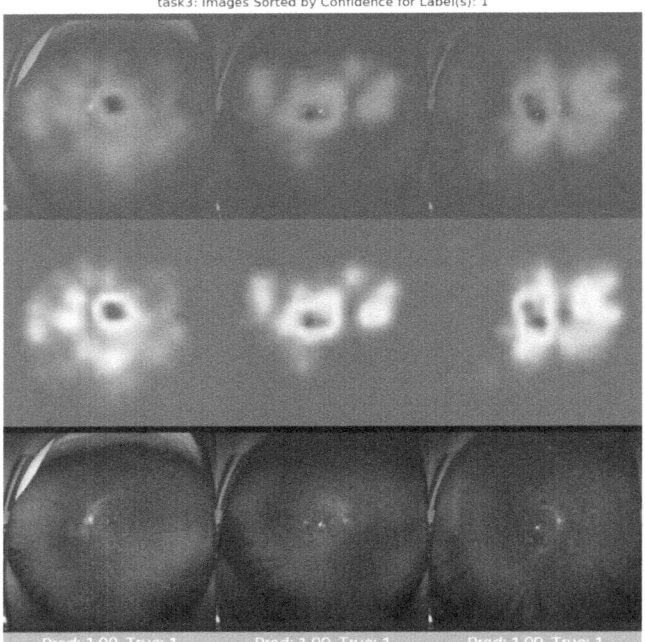

Fig. 14. Training Phase: Grad-CAM of Task 3 - DME (labeled 1): overlay, grad-CAM, and original image (from top to bottom).

References

1. Teo, Z.L., et al.: Global prevalence of diabetic retinopathy and projection of burden through 2045: Systematic review and meta-analysis. Ophthalmology **128**(11), 1580–1591 (2021)
2. Ning, C., Paul, M., Tien, Y.W.: Diabetic retinopathy. Lancet (London, Engl.) **376**, 124–136 (2010)
3. Chetoui, M., Akhloufi, M.A.: Explainable end-to-end deep learning for diabetic retinopathy detection across multiple datasets. J. Med. Imaging (Bellingham, Wash.) **7**(8) (2020)
4. Farahat, Z., et al.: A Systematic Review. Survey of Ophthalmology, Diabetic Retinopathy Screening through Artificial Intelligence Algorithms (2024)
5. Ting, D., et al.: Development and validation of a deep learning system for diabetic retinopathy and related eye diseases using retinal images from multiethnic populations with diabetes. JAMA **318**(12), 2211–2223 (2017)
6. Lin, D., et al.: Application of comprehensive artificial intelligence retinal expert (care) system: a national real-world evidence study. Lancet Digit. Health **3**(8), e486–e495 (2021)
7. Liu, R., et al.: Diabetic retinopathy-grading and image quality estimation challenge. Patterns **3**(6), 100512 (2022)
8. Zhou, Y., et al.: Automorph: automated retinal vascular morphology quantification via a deep learning pipeline. Transl. Vis. Sci. Technol. **11**(7) (2022)

9. Tan, M., Le, Q.: Efficientnet: rethinking model scaling for convolutional neural networks. In: 36th International Conference on Machine Learning, vol. 5 ,pp. 10691–10700. ICML 2019, 2019-June (2019)
10. Fu, H., et al.: Evaluation of retinal image quality assessment networks in different color-spaces. In: Medical Image Computing and Computer Assisted Intervention – MICCAI 2019, pages 48–56. Springer, Cham (2019)
11. Li, T., Gao, Y., Wang, K., Guo, S., Liu, H., Kang, H.: Diagnostic assessment of deep learning algorithms for diabetic retinopathy screening. Inf. Sci. **501**, 511–522 (2019)
12. Zhang, X., Zhou, X., Lin, M., Sun, J.: Shufflenet: an extremely efficient convolutional neural network for mobile devices. In: Proceedings of the IEEE Computer Society Conference on Computer Vision and Pattern Recognition, vol. 7, pp. 6848–6856 (2017)
13. Deng, J., Dong, W., Socher, R., Li, L.J., Li, K., Fei, L.F.: Imagenet: a large-scale hierarchical image database. In: 2009 IEEE Conference on Computer Vision and Pattern Recognition, CVPR 2009, pp. 248–255 (2009)
14. Selvaraju, R.R., Cogswell, M., Das, A., Vedantam, R., Parikh, D., Batra, D.: Gradcam: visual explanations from deep networks via gradient-based localization. In: 2017 IEEE International Conference on Computer Vision (ICCV), pp. 618–626 (2017)
15. Loshchilov, I., Hutter, F.: Decoupled weight decay regularization. In: International Conference on Learning Representations (2017)

Efficient Deep Learning Models for Ultra-widefield Fundus Imaging for Diabetic Retinopathy

Abdul Qayyum[1]($\boxtimes$), Moona Mazher[2], and Steven A. Niederer[1]

[1] National Heart and Lung Institute, Faculty of Medicine, Imperial College London, London, UK
a.qayyum@imperial.ac.uk
[2] Centre for Medical Image Computing, Department of Computer Science, University College London, London, UK

Abstract. Diabetic retinopathy (DR) is a leading cause of preventable blindness among working-age adults, with global cases expected to rise from 103 million in 2020 to 161 million by 2045. Early detection and treatment are essential for preventing vision loss. While color fundus photography (CFP) is the gold standard for DR diagnosis, ultra-widefield (UWF) fundus imaging, which provides up to a 200-degree view of the retina, is gaining traction as an alternative. However, classifying UWF images remains labor-intensive, and research on automated analysis is limited. In this study, we trained several deep-learning models for DR detection and assessment using UWF imaging. For Task 1, Image Quality Assessment, we utilized the DINOv2 models due to their ability to efficiently manage complex features while maintaining computational efficiency. For Task 2, Identification of Referable DR, we employed MobileNetV3, which stood out for its lightweight architecture and advanced features like Squeeze-and-Excitation modules and H-Swish activation. MobileNetV3 achieved high accuracy with minimal computational requirements, making it well-suited for clinical deployment in resource-limited environments. To further enhance the model performance, we applied test-time augmentation (TTA) during inference, improving robustness and accuracy in challenging cases. This approach offers a powerful and efficient solution for DR classification and detection in UWF fundus images. Our proposed model ranked second in identifying referable DR on the final test dataset. Souce code is available at https://github.com/RespectKnowledge/UWF4DR_Challenge_2nd_place.

Keywords: MobileNetV3 · DINOv2 · Pretrained Deep Learning models · Ultra-Widefield Fundus Imaging · Test-Time Augmentation

1 Introduction

Diabetic retinopathy (DR), a common complication of diabetes, is a leading cause of preventable blindness in working-age adults [1]. In 2020, an estimated 103 million people worldwide had DR, with this number expected to rise to 130 million by 2030 and

161 million by 2045 [2, 3]. DR is classified into five stages based on the International Clinical Diabetic Retinopathy (ICDR) system, with a referable DR (RDR) including moderate nonproliferative DR and diabetic macular edema (DME) [4]. Early screening, timely referral, and treatment are crucial to prevent vision loss [5]. Standard color fundus photography (CFP), covering 30 to 50 degrees of the retina, remains the gold standard for DR classification [6].

Deep learning techniques for DR classification using color fundus photography (CFP) have made significant progress [7, 8]. However, ultra-widefield (UWF) fundus imaging, which captures up to 200 degrees of the retina, offers a promising alternative for DR management. UWF imaging aligns with the standard 7-field images from the Early Treatment Diabetic Retinopathy Study and reduces ungradable images compared to CFP [9–11]. Yet, classifying UWF images is labor-intensive and time-consuming for human graders, and research on computer-aided analysis for UWF imaging remains limited.

To advance automatic diabetic retinopathy (DR) analysis using ultra-widefield (UWF) fundus images, a challenge has been organized, inviting researchers to develop algorithms for key DR-related tasks. These tasks include image quality assessment, DR classification, and diabetic macular edema (DME) classification. Image quality assessment ensures that only high-quality images are used for further analysis, while the classification of DR and DME forms the foundation for automated diagnosis, significantly aiding DR patient management. This challenge marks an important milestone in DR analysis with UWF imaging, aiming to foster innovation and progress in medical image analysis. Our proposed approach leverages various pre-trained deep learning models [12–17] for DR classification and image quality assessment. These models, originally trained on ImageNet, were fine-tuned using the challenge dataset to enhance performance and accuracy in this critical domain.

2 Proposed Method

2.1 Dataset

For the UWF4DR challenge, we used two distinct datasets tailored to the specific tasks of Image Quality Assessment and the Identification of Referable Diabetic Retinopathy (DR).

2.2 Task 1: Image Quality Assessment

Training Data: The dataset for training comprised 434 ultra-widefield fundus images. This set was designed to teach the model how to evaluate the quality of fundus images, determining whether they are suitable for further diagnostic analysis. Notably, 201 of these images were shared with the dataset for Task 2, ensuring that the model was exposed to a consistent set of images for both tasks.

Validation Data: A separate set of 61 images was used for validation, allowing us to assess the model's performance on image quality assessment independently of the training data.

2.3 Task 2: Identification of Referable Diabetic Retinopathy

Training Data: The training dataset for this task included 201 images. These images were specifically selected to train the model in identifying cases of referable diabetic retinopathy, where the disease has progressed to a stage that requires medical intervention. This dataset overlaps with Task 1, utilizing the same 201 images to ensure consistency in how the images were presented to the model.

Validation Data: For validation, a distinct set of 50 images was employed. This smaller set was used to evaluate the model's ability to accurately identify referable diabetic retinopathy in new, unseen images, providing a measure of its generalization capability.

These datasets were carefully curated and split to ensure that the model could effectively learn and generalize the tasks of image quality assessment and the identification of referable diabetic retinopathy.

2.4 Model Selection and Training

2.5 ResNet

ResNet (Residual Networks) is known for its deep architecture that addresses the vanishing gradient problem using residual connections. Despite its depth and powerful feature extraction capabilities, ResNet did not perform as well as other models in our experiments, particularly on Task 1 (Image Quality Assessment) and Task 2 (Identification of Referable DR).

2.6 DenseNet

DenseNet (Densely Connected Convolutional Networks) builds on the concept of dense connections between layers, which allows for improved information flow and gradient propagation. Although DenseNet provided decent results, it still fell short of the performance achieved by MobileNetV3.

2.7 EfficientNet

EfficientNet, which scales the depth, width, and resolution of networks in a balanced manner, offers competitive performance. Its efficiency in balancing accuracy and computational cost made it a strong contender, yet MobileNetV3 [16] still outperformed it in our tasks.

2.8 MobileNetV3

MobileNetV3 emerged as the top performer among the models tested. Designed for mobile and edge devices, MobileNetV3 combines depthwise separable convolutions and squeeze-and-excitation modules to optimize both accuracy and efficiency. When fine-tuned on our ultra-widefield fundus imaging dataset, MobileNetV3 achieved superior performance on both the validation and test datasets for Task 2.

2.9 Transformer-Based Models

While Transformer-based models, particularly Vision Transformers (ViTs), have shown great promise in recent computer vision tasks [13], their performance in our study did not surpass that of MobileNetV3. Transformers are typically more data-hungry and computationally intensive, which may have contributed to their relatively lower performance in this context.

2.10 Performance Improvement with Test-Time Augmentation (TTA)

To further enhance the performance of MobileNetV3, we implemented Test-Time Augmentation (TTA), a technique that generates multiple augmented versions of each test image—through methods like rotations, flips, and scaling—and averages the predictions across these variations. This approach increases the model's robustness by accounting for variations in image appearance that may affect predictions. During TTA implementation, we applied augmentations such as horizontal and vertical flips, slight rotations, and adjustments to brightness and contrast, creating diverse perspectives of the same image. This allowed the model to make more informed predictions by aggregating results from these different views. The inclusion of TTA led to a noticeable improvement in performance metrics, including accuracy, sensitivity, and specificity, particularly in Task 2. This improvement was most significant in cases where the original image quality was suboptimal or when subtle features needed to be identified for accurate classification of diabetic retinopathy.

2.11 Model Architecture

MobileNetV3 comes in two versions: MobileNetV3-Large and MobileNetV3-Small, each tailored for different levels of resource constraints. Here, we'll focus on the general architecture and key components that make MobileNetV3 particularly effective. Figure 1 shows the overall diagram of the proposed solution.

2.12 Inverted Residuals with Linear Bottlenecks

This concept was introduced in MobileNetV2 and continues to play a central role in MobileNetV3. Inverted residuals reduce the computational burden by applying convolutions in a high-dimensional space (expanding the input channels) and then projecting back to a low-dimensional space. The linear bottleneck layer helps maintain the expressiveness of the network while reducing the dimensionality of the feature space, which is critical for efficient computation.

2.13 Squeeze-and-Excitation (SE) Modules

SE modules are integrated into the network to adaptively recalibrate channel-wise feature responses. This is achieved by weighting each channel according to its importance, which enhances the model's ability to focus on relevant features. In MobileNetV3, SE modules are selectively applied in certain layers, balancing the trade-off between complexity and accuracy.

2.14 Hard-Swish Activation

While previous versions used ReLU as the activation function, MobileNetV3 introduces Hard-Swish (H-Swish), which is a computationally efficient approximation of the Swish activation function. H-Swish is defined as H-Swish(x) = x * ReLU6(x + 3)/6, where ReLU6 clamps the input to the range [0, 6]. This activation function retains the smoothness of Swish while being easier to compute, especially on low-power devices.

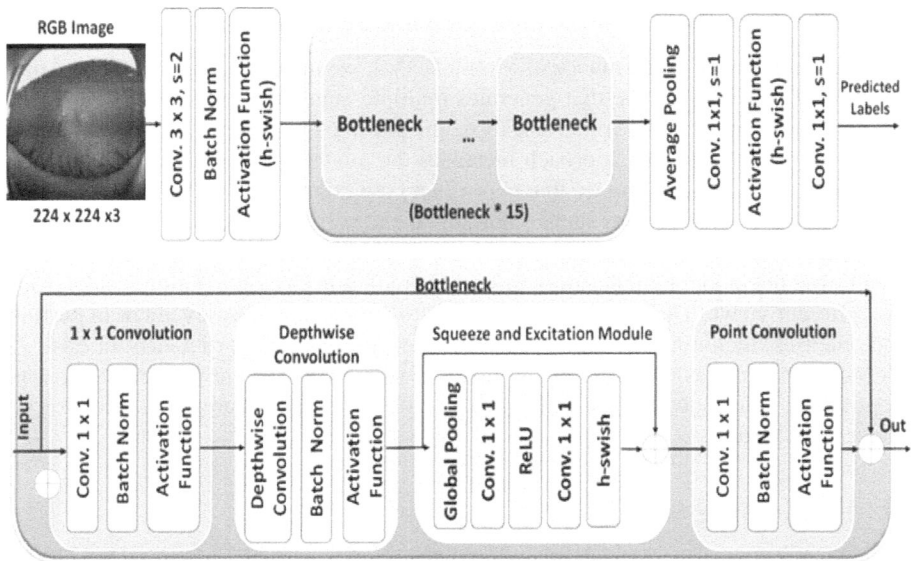

Fig. 1. The MobileNetV3 model for Image Quality Assessment and Identification of Referable Diabetic Retinopathy.

2.15 Network Scaling

MobileNetV3 employs a compound scaling strategy where the network's depth, width, and resolution are scaled uniformly. This allows for more flexibility in optimizing the network for various deployment scenarios, depending on the available computational resources. The final stages of MobileNetV3 [18] include a lightweight head that consists of a pooling layer followed by a fully connected layer. This design is optimized for efficiency while ensuring that the network captures high-level features effectively. A significant portion of MobileNetV3's design was informed by Neural Architecture Search (NAS), which systematically explores different network configurations to identify the most efficient structure for mobile devices.

2.16 Training Process and Fine-Tuning

For the UWF4DR challenge, we fine-tuned MobileNetV3, initially pretrained on the ImageNet dataset, for the specific tasks of ultra-widefield fundus image analysis. The training process began with dataset preparation, where the ultra-widefield fundus images were standardized in size and resolution to match the input dimensions required by MobileNetV3. Data augmentation techniques, including random rotations, flips, and adjustments to brightness and contrast, were applied to enhance the model's robustness. We employed transfer learning by initializing MobileNetV3 with ImageNet-pretrained weights, leveraging the model's general feature extraction capabilities, and adapting them to the specific characteristics of fundus images. The deeper layers of the network, containing more task-specific features, were fine-tuned with a lower learning rate to prevent catastrophic forgetting of the pretrained features. Optimization was carried out using the Adam optimizer, supplemented by a learning rate scheduler that adjusted the learning rate based on validation loss plateaus, ensuring effective convergence while minimizing the risk of overfitting. Cross-entropy loss was employed for classification tasks, along with regularization techniques like dropout and L2 weight regularization to improve generalization. Model performance was evaluated on both validation and test datasets, with metrics such as accuracy, precision, recall, and F1-score being tracked to assess the model's ability to identify referable diabetic retinopathy and evaluate image quality. To further boost performance, Test-Time Augmentation (TTA) was applied during inference, where each test image underwent multiple augmentations (e.g., rotations, flips, brightness changes), and the model's predictions were averaged across these augmented versions. This technique improved prediction robustness by mitigating the effects of minor image variations.

We employed a comprehensive data augmentation strategy to enhance model generalization for medical image analysis, particularly given the dataset's limitations. The training phase included resizing all images to 224×224 pixels to match the input size of MobileNetV3, followed by random cropping of the same dimensions to introduce slight positional variations. Horizontal and vertical flips, each with a 50% probability, were applied to account for orientation variability, along with random 90-degree rotations to improve the robustness of image orientation. A blur effect (30% probability) and coarse dropout (up to 12 holes of 20×20 pixels, 30% probability) were also included to simulate image quality variations and encourage reliance on broader features. For validation, only resizing was applied to ensure consistent evaluation. The model was trained for 200 epochs using the Adam optimizer, with weighted cross-entropy loss to address class imbalance. Although normalization and tensor conversion were part of the initial pipeline, they were ultimately not applied; however, they remain critical steps for ensuring faster convergence and optimal model performance in deep learning frameworks like PyTorch [19].

Throughout training, the model's performance was closely monitored on the validation set. Adjustments were made to the learning rate dynamically (using learning rate schedulers), particularly when the model seemed to plateau. This helped in fine-tuning the model further to achieve better accuracy. The combination of these data augmentation techniques, the use of a robust optimizer like Adam, and a carefully chosen loss function like weighted cross-entropy played a crucial role in the effective training and optimization of the MobileNetV3 model, leading to superior performance in the tasks at hand.

2.17 DINOv2 for Image Quality Assessment

The DINOv2 [20] models are a family of deep learning models pretrained for image classification tasks. These models are designed to classify images by extracting and analyzing key features, making them suitable for a range of visual tasks, including medical image analysis. DINOv2 models use lightweight, efficient architecture, balancing performance and computational resources. This enables them to handle complex visual features while remaining fast and scalable, making them ideal for real-time applications. In classification tasks, the DINOv2 models process input images through a series of convolutional layers that capture essential patterns and features. These layers help in distinguishing between different image quality levels or categories, such as in medical imaging or other quality assessment applications. Being pretrained on large datasets, DINOv2 models come with learned feature representations that improve their ability to generalize well across new tasks, such as image quality assessment, where image clarity and feature consistency are critical for making accurate classifications. These models are especially useful in applications requiring reliable and efficient image classification with minimal computational overhead, making them suitable for resource-constrained environments like clinical settings. For Task 1: Image Quality Assessment, the same training and optimization settings were applied to the DINOv2 models as those used for the MobileNetV3 models in Task 2. This included consistent configurations for learning rate, batch size, optimizer type, and data augmentation techniques across both tasks. By maintaining uniform training and optimization parameters, we ensured a fair comparison between models, allowing for accurate evaluation of their respective performances in image quality assessment and diabetic retinopathy detection tasks.

3 Results

The performance analysis of the models across two key tasks—Image Quality Assessment and Identification of Referable Diabetic Retinopathy (DR)—demonstrates the superiority of the DINOv2 and MobileNetV3 model families.

For Task 1: Image Quality Assessment, the DINOv2 models exhibited impressive performance, with the DINOv2_base model achieving an AUROC of 0.8671 and an AUPRC of 0.9093. This model also recorded a sensitivity of 0.7567 and a specificity of 0.8333, while maintaining a relatively low CPU time of 0.3016. The lightweight architecture of the DINOv2_base model was crucial in enabling its efficient processing of complex image features, making it highly suitable for deployment in resource-constrained clinical settings. Notably, the incorporation of Test-Time Augmentation (TTA) further boosted the model's performance, particularly in scenarios where image quality varied or DR-related features were difficult to discern. The DINOv2_base_TTA model achieved a significant sensitivity of 0.9459, reflecting its ability to accurately detect subtle features in challenging images, though with a slight drop in specificity (0.6666). Despite the increase in CPU time to 0.9869, the overall performance was enhanced, reducing prediction errors and increasing the confidence of the model's outputs. The DINOv2_small model, although slightly less performant than the base model, still demonstrated competitive results with an AUROC of 0.7792 and a CPU time of 0.259, further supporting its viability in real-time clinical use.

Table 1. Performance Analysis for Image Quality Assessment using DINOv2 models family.

Methods	AUROC	AUPRC	Sensitivity	Specificity	CPU-Time
DINOv2_base	0.8671	0.9093	0.7567	0.8333	0.3016
DINOv2_base_TTA	0.8085	0.8424	0.9459	0.6666	0.9869
DINOv2_small	0.7792	0.8089	0.6486	0.8750	0.259

For Task 2: Identification of Referable Diabetic Retinopathy, the MobileNetV3 family showed exceptional results, outperforming other deep learning models in both accuracy and computational efficiency. The MobileNetV3_large_TTA model achieved the highest scores across all metrics, with an AUROC of 0.9802, AUPRC of 0.9856, and perfect sensitivity (1.0), alongside a specificity of 0.8571. Despite the model's high performance, it maintained an extremely low CPU time of just 0.0433, indicating its capability for rapid, real-time predictions. Similarly, the MobileNetV3_small_TTA model also performed admirably, with an AUROC of 0.9704, AUPRC of 0.9784, and a sensitivity of 0.9310, while preserving a slightly higher specificity of 0.9523 and a CPU time of 0.0424. Even without TTA, the MobileNetV3_small model still delivered strong results, achieving an AUROC of 0.9573 and a CPU time of 0.0190, making it a highly efficient option for referable DR detection in resource-limited environments.

In conclusion, the DINOv2 models demonstrated superior performance in Image Quality Assessment, particularly with the use of TTA, while the MobileNetV3 models excelled in the Identification of Referable DR tasks, providing a robust, efficient solution with minimal computational overhead. The performance analysis for Task 1 is presented in Table 1, while the performance analysis for Task 2 is displayed in Table 2.

Table 2. Performance Analysis for Identification of Referable Diabetic Retinopathy MobileNetV3 models family.

Methods	AUROC	AUPRC	Sensitivity	Specificity	CPU-Time
MobileNetV3_large_TTA	0.9802	0.9856	1.0	0.8571	0.0433
MobileNetV3_small_TTA	0.9704	0.9784	0.9310	0.9523	0.0424
MobileNetV3_small	0.9573	0.9722	0.9310	0.9047	0.0190

Figure 2 presents the ROC and Precision-Recall (PR) curves for both Task 1 and Task 2. Figure 2 is organized into two rows: the first row illustrates the ROC and PR curves for Task 1, while the second row showcases these metrics for Task 2. For Task 1, the DINOv2_small model exhibited comparatively lower performance on both the ROC and PR curves, indicating reduced effectiveness in classification compared to the DINOv2_base and DINOv2_base+TTA models. The latter models demonstrate higher true positive rates and precision, highlighting their superior performance in distinguishing between classes. In contrast, the second row reveals that the MobileNetV3_large

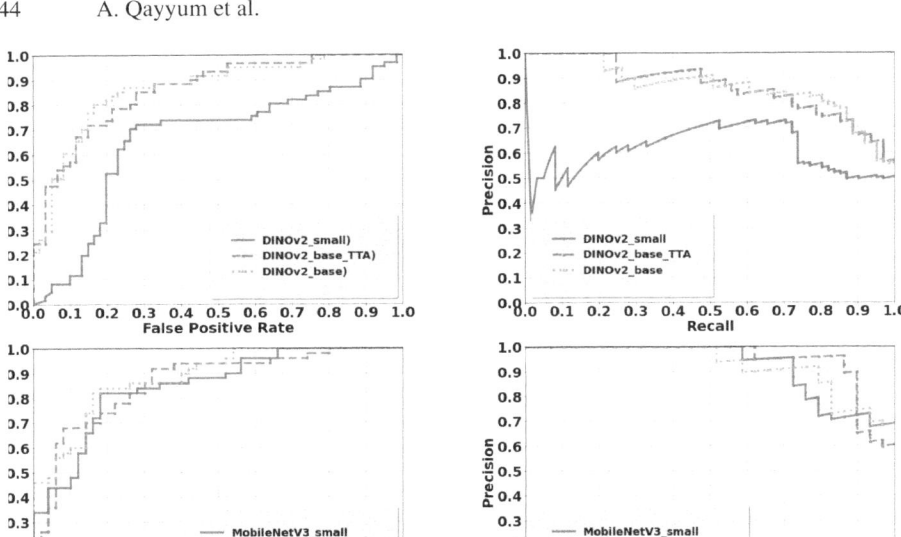

Fig. 2. The ROC and Precision-Recall (PR) curves for both Task 1 and Task 2.

model delivered exceptional results for Task 2, with its ROC and PR curves showing markedly improved performance. This model consistently achieved higher true positive rates and precision, underscoring its robust classification capability and effectiveness in Task 2. Overall, these results emphasize the varying performance of different models across tasks, providing a clear view of their strengths and limitations.

4 Conclusion

MobileNetV3 and DINOv2 models demonstrated strong performance in the UWF4DR challenge tasks, each excelling in different areas. MobileNetV3 proved to be the most effective model for referable DR identification, combining high accuracy with computational efficiency. Its advanced architecture, featuring Squeeze-and-Excitation (SE) modules, inverted residuals, and H-Swish activation, allowed it to achieve superior results while maintaining a lightweight footprint. The application of Test-Time Augmentation (TTA) further boosted its performance, making it a promising tool for practical diabetic retinopathy screening and management.

On the other hand, DINOv2 models excelled in the task of image quality assessment, effectively managing complex visual features with minimal computational resources. DINOv2's lightweight design makes it particularly suitable for clinical environments where computational efficiency is crucial. Together, these models offer a robust and efficient solution for automated DR detection and image quality assessment using ultra-widefield (UWF) imaging, paving the way for their application in real-world clinical settings.

For future research and development, several recommendations can be made to further improve the performance and clinical applicability of models like MobileNetV3 and DINOv2 for diabetic retinopathy (DR) detection and assessment. Incorporating additional data such as patient demographics, medical history, or optical coherence tomography (OCT) images could enhance model accuracy, providing more comprehensive insights into DR progression and improving diagnostic performance. Applying domain adaptation techniques could help the models generalize better across different imaging devices, clinical settings, and population groups, making them more robust in real-world applications. Future models should focus on increasing interpretability to provide clear visual explanations for predictions. This will help clinicians trust and adopt AI solutions more readily in clinical practice. Implementing a continuous learning framework where models can be fine-tuned over time with new data could help maintain high performance and adapt to emerging clinical trends and challenges. Future studies should aim to validate these models across different geographic regions and healthcare settings to ensure their global applicability, particularly in low-resource environments where DR screening is critical. Developing models that can run efficiently on edge devices, such as portable fundus cameras or smartphones, would enable wider access to DR screening in remote or resource-constrained areas. Exploring the combination of ultra-widefield (UWF) imaging with standard color fundus photography (CFP) could provide more comprehensive assessments and reduce cases of ungradable images, leading to more accurate diagnoses. By addressing these areas, future research could further improve the accuracy, efficiency, and accessibility of AI-based solutions for diabetic retinopathy detection and assessment.

References

1. Cheung, N., Mitchell, P., Wong, T.Y.: Diabetic retinopathy. Lancet **376**(9735), 124–36 (2010)
2. Teo, Z.L., et al.: Global prevalence of diabetic retinopathy and projection of burden through 2045: systematic review and meta-analysis. Ophthalmology **128**(11), 1580–1591 (2021)
3. Wilkinson, C.P., et al.: Proposed international clinical diabetic retinopathy and diabetic macular edema disease severity scales. Ophthalmology **110**(9), 1677–82 (2003)
4. Bellemo, V., et al.: Artificial intelligence using deep learning to screen for referable and vision-threatening diabetic retinopathy in Africa: a clinical validation study. Lancet Digit Health **1**(1), e35–e44 (2019)
5. Ting, D.S., Cheung, G.C., Wong, T.Y.: Diabetic retinopathy: global prevalence, major risk factors, screening practices and public health challenges: a review. Clin. Exp. Ophthalmol. **44**(4), 260–77 (2016)
6. Grading diabetic retinopathy from stereoscopic color fundus photographs--an extension of the modified Airlie House classification. ETDRS report number 10. Early Treatment Diabetic Retinopathy Study Research Group. Ophthalmology **98**(5 Suppl), 786–806 (1991)
7. Ting, D.S.W., et al.: Development and validation of a deep learning system for diabetic retinopathy and related eye diseases using retinal images from multiethnic populations with diabetes. JAMA **318**(22), 2211–2223 (2017)
8. Lin, D., et al.: Application of Comprehensive Artificial intelligence Retinal Expert (CARE) system: a national real-world evidence study. Lancet Digit Health **3**(8), e486–e495 (2021)
9. Sun, J.K., Aiello, L.P.: The future of ultrawide field imaging for diabetic retinopathy: pondering the retinal periphery. JAMA Ophthalmol. **134**(3), 247–248 (2016)

10. Silva, P.S., et al.: Identification of diabetic retinopathy and ungradable image rate with ultra-wide field imaging in a national teleophthalmology program. Ophthalmology **123**(6), 1360–7 (2016)
11. Aiello, L.P., et al.: Comparison of early treatment diabetic retinopathy study standard 7-field imaging with ultrawide-field imaging for determining severity of diabetic retinopathy. JAMA Ophthalmol. **137**(1), 65–73 (2019)
12. Das, A., et al.: Pitvis-2023 challenge: workflow recognition in videos of endoscopic pituitary surgery. arXiv preprint arXiv:2409.01184 (2024)
13. Qayyum, A., Razzak, I., Tanveer, M., Mazher, M., Alhaqbani, B.: High-density electroencephalography and speech signal based deep framework for clinical depression diagnosis. IEEE/ACM Trans. Comput. Biol. Bioinf. **20**(4), 2587–2597 (2023)
14. Li, X., et al.: The state-of-the-art 3D anisotropic intracranial hemorrhage segmentation on non-contrast head CT: The INSTANCE challenge. arXiv preprint arXiv:2301.03281 (2023)
15. Qayyum, A., Malik, A., Saad, N.M., Mazher, M.: Designing deep CNN models based on sparse coding for aerial imagery: a deep-features reduction approach. Eur. J. Remote Sens. **52**(1), 221–239 (2019)
16. Mazher, M., et al.: Self-supervised spatial–temporal transformer fusion based federated framework for 4D cardiovascular image segmentation. Inf. Fusion **106**, 102256 (2024)
17. Ahmad, R.F., et al.: Discriminating the different human brain states with EEG signals using Fractal dimension: a nonlinear approach. In: 2014 IEEE International Conference on Smart Instrumentation, Measurement and Applications (ICSIMA), pp. 1–5. IEEE (2014)
18. Howard, A., et al.: Searching for mobilenetv3. In: Proceedings of the IEEE/CVF International Conference on Computer Vision, pp. 1314–1324 (2019)
19. Qayyum, A., Benzinou, A., Mazher, M., Meriaudeau, F.: Efficient multi-model vision transformer based on feature fusion for classification of dfuc2021 challenge. In: Diabetic Foot Ulcers Grand Challenge, pp. 62–75. Springer, Cham (2021)
20. Oquab, M., et al.: Dinov2: learning robust visual features without supervision. arXiv preprint arXiv:2304.07193 (2023)

Bag of Tricks for Ultra-widefield Fundus Image Quality Assessment

Junfeng Sun, Xinliang Wang, and Yunchao Gu[✉]

State Key Laboratory of Virtual Reality Technology and Systems, Beihang University, 100191 Beijing, China
guyunchao@buaa.edu.cn

Abstract. Ultra-widefield fundus images provide a broad view and play an important role in the integration of deep learning and healthcare. Therefore, it is important to obtain high-quality ultra-widefield fundus image data. We participated in Task 1 of the Ultra-Widefield Fundus Imaging for Diabetic Retinopathy Challenge, focusing on ultra-widefield fundus image quality assessment. The performance of the image quality assessment can be improved by tricks in the training and inference procedure, such as data augmentation, label smoothing, image resizing, and integration of deep learning models. We employ the bag of tricks to enhance the performance of ultra-widefield fundus image quality assessment. In this paper, we examine a series of such tricks and empirically assess their impact on the final model through experiments. The experiments demonstrate that by combining these improvements, significant improvements in prediction performance can be achieved. We achieve a test score of 0.9644 in the image quality assessment task of the challenge.

Keywords: Ultra-widefield fundus image · Deep learning · Computer vision

1 Introduction

Diabetic retinopathy (DR) is one of the most common microvascular complications of diabetes mellitus and a major cause of preventable blindness among working-aged people [1]. In 2020, an estimated 103 million adults globally were affected by diabetic retinopathy. This number is projected to rise significantly, reaching 130 million by 2030 and 161 million by 2045 [2]. DR leads to retinal microvascular leakage and obstruction thus causing a series of fundus lesions such as microangiomas, hard exudates, cotton-wool spots, neovascularization, vitreous proliferation, macular edema and even retinal detachment. Prompt detection, timely referral, and early treatment are widely recognized as crucial measures to prevent vision loss [3].

With the development of computer vision technology, the application of deep learning to auxiliary diagnosis of DR has become increasingly mature. Standard color fundus photography (CFP) captures optic nerve within a field of view ranging from 30 to 50°, serving as the gold standard imaging technique for classifying

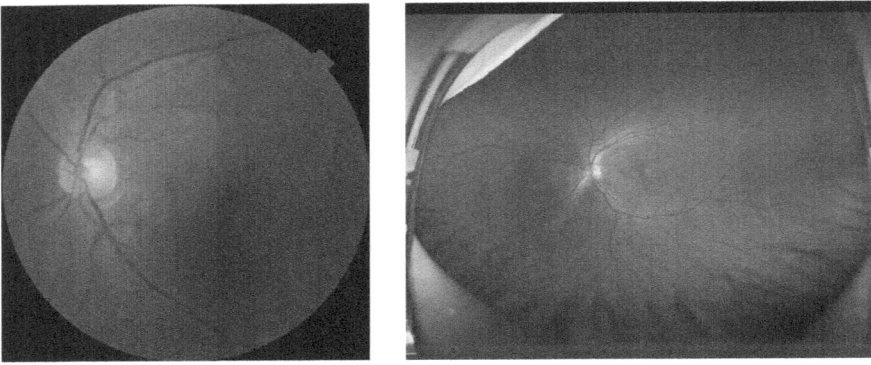

Fig. 1. Comparison of CFP and UWF image. The left is a CFP image, and the right is an UWF image.

DR. As shown in the Fig. 1, compared to CFP, ultra-widefield (UWF) fundus images provide a wider view of the retina up to 200°. Because of wider field of view, UWF is more likely to capture lesions of DR. By combining UWF with deep learning, it is possible to detect DR earlier and plan more effective treatments, thereby preventing the vision loss. Typically, high-quality data plays a significant role in enhancing the performance of deep learning models. Therefore, evaluating the quality of UWF images is a crucial task.

In this paper, we introduce a bag of tricks used in the ultra-widefield fundus image quality assessment task. Extensive experiments have shown the effectiveness of our methods.

2 Method

2.1 Data Augmentation

Data augmentation is a commonly used technique for training deep learning models. Its purpose is to apply various transformations and processing methods to the existing dataset to generate new training samples, thereby increasing the diversity and size of the dataset. This helps the model generalize better, improve its performance on the unseen data, and reduce the risk of overfitting.

The task of UWF image quality assessment requires a comprehensive assessment of factors such as image clarity, contrast, brightness, lighting uniformity, image alignment and registration. Therefore, commonly used augmentation methods such as adjusting contrast and brightness, image translation and vertical flipping are not applicable in this task. Considering that the human eye has a left-right symmetrical structure, we use horizontal flipping as an augmentation method during the training process, implemented through Albumentations which is a Python library for image augmentation [4].

2.2 Label Smoothing

Label Smoothing is a regularization technique. It converts hard labels into soft labels, thereby preventing the model from being overly confident in its predictions during training and enhancing generalization. Label smoothing can make the clusters between classes more compact, increase the inter-class distance, reduce the intra-class distance and increase the alignment between model's prediction confidences and actual accuracies [5].

UWF image quality assessment is a binary classification task. Therefore, we choose binary cross-entropy function (BCE) as the loss function. Equation (1) demonstrates the combination of label smoothing and the BCE loss function. Label smoothing hyperparameter ϵ is used to control the extent to which the original label distribution (typically one-hot encoded) is smoothed. Under normal circumstances, ϵ is set to 0.1. N is the number of samples and y_{pred} is the model's predicted output.

$$L_{BCEwithLabelSmoothing} = (1-\epsilon) \times L_{BCE} - \frac{\epsilon}{N} \times \sum_{i=1}^{n} log y_{pred} \qquad (1)$$

2.3 K-Fold Cross-Validation

K-fold cross-validation can reduce the risk of overfitting, enhance the robustness of the model, and is suitable for situations with a small amount of data. To fully utilize the data, we use stratified K-fold cross-validation during the training process. We utilize the StratifiedKFold from the sklearn library to split the original dataset into K-1 subsets. Each subset maintains a similar class distribution as the original dataset. Each fold is sequentially used as test set while the remaining folds serve as the training set. During the validation phase of the challenge, we integrate the K-fold models from the training process and average their predictions to obtain the final predictions. We compare multi-fold integrated models with individual models and the results indicate that the ensemble model performances better.

2.4 Architectures

During the validation phase of the challenge, we experiment with several classical models, including ResNet [6], ResNext [7], GhostNet [8], MobileNet [9], and VANnet [10]. We optimize different models and select the approach used in the test phase based on online evaluation results.

The ResNet series models have three variants: B, C, and D. ResNet-B moves the downsampling in the residual branch to the subsequent 3×3 convolution, avoiding significant information loss caused by the original 1×1 convolution. ResNet-C replaces the 7×7 convolution kernel in the input part with three 3×3 convolution kernels, aiming to significantly reduce the number of parameters and computation. ResNet-D, based on ResNet-B, decouples the downsampling of the identity part by using an average pool to handle it, thus avoiding information loss caused by simultaneous 1×1 convolution and downsampling. In our experiments, we mainly used the structure of ResNet-D.

In addition to ensembling multiple folds of a single model, we also test the effect of ensemble models during the validation phase. To limit model inference time, we experiment with ensembling 2 models or 3 models only. Online evaluation results indicate that ensembling multiple models effectively improves prediction performance.

2.5 Image Size

Proper adjustment of image size can enhance model performance, especially in detail-rich tasks such as medical imaging or high-resolution image quality assessment. During training, we adjust image sizes for each model and select the optimal value based on the best evaluation results of online validation phases.

During inference, We enlarge image size to enable models to capture more details and compensate for the changes in statistical properties caused by scale variations during training, thereby improving the prediction performance. Based on the work by Touvron, due to the presence of preprocessing and image augmentation, the image size perceived by the model during training is larger than during the testing phase. The Touvron team estimates that the ratio between the two phases is 1.25 [11]. During the validation phase, we adjust image sizes of the Resize operation according to this ratio. Additionally, we experiment with larger image sizes. The results of online submissions indicate that increasing the image size can significantly enhance predictive performance.

2.6 Test-Time Augmentation

Test-Time Augmentation (TTA) is a data augmentation technique used during the inference phase. TTA applies various transformations to input to generate multiple images, then performing inference on each transformed image, and finally aggregating all the prediction results to obtain a more reliable prediction. For the same reason mentioned in Sect. 2.1, we only use horizontal flipping for TTA in the UWF image quality assessment task.

3 Experiments

3.1 Dataset and Metrics

For the UWF image quality assessment task, we utilized solely the official UWF image dataset provided by the Challenge, comprising 434 images. In order to comprehensively evaluate the performance of the model, the challenge combines the AUC and the average inference time per image as evaluation metrics. The evaluation metric is AUC - 5% × time(seconds).

3.2 Implementation Details

We do experiments using the bag of tricks as described in the Sect. 2 an NVIDIA RTX A5000 card. During training, we use the Adam optimizer with an initial learning rate of 6e-5. Label smoothing hyperparameter ϵ is set to 0.1. Because the amount of data is small, we use 4-fold cross validation for experiments. After extensive experiments, we choose to integrate ResNet34d, ResNet50d and ResNext50d to obtain better results. Note that the image size for our training pipeline is 448 × 448, and the image size for inference is 576 × 576. The overall framework is shown in Fig. 2.

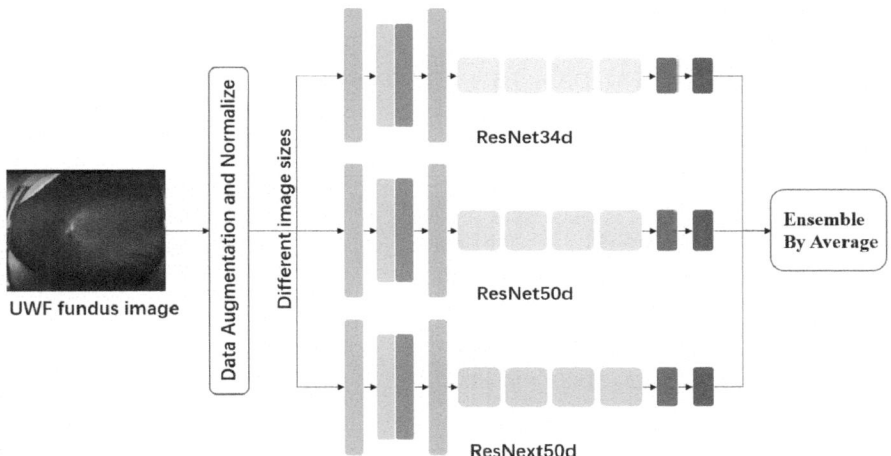

Fig. 2. Overall framework of our method

3.3 Results

Table 1 shows the quantitative evaluation results of tricks we use. Since the submission results of the testing phase are not visible, we show here the AUROC of the validation phase. KF, DA, and LS represent ensemble of K-fold integrated models, data augmentation, and label smoothing respectively. We incrementally apply these tricks, adding one technique at each step to verify its effectiveness. The architectures used in the experiment are ResNet34d and ResNet50d. The online evaluation results indicate that the tricks we used can effectively improve the model's performance.

Table 2 shows the quantitative evaluation results of part of the models we use. These models utilize the tricks validated in Table 1. ResNet34d, ResNet50d, and ResNext50d perform well. Therefore, for integration and submission, we use these three models.

Table 1. Quantitative evaluation results of tricks

Model	AUROC in validation phase
ResNet34d	0.8029
ResNet34d + KF	0.8333
ResNet34d + KF + DA	0.8490
ResNet34d + KF + DA + LS	0.8547
ResNet34d + KF + DA + LS + TTA	**0.8738**
ResNet50d	0.8034
ResNet50d + KF	0.8355
ResNet50d + KF + DA	0.8378
ResNet50d + KF + DA + LS	0.8693
ResNet50d + KF + DA + LS + TTA	**0.8840**

Table 2. Quantitative evaluation results of different models

Model	AUROC in validation phase
ResNet34d	0.8738
ResNet50d	**0.8840**
ResNext50d	0.8648
SeResNext26d	0.8536
GhostNet130	0.8434
MobileNetv2 140	0.8455

Table 3. Quantitative evaluation results of integrated models

Model	AUROC in validation phase
ResNet34d	0.8738
ResNet50d	0.8840
ResNext50d	0.8648
ResNet50d + ResNext50d	0.8896
ResNet34d + ResNet50d	**0.9099**
ResNet34d + ResNet50d + ResNext50d	0.9065

Table 3 shows the quantitative evaluation results of integrated models. We center our approach around ResNet50d, which performs the best, integrating it with ResNet34d and ResNext50d. The results indicate that the integrated models have better predictive performance.

Table 4. The impact of increasing image size during inference

Image Size	AUROC in validation phase
448 × 448	0.8851
512 × 512	0.9020
576 × 576	**0.9099**
608 × 608	0.9020

Table 4 shows the impact of increasing image size during inference. We use the ensemble of ResNet34d and ResNet50d models trained on 448x448. The results indicate that increasing the image size during inference improves prediction performance.

4 Conclusion

This paper demonstrates the bag of tricks we use in the Ultra-Widefield Fundus Imaging for Diabetic Retinopathy Challenge. These improvements bring solid progress and positivity to UWF image quality assessment task. In the future, we will pre-train the models using additional image datasets to further improve performance.

References

1. Cheung, N., Mitchell, P., Wong, T.Y.: Diabetic retinopathy. Lancet **376**(59735), 124–36 (2010)
2. Teo, Z.L., et al.: Global prevalence of diabetic retinopathy and projection of burden through 2045: systematic review and meta-analysis. Ophthalmology **128**(11), 1580–1591 (2021)
3. Ting, D.S., Cheung, G.C., Wong, T.Y.: Diabetic retinopathy: global prevalence, major risk factors, screening practices and public health challenges: a review. Clin. Exp. Ophthalmol. **44**(4), 260–77 (2016)
4. Buslaev, A., Iglovikov, V.I., Khvedchenya, E., et al.: Albumentations: fast and flexible image augmentations. Information **11**(2), 125 (2020)
5. Müller, R., Kornblith, S., Hinton, G.E..: When does label smoothing help?. Adv. Neural Inform. Process. Syst. **32** (2019)
6. He, K., Zhang, X., Ren, S., et al.: Deep residual learning for image recognition. In: Proceedings of the IEEE Conference on Computer Vision and Pattern Recognition, pp. 770–778 (2016)
7. Xie, S., Girshick, R., Dollár, P., et al.: Aggregated residual transformations for deep neural networks. In: Proceedings of the IEEE Conference on Computer Vision and Pattern Recognition, pp. 1492–1500 (2017)
8. Han, K., Wang, Y., Tian, Q., et al.: Ghostnet: more features from cheap operations. In: Proceedings of the IEEE/CVF Conference on Computer Vision and Pattern Recognition, pp. 1580–1589 (2020)

9. Howard, A.G., Zhu, M., Chen, B., et al.: Mobilenets: efficient convolutional neural networks for mobile vision application. arxiv preprint arxiv:1704.04861 (2017)
10. Guo, M.H., Lu, C.Z., Liu, Z.N., et al.: Visual attention network. Comput. Vis. Media **9**(4), 733–752 (2023)
11. Touvron, H., Vedaldi, A., Douze, M., et al.: Fixing the train-test resolution discrepancy. Adv. Neural Inform. Process. Syst. **32** (2019)

Bag of Tricks for Diabetic Retinopathy and Diabetic Macular Edema Classification in Ultra-widefield Imaging

Hyeonmin Kim[1,2], Yunnie Cho[1,3], Ohhyun Kwon[1], and Dongha Lee[4(✉)]

[1] Mediwhale, Gangnam, South Korea
{luke.kim,yunnie.cho,carl.kwon}@mediwhale.com
[2] Pohang University of Science and Technology (POSTECH), Pohang, South Korea
[3] Seoul National University Hospital, Jongno, South Korea
[4] Yonsei University, Seoul, South Korea
donalee@yonsei.ac.kr

Abstract. Diabetic retinopathy (DR) is a common complication of diabetes mellitus that can result in significant vision loss or blindness if left untreated, making early detection and effective management crucial. Ultra-widefield fundus (UWF) imaging, which captures up to 200 degrees of the retina, provides a broader and more comprehensive view for diagnosing and monitoring DR compared to traditional color fundus photography (CFP), which captures only 30 to 60 degrees. Despite its advantages, annotating UWF images remains labor-intensive, and the availability of open datasets for UWF imaging is limited compared to CFP. To address these challenges, two key methods are applied: 1) Multitask Learning with Pseudo-labeling, which enables the model to perform multiple tasks simultaneously and generalize more effectively by distilling knowledge from unlabeled data across various open datasets; and 2) UWF transformation, which makes UWF images resemble CFP images by focusing on common retinal structures despite differences in field of view. Our model achieved first place in two tasks-identification of diabetic macular edema and diabetic retinopathy-at MICCAI 2024 UWF4DR, demonstrating the effectiveness of these approaches in overcoming challenges in UWF image analysis. Our code, along with our data augmentation library that includes UWF preprocessing, is available at https://github.com/medi-whale/UWF4DR_mediwhale.

Keywords: Ultra-widefield fundus · Diabetic retinopathy classification

1 Introduction

Diabetic retinopathy (DR) is a common and specific complication of diabetes mellitus, and it is one of the leading causes of preventable blindness in working-age adults worldwide. As the incidence of diabetes continues to rise, so does the burden of DR. In 2020, 103.12 million adults were affected by DR, and by

2045, this number is projected to increase to 160.50 million globally [12]. In the United States, the prevalence of DR among adults with diabetes was estimated to be approximately 27.0% in 2021 [10], highlighting the significant impact of DR even in developed countries. The disease is characterized by progressive damage to the retinal blood vessels, which can lead to vision impairment and, if left untreated, irreversible blindness. The global prevalence of vision-threatening diabetic retinopathy (VTDR) was 6.17% in 2020, and diabetic macular edema (DME) was reported at 4.07%, with projections similarly increasing by 2045. Early detection and appropriate intervention are critical to preventing vision loss in individuals with DR.

DR is classified into several stages according to the International Clinical Diabetic Retinopathy (ICDR) Severity Scale, ranging from no apparent retinopathy to proliferative diabetic retinopathy (PDR). Effective management of DR requires regular screening and timely intervention, especially in cases of moderate nonproliferative DR (NPDR) or more severe stages, including DME. Traditional methods, such as standard color fundus photography (CFP), have played a key role in detecting and monitoring the progression of the disease. However, CFP has limitations, including a relatively narrow field of view and potential ungradable images, which highlights the need for more advanced imaging techniques.

Ultra-widefield (UWF) fundus imaging has emerged as a valuable tool in the management of DR, offering a panoramic view of the retina with up to a 200-degree field of view, capturing up to 82% of the retinal surface in one image. This is a significant improvement over traditional CFP, which captures only the central third of the retina [1]. UWF imaging enhances the detection of peripheral retinal lesions, which are often associated with a higher risk of DR progression, and reduces the rate of ungradable images compared to CFP [6]. UWF imaging has shown significant potential in improving the accuracy of DR severity assessments and facilitating better patient management. Despite these advantages, the interpretation and classification of UWF images remain complex and labor-intensive, which emphasizes the need for advanced automated methods to fully utilize its capabilities in clinical practice.

To mitigate the issue of data scarcity, we introduce two key strategies: 1) Multitask Learning with Pseudo-labeling, and 2) UWF transformation. By addressing multiple tasks simultaneously, our model not only increase the available data but also learn generalized features. Specifically, datasets such as DeepDRiD [7], DR EyePACS [3], MSHF [5], and JustRAIGS [13], were incorporated, with tasks including DR, DME, glaucoma detection, and age classification. Pseudo-labeling was employed to leverage unlabeled datasets, distilling the knowledge from models trained on high-resolution images into a student model trained on lower-resolution images. This process enhances inference speed without sacrificing accuracy. By combining Multitask Learning with Pseudo-labeling, we significantly improved our model's performance.

In addition to Multitask Learning, we applied UWF transformation method to make UWF images resemble CFP images, as both target the same retinal structures. By considering features like the optic disc and vessel size, we set the center cropping range between 0.3 and 1.0, applied randomly during the training phase. This alignment process further enhances model performance by focusing on shared anatomical structures. Through the integration of these techniques, our model demonstrated competitive performance, securing first place in Task 2 (Identification of referable diabetic retinopathy) and Task 3 (Identification of diabetic macular edema).

To support further research, we provide an Image Transformation library that includes UWF-to-CFP alignment, available alongside the model training code on our GitHub.[1]

2 Related Work

Addressing multiple tasks simultaneously, known as Multitask Learning [11], has gained attention for its ability to learn generalized features from multiple tasks or datasets. Specifically, Multitask Learning enables models to share knowledge across related tasks, improving performance by leveraging complementary information from each task. Notably, MUST (Multi-Task Self-Training) [4] proposed training a general student model from multiple specialized teacher models for tasks such as classification, detection, segmentation, and depth estimation, demonstrating the superiority of a versatile model. Another study [2] addressed the classification of conditions such as melanoma, glaucoma, AMD (Age-related Macular Degeneration), and DR to reduce reliance on large amounts of labeled data for individual tasks. In summary, these studies emphasize the potential of multitask learning to improve model performance and address the challenges associated with limited labeled data.

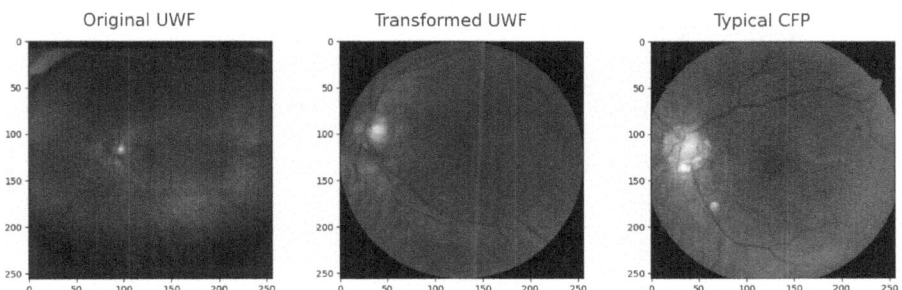

Fig. 1. Comparison between Original UWF, Transformed UWF (aligned to CFP), and Typical CFP.

---

[1] https://github.com/medi-whale/UWF4DR_mediwhale.

3 Method

3.1 UWF Transformation: Aligning UWF to CFP for Adaptation

To fully leverage DR-related CFP datasets, we apply a UWF transformation method that aligns UWF images with CFP images, as both modalities capture the same anatomical structures. This transformation process includes random scaling and center cropping to resize UWF images and focus on key retinal regions. This alignment bridges the gap between UWF and CFP datasets, enabling the model to generalize more effectively across both modalities. In Fig. 1, the left image shows the original UWF, the middle image depicts the transformed UWF after alignment, and the right image represents a typical CFP.

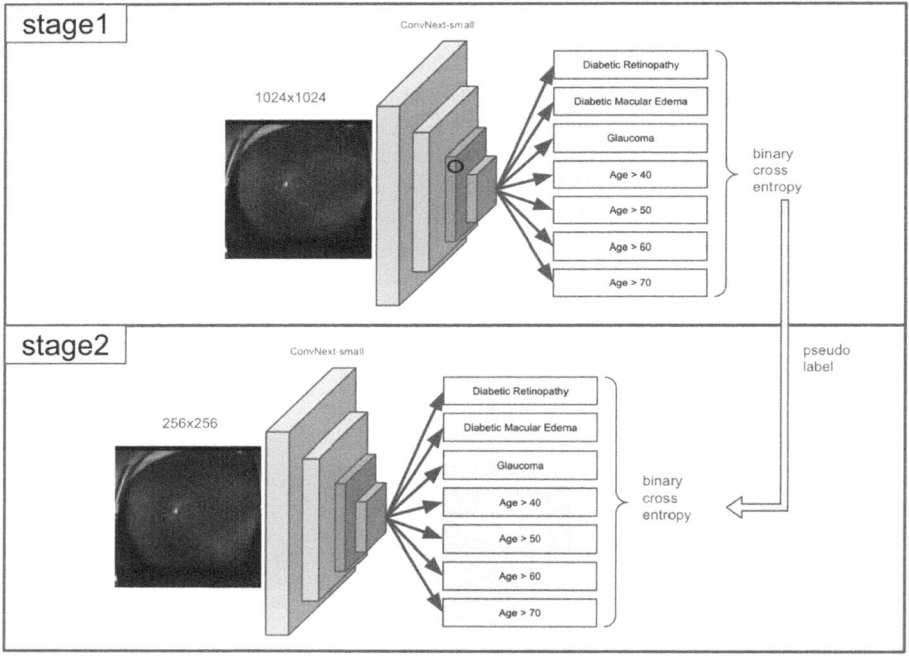

Fig. 2. Overview of training multitask classification using ConvNeXt-Small.

3.2 Multitask Learning with Pseudo-labeling

To address the issue of insufficient UWF DR datasets, we introduce two well-established approaches: Multitask Learning with Pseudo-labeling. We gather various public datasets, including DeepDRiD [7], DR EyePACS [3], MSHF [5], and JustRAIGS [13], to train a model capable of solving multiple tasks, such as detecting DR, DME, and glaucoma, as well as classifying gender and age groups (>40, >50, >60, >70). By integrating these tasks, our model learns more generalized features.

Additionally, Pseudo-labeling is incorporated to further enhance generalization by training a teacher model and distilling its knowledge into a student model. As shown in Fig. 2, the teacher model is trained using Multitask Learning with high-resolution images (1024×1024). Pseudo-labels generated by the teacher model are then used to train the student model with lower-resolution images (256×256), reducing computational overhead while maintaining performance. This two-stage process ensures efficient training and effective generalization across tasks such as DR, DME, glaucoma detection, and age classification. By reducing the resolution in the student model, our approach effectively addresses the CPU time constraints in the challenge metric.

3.3 Implementation Detail

ConvNeXt [8] is used as the backbone, with the learning rate set to 2e–4, optimized using the AdamW optimizer [9]. The teacher model is trained with a batch size of 16 using 1024×1024 resolution images, while the student model is trained with a batch size of 128 on 256×256 resolution images. During training, the UWF transformation's cropping ratio is randomly sampled between 0.3 and 1.0 and the same augmentation used for CFP is applied after the transformation. For data augmentation, we apply a variety of geometric transformations (i.e., scaling, rotation, translation, shearing, and flipping) and photometric adjustments (i.e., color jitter, blur, noise, and contrast enhancement) to improve model generalization. We also employ coarse dropout to simulate occlusion by randomly removing parts of the image. Furthermore, our model is converted to an ONNX file for further optimization.

4 Experiments

4.1 Datasets and Evaluation Metrics

Our main dataset is the UWF4DR dataset, released specifically for this competition, consisting of 251 training images and 183 validation images annotated for DR and DME. In addition to this dataset, we incorporated several publicly available datasets, including DeepDRiD [7], DR EyePACS [3], MSHF [5], and JustRAIGS [13]. The combined training dataset consists of 189,477 images, with 52,505 labeled for DR, 97 for DME, 99,476 for glaucoma, and 99,410 for age classification. The internal validation set includes 4,342 images, similarly distributed across these tasks. These datasets enable the evaluation of multiple tasks, which are DR, DME, glaucoma, and age classification. Table 1 and Table 2 summarize the organization of the datasets used for training and internal validation.

For evaluation, we used the Area Under the Receiver Operating Characteristic curve (AUROC) as the primary metric. AUROC effectively measures

Table 1. Details of training datasets, including total image counts for various tasks: DR, DME, glaucoma, and age classification.

Dataset	Images	DR	DME	Glaucoma	Age
UWF4DR	251	121	97	0	0
DeepDRiD	2176	2168	0	0	0
DR EyePACS	86702	49375	0	0	0
MSHF	894	841	0	52	0
JustRAIGS	99424	0	0	99424	99410
Total	189477	52505	97	99476	99410

Table 2. Details of internal validation datasets, including total image counts for various tasks: DR, DME, glaucoma, and age classification.

Dataset	Images	DR	DME	Glaucoma	Age
UWF4DR	183	80	70	0	0
DeepDRiD	80	80	0	0	0
DR EyePACS	2000	2000	0	0	0
MSHF	80	80	0	0	0
JustRAIGS	1999	0	0	1999	1999
Total	4342	2240	70	1999	1999

the model's ability to differentiate between classes, offering reliable performance insights across tasks, even in the presence of class imbalances.

4.2 Results and Ablation Study

In this study, we validate the effectiveness of UWF transformation, Multitask Learning, and Pseudo-labeling for detecting DR and DME by evaluating ablated models using the AUROC curve. In Table 3, the results demonstrate that these techniques enhance performance for both tasks, yielding improved AUROC scores across various configurations. For DR, the baseline model (i.e., one that employs none of the techniques) achieves an AUROC of 0.9769, while incorporating Multitask Learning and UWF transformation boosts the score to 0.9905. The highest performance is reached with the incorporation of Pseudo-labeling, achieving an AUROC of 0.9983. Similarly, for DME, the baseline model achieves an AUROC of 0.9746. By introducing Multitask Learning and UWF transformation, the AUROC improves to 0.9926, while the highest score of 0.9975 is attained with the additional use of Pseudo-labeling. These results show that combining these techniques enhances model performance for both DR and DME.

In summary, the ablation study demonstrates the significant effectiveness of each technique. UWF transformation, Multitask Learning, and Pseudo-labeling, particularly when used in combination, contribute to substantial improvements

Table 3. Comparison of test AUROC scores for DR and DME using various configurations of Multitask learning, UWF transformation, and pseudo-labeling from a high-resolution trained teacher.

	Multi-task Learning	UWF Transformation	Pseudo-labeling	AUROC
DR				0.9769
	✓			0.9879
	✓	✓		0.9905
	✓	✓	✓	0.9983
DME				0.9746
	✓			0.9884
	✓	✓		0.9926
	✓	✓	✓	0.9975

in AUROC scores. These findings suggest that integrating these techniques is highly effective for improving the detection of both DR and DME.

5 Conclusion

In this study, we present a DR and DME classification framework combining Multitask Learning with Pseudo-labeling and UWF transformation. Our proposed methods demonstrate significant effectiveness, securing first place in both tasks at the MICCAI 2024 UWF4DR challenge. Beyond improving classification accuracy, our framework offers a scalable solution for multi-task datasets, making it adaptable for broader use. Future work could extend the application of this approach to other retinal diseases, further enhancing its potential in medical image analysis.

References

1. Cai, S., Liu, T.A.: The role of ultra-widefield fundus imaging and fluorescein angiography in diagnosis and treatment of diabetic retinopathy. Curr. Diab. Rep. **21**(9), 30 (2021)
2. Chelaramani, S., Gupta, M., Agarwal, V., Gupta, P., Habash, R.: Multi-task knowledge distillation for eye disease prediction. In: Proceedings of the IEEE/CVF winter conference on applications of computer vision, pp. 3983–3993 (2021)
3. Dugas, E., Jared, J., Cukierski, W.: Diabetic retinopathy detection (2015). https://kaggle.com/competitions/diabetic-retinopathy-detection
4. Ghiasi, G., Zoph, B., Cubuk, E.D., Le, Q.V., Lin, T.Y.: Multi-task self-training for learning general representations. In: Proceedings of the IEEE/CVF International Conference on Computer Vision, pp. 8856–8865 (2021)
5. Jin, K., et al.: MSHF: a multi-source heterogeneous fundus (MSHF) dataset for image quality assessment. Sci. Data **10**(1), 286 (2023)

6. Li, J., et al.: Ultra-widefield color fundus photography combined with high-speed ultra-widefield swept-source optical coherence tomography angiography for non-invasive detection of lesions in diabetic retinopathy. Front. Public Health **10**, 1047608 (2022)
7. Liu, R., et al.: Deepdrid: diabetic retinopathy-grading and image quality estimation challenge. Patterns **3**(6) (2022)
8. Liu, Z., Mao, H., Wu, C.Y., Feichtenhofer, C., Darrell, T., Xie, S.: A convnet for the 2020s. In: Proceedings of the IEEE/CVF conference on computer vision and pattern recognition, pp. 11976–11986 (2022)
9. Loshchilov, I., Hutter, F.: Decoupled weight decay regularization. In: Proceedings of the International Conference on Learning Representations (ICLR) (2019)
10. Lundeen, E.A., et al.: Prevalence of diabetic retinopathy in the us in 2021. JAMA Ophthalmol. **141**(8), 747–754 (2023). https://doi.org/10.1001/jamaophthalmol.2023.2289
11. Nam, H., Han, B.: Learning multi-domain convolutional neural networks for visual tracking. In: Proceedings of the IEEE Conference on Computer Vision and Pattern Recognition, pp. 4293–4302 (2016)
12. Teo, Z.L., et al.: Global prevalence of diabetic retinopathy and projection of burden through 2045: systematic review and meta-analysis. Ophthalmology **128**(11), 1580–1591 (2021)
13. Yousefi, S., Madadi, Y., Raja, H., Vermeer, K.A., Lemij, H.G.: Justraigs (2024). https://justraigs.grand-challenge.org/justraigs/

Deep Self-supervised Learning for Ultra-widefield Fundus Image Quality Assessment

Ammar M. Okran[1](✉)[iD], Saif Khalid Musluh[1,2][iD], Saddam Abdulwahab[1][iD], Domenec Puig[1][iD], and Hatem A. Rashwan[1][iD]

[1] Universitat Rovira i Virgili, 43007 Tarragona, Spain
{ammar.okran,saifkhalidmusluh.al-khalidy,saddam.abdulwahab, domenec.puig,hatem.abdellatif}@urv.cat
[2] University of Al-Qadisiyah, Al Diwaniyah, Iraq
saif.khalid@qu.edu.iq

Abstract. Ultra-widefield fundus imaging (UWF) enhances retinal diagnostics by offering comprehensive retinal views, crucial for detecting and managing diabetic retinopathy (DR). This study introduces a deep learning method utilizing self-supervised learning through an Autoencoder network to assess the quality of UWF images. The classification task distinguishes between gradable and ungradable images, a critical component for effective DR screening. The model was evaluated using the MICCAI UWF4DR 2024 dataset, which included 434 training images (with 201 images shared with Task 2) and 61 validation images. The system demonstrated excellent performance during the validation phase, achieving an AUROC of 0.8863, sensitivity of 0.9730, and specificity of 0.7500. In the test phase, the model achieved an AUROC of 0.8979, AUPRC of 0.9371, sensitivity of 0.7627, and specificity of 0.9000. These results highlight the model's effectiveness in accurately classifying images as gradable or ungradable, demonstrating robust performance in UWF image quality assessment. This approach shows great potential for integration into large-scale DR screening programs, improving diagnostic efficiency and consistency in teleophthalmology.

Keywords: diabetic retinopathy · ultra-widefield fundus imaging · image quality assessment · self-supervised learning · automated diagnostics

1 Introduction

Diabetic retinopathy (DR) is a leading cause of blindness, affecting nearly one-third of people with diabetes [12,15]. With rising diabetes prevalence, DR's burden is expected to grow. Early detection is crucial to prevent vision loss, but widespread DR screening faces challenges, especially in areas with limited healthcare resources. Automated systems powered by artificial intelligence (AI), mainly based on deep learning (DL), could enhance DR screening's accessibility and efficiency.

Ultra-widefield (UWF) fundus imaging is highly valuable for DR grading as it captures a significantly larger retinal area, including the periphery, allowing for detecting lesions often missed by standard imaging methods. This broader view enhances diagnostic accuracy and supports better disease monitoring without requiring pupil dilation, making it more efficient and comfortable for patients. UWF imaging is particularly useful for identifying peripheral lesions associated with more severe DR and is critical for accurate grading and treatment decisions [11,16].

The success of AI-based screening hinges on the quality of UWF images. Poor-quality images can impair diagnostic accuracy and reliability. Traditional image quality assessment (IQA) methods, like manual ophthalmologist evaluations, are subjective and time-consuming. Therefore, there is a need for efficient, automated IQA systems to ensure high-quality images are used and Fig. 1 presents examples of fundus images acquired by retinography devices. These images suffer from different distortions, such as color distortion, uneven illumination, and low contrast. Reliable screening of eye diseases requires fundus images of sufficient quality to analyze and extract disease biomarkers.

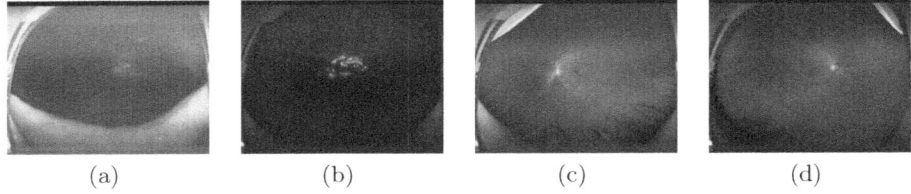

Fig. 1. Samples from MICCAI UWF4DR database: EyeQuality (Rejected (a), (b) and Accepted (c), (d)) respectively for retinal fundus images.

Consequently, in this paper, our work introduces a DL-based IQA system for UWF imaging designed for IQA using the dataset of Task 1 of the MICCAI UWF4DR 2024 challenge. Key contributions include:

- Development of a DL-based IQA system that combines image reconstruction with quality classification for UWF. We integrate two networks into a unified pipeline that combines both local and global features. These merged features are then utilized by the decoder to reconstruct the input image, enhancing the model's learning process using self-supervised learning. We then use a Convolutional Neural Network (CNN) classifier that leverages the latent features learned by the encoder to classify UWF images as either gradable or ungradable.
- Demonstration of the high performance and the competitive computational efficiency of the proposed model on Task 1 of the UWF4DR dataset, achieving high sensitivity, specificity, and AUROC.

- Various off-the-shelf interpretability methods are integrated with our model to provide interpretable visual feedback, helping ophthalmologists understand the reasoning behind the model's grading of UWF image quality.

2 Related Work

The evaluation of UWF image quality has become increasingly crucial with the rise of AI-based DR screening programs. Traditionally, ophthalmologists manually assessed image quality, a subjective and variable process. The Early Treatment Diabetic Retinopathy Study (ETDRS) grading system introduced more objective criteria [1], but manual grading remains time-consuming and prone to interpretation biases.

Earlier automated image quality assessment (IQA) methods used hand-crafted features such as brightness, sharpness, and color consistency to distinguish between gradable and ungradable images [14]. While these methods improved over manual grading, they often struggled with dataset variability and failed to fully capture the complexity of fundus images. For example, [10] emphasized the need for effective filtering of low-quality images to improve diagnostic accuracy in large-scale teleophthalmology programs.

DL has significantly advanced IQA by learning complex image quality representations from data [2]. A notable development by [13] demonstrated a deep learning-based system that incorporated an IQA module for automatic detection of ungradable images. This advancement marked a shift from manual feature extraction to automated learning of subtle image patterns.

Further, [6] applied DL to assess image quality in real-world settings, showing that DL can enhance the consistency and reliability of assessments across diverse conditions. This is especially important as teleophthalmology and UWF imaging become more prevalent.

Recent innovations have introduced advanced architectures such as VISTA, which employs a split-and-reconstruct deep neural network for fundus image quality assessment, enhancing both the detection of ungradable images and the reconstruction of degraded images [5]. These approaches address challenges such as dataset variability and feature complexity by leveraging DL's ability to capture intricate image representations. Similarly, [7] integrated pathological indicator segmentation and morphological feature analysis, illustrating the potential of combining image quality assessment with diagnostic capabilities for diabetic retinopathy (DR) classification. Additionally, the ensemble-based approach proposed by [4] demonstrated a simple yet robust deep learning framework for assessing DR in fundus images, which effectively complements IQA advancements by improving DR classification accuracy through ensemble techniques.

Thus, our work in this paper focuses on exploiting DL models to build a robust IQA system capable of detecting nuanced features in complex UWF imaging. Our approach achieves state-of-the-art performance on the UWF4DR dataset, significantly improving accuracy and sensitivity in image quality classification, while paving the way for more consistent and reliable applications in teleophthalmology and large-scale DR screening programs.

3 Methodology

The proposed IQA model utilizes a hybrid deep learning architecture combining EfficientNet-B5 and U-Net-based components, as depicted in Fig. 2. This design leverages EfficientNet-B5 for feature extraction and U-Net for image reconstruction and quality classification, effectively capturing and preserving both spatial and contextual information.

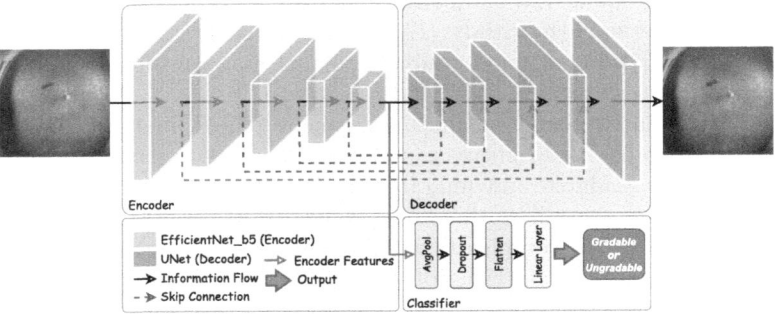

Fig. 2. Overview of the model architecture.

3.1 The Proposed Model

Figure 2 depicts the proposed model for fundus image gradability assessment. The first (top) part of the network is an autoencoder trained to learn robust feature representations of fundus images. The intermediate representations learned by the autoencoder are fed into a classifier to predict the gradability of the input fundus images as two labels: " Gradable" or " Ungradable ".

In Our Model, we present a self-supervised approach for image-image translation. To formulate the reconstruction for the fundus image, let $A \in \mathbb{A}$ be a fundus image. The problem of generating a reconstructed image, $B \in \mathbb{A}$, can be formally defined as a function: $f : \mathbb{A} \to \mathbb{A}$, that maps elements from a domain $\mathbb{A}$ to the same domain $\mathbb{A}$, under a constraint of that the representation of the input image must be encoded into a lower-dimensional manifold to force the compression of the input features. To optimize the autoencoder network, it is trained via backpropagation using as a loss function minimizing the distance between the reconstructed image and the input image (i.e., target).

The autoencoder network helps to learn the fundus image-relevant features of the input fundus image, including the visible quality features. Thus, the input to our autoencoder is an RGB fundus image, and the target is the same as the input fundus image. We propose that if the autoencoder network succeeds in reconstructing the same input image, the network succeeds in learning the input image's key features, including visual quality features. In this way, we can ensure that the intermediate representations preserve the information required for the gradability classification task. The experiments support our hypothesis. The proposed autoencoder network contains two sub-networks: encoder and decoder.

Encoder: The encoder comprises 9 stages, processing inputs of size $448 \times 448 \times 3$ into a final feature map of $14 \times 14 \times 2048$. The first stage includes a single Conv2dNormActivation0 layer (Conv2d + BatchNorm2d + SiLU). Stages 2 through 8 utilize MBConv blocks, combining Conv2dNormActivation0 layers, Squeeze-and-Excitation layers [3], Conv2dNormActivation1 layers (Conv2d + BatchNorm2d), and Stochastic Depth. These MBConv blocks are repeated [3, 5, 7, 7, 9] times, progressively increasing feature depth and reducing spatial resolution. The final stage, like the first, consists of a Conv2dNormActivation0 layer for output refinement. Table 1 details the full architecture.

Table 1. The detailed structure of the encoder network.

Stages	Block	Input	Layer Type	filters	kernel size	strice and padding	groups	Output shape
0	Conv2dNormActivation0	$448 \times 448 \times 3$	Conv2d + BatchNorm2d + SiLU	48	3	(2, 2),(1, 1)	1	$224 \times 224 \times 48$
1	Conv2dNormActivation0	$224 \times 224 \times 48$	Conv2dNormActivation0	48	3	(1, 1),(1, 1)	48	$224 \times 224 \times 48$
	SqueezeExcitation	$224 \times 224 \times 48$	AdaptiveAvgPool2d	-	-	-	-	$1 \times 1 \times 48$
		$1 \times 1 \times 48$	Conv2d + SiLU	12	1	(1, 1),(0, 0)	1	$1 \times 1 \times 12$
		$1 \times 1 \times 12$	Conv2d + Sigmoid	48	1	(1, 1),(0, 0)	1	$1 \times 1 \times 48$
		$1 \times 1 \times 48$	$\times$ input($224 \times 224 \times 48$)	48	1	(1, 1),(0, 0)	1	$224 \times 224 \times 48$
	Conv2dNormActivation1	$224 \times 224 \times 48$	Conv2d + BatchNorm2d	48	1	(1, 1),(0, 0)	1	$240 \times 240 \times 24$
	stochastic-depth	$224 \times 224 \times 24$	StochasticDepth	-	-	-	-	$240 \times 240 \times 24$
	MBConv	$224 \times 224 \times 24$	Conv2dNormActivation0	24	1	(1, 1),(1, 1)	24	$224 \times 224 \times 24$
		$224 \times 224 \times 24$	SqueezeExcitation	12	1	(1, 1),(0, 0)	1	$224 \times 224 \times 24$
		$224 \times 224 \times 24$	Conv2dNormActivation1	12	1	(1, 1),(0, 0)	1	$224 \times 224 \times 24$
		$224 \times 224 \times 24$	stochastic-depth	-	-	-	-	$224 \times 224 \times 24$
	MBConv	$224 \times 224 \times 24$	MBConv	24	1	(1, 1),(1, 1)	24	$224 \times 224 \times 24$
2	MBConv2	$224 \times 224 \times 24$	(MBConv(Conv2dNormActivation0 $\times$ 2)) $\times$ 5	-	-	-	-	$112 \times 112 \times 40$
3	MBConv2	$112 \times 112 \times 40$	MBConv2 $\times$ 5	-	-	-	-	$56 \times 56 \times 64$
4	MBConv2	$56 \times 56 \times 64$	MBConv2 $\times$ 7	-	-	-	-	$28 \times 28 \times 128$
5	MBConv2	$28 \times 28 \times 128$	MBConv2 $\times$ 7	-	-	-	-	$28 \times 28 \times 176$
6	MBConv2	$28 \times 28 \times 176$	MBConv2 $\times$ 9	-	-	-	-	$14 \times 14 \times 304$
7	MBConv2	$14 \times 14 \times 304$	MBConv2 $\times$ 3	-	-	-	-	$14 \times 14 \times 512$
8	Conv2dNormActivation0	$14 \times 14 \times 512$	Conv2dNormActivation0	2048	1	(1, 1), (0, 0)	1	$14 \times 14 \times 2048$

Decoder: The decoder consists of a centre layer (i.e., a convolutional layer with a kernel of 3×3) and four deconvolution layers (i.e., upsampling using bilinear interpolation and a convolutional layer with a kernel of 3×3) on the top-level feature map extracted from the encoder network to combine different features in the downsampling process and restore the input fundus image. Skip connections were used to connect the corresponding layers between the encoder and decoder networks to preserve the spatial information and the anatomical structures in fundus images. At the top of the decoder, a convolutional layer with a kernel size of 3×3 is used to refine the feature maps, followed by upsampling using bilinear interpolation with a factor of 2 to reconstruct the image. The detailed structure is shown in Table 2.

3.2 Classifier

After reconstruction, the features extracted by the encoder are processed through the following combined steps (Table 3):

Table 2. The detailed structure of the decoder network

Layers	Input	Layer Type	filters	kernel size	stride and padding	Output shape
Cent	14 × 14 × 512	Conv2d + BatchNorm2d + ReLU	512	3	(1, 1),(1, 1)	14 × 14 × 512
	14 × 14 × 512	Conv2d + BatchNorm2d + ReLU	512	3	(1, 1),(1, 1)	14 × 14 × 512
B4	14 × 14 × 512	Upsampling	-	-	-	28 × 28 × 512
	28 × 28 × 688	Conv2d + BatchNorm2d + ReLU	256	3	(1, 1),(1, 1)	28 × 28 × 256
	28 × 28 × 256	Conv2d + BatchNorm2d + ReLU	256	3	(1, 1),(1, 1)	28 × 28 × 256
B3	28 × 28 × 256	Upsampling	-	-	-	56 × 56 × 256
	56 × 56 × 320	Conv2d + BatchNorm2d + ReLU	128	3	(1, 1),(1, 1)	56 × 56 × 128
	56 × 56 × 128	Conv2d + BatchNorm2d + ReLU	128	3	(1, 1),(1, 1)	56 × 56 × 128
B2	56 × 56 × 128	Upsampling	-	-	-	112 × 112 × 128
	112 × 112 × 168	Conv2d + BatchNorm2d + ReLU	64	3	(1, 1),(1, 1)	112 × 112 × 64
	112 × 112 × 64	Conv2d + BatchNorm2d + ReLU	64	3	(1, 1),(1, 1)	112 × 112 × 64
B1	112 × 112 × 64	Upsampling	-	-	-	224 × 224 × 64
	224 × 224 × 88	Conv2d + BatchNorm2d + ReLU	32	3	(1, 1),(1, 1)	224 × 224 × 32
	224 × 224 × 32	Conv2d + BatchNorm2d + ReLU	32	3	(1, 1),(1, 1)	224 × 224 × 32
final	224 × 224 × 32	Conv2d	3	3	(1, 1),(1, 1)	224 × 224 × 3
	224 × 224 × 32	Upsampling by factor 2	-	-	-	448 × 448 × 3

Table 3. The detailed structure of the classifier network.

Layers	Layer type	Input features	Output features	Bias
avgpool	AdaptiveAvgPool2d	14 × 14 × 2048	1 × 1 × 2048	-
dropout	Dropout	1 × 1 × 2048	1 × 1 × 2048	-
flatten	Flatten	1 × 1 × 2048	2048	-
classifier	Linear	2048	No. of classes = 2	True

$$y_{\text{pred}} = \sigma\left(W \cdot \mathcal{F}\left(\mathcal{D}\left(\mathcal{P}\left(E(I)\right)\right)\right) + b\right) \quad (1)$$

where $E(I)$ represents the output features from the encoder E, $\mathcal{P}$ performs pooling on these features, $\mathcal{D}(p)$ applies dropout regularization with a dropout probability p, $\mathcal{F}$ flattens the pooled feature map into a one-dimensional vector, W is the weight matrix of the linear layer, b is the bias term, σ is the sigmoid activation function, and y_{pred} is the predicted probability of the image being of "Gradable" or "Ungradable" quality.

3.3 Training and Optimization

The model is trained using the AdamW optimizer with a learning rate of 1×10^{-4} and a learning rate scheduler. The training objective is to minimize the cross-entropy loss function, which is defined as:

$$\mathcal{L}(\theta) = -\frac{1}{N}\sum_{i=1}^{N}\left[y_i \log(p(y_i|\mathbf{z}_i)) + (1 - y_i)\log(1 - p(y_i|\mathbf{z}_i))\right] \quad (2)$$

where θ represents the model parameters, N is the number of training samples, y_i is the ground truth label for the i-th image, and $\mathbf{z}_i$ is the predicted probability for that image.

The AdamW optimizer updates the model parameters θ to minimize the loss function by incorporating weight decay to prevent overfitting. The parameter updates can be represented as:

$$\theta_{t+1} = \theta_t - \eta_t \left(\frac{\hat{m}_t}{\sqrt{\hat{v}_t} + \epsilon} + \lambda \theta_t \right) \tag{3}$$

where η_t is the learning rate at time step t, $\hat{m}_t$ and $\hat{v}_t$ are the bias-corrected first and second-moment estimates of the gradients at time step t, ϵ is a small constant added for numerical stability and λ is the weight decay factor.

4 Experimental Results

4.1 Dataset Description

For the MICCAI challenge, we used the UWF4DR dataset for Task 1: Image Quality Assessment, comprising:

- **Training Set:** 434 images, with 201 shared between Task 1 and Task 2.
- **Validation Set:** 61 images.
- **Test Set:** Private Data for Miccai challenges.

The dataset, sourced from the Diabetic Retinopathy Clinical Research Network (DRCR.net), features images of varying quality, crucial for developing robust IQA algorithms.

4.2 Evaluation Metrics

Model performance is assessed using:

- **AUROC**: Measures the model's ability to distinguish between classes.
- **Sensitivity**: Proportion of correctly identified "Gradable" quality images.
- **Specificity**: Proportion of correctly identified "Ungradable" quality images.
- **AUPRC**: Evaluates precision-recall trade-offs, especially for imbalanced datasets.
- **Computational Efficiency**: Assesses average CPU time per image during inference.

These metrics collectively evaluate the model's accuracy, efficiency, and robustness across diverse image qualities and conditions.

4.3 UWF Images Preprocessing

UWF images were captured using devices like Optos, covering a 200-degree retina view. Image quality varies due to factors like camera settings and ocular conditions. We applied data augmentation techniques:

- **Resizing:** To 512×512 pixels.
- **Flipping and Cropping:** Random horizontal flips and crops to 448×448 pixels.
- **Blur and Transformations:** Gaussian blur, random translations, and scaling.
- **Normalization:** Images normalized to ImageNet standards.

4.4 Results and Discussion

Validation Stage: Table 4 presents the performance of various teams during the validation stage. Our team participated with two entries: IRCVG-OMZ and IRCVG-URV. IRCVG-OMZ demonstrated strong results, achieving an AUROC of 0.8998, placing 3rd overall, and the highest sensitivity of 0.9730 (1st place), highlighting its effectiveness in identifying true positives. Meanwhile, IRCVG-URV showcased solid performance, emphasizing the collective strength of our team in tackling the validation phase. These results underline the robustness of our models compared to leading teams such as *AIFUTURE* and *group*.

Table 4. Validation Set Performance Evaluation Based on the IRCVG-URV Model.

Team Name	AUROC	AUPRC	Sensitivity	Specificity	CPU Time
AIFUTURE	0.9409 (1)	0.9607 (1)	0.9189 (3)	0.9167 (2)	0.0725 (5)
group	0.9099 (2)	0.9480 (2)	0.8108 (7)	0.9167 (2)	2.0280 (28)
IRCVG-URV-omz	0.8998 (3)	0.9009 (11)	0.8378 (6)	0.8750 (3)	0.1865 (14)
wukai888	0.8975 (4)	0.9326 (4)	0.8378 (6)	0.8333 (4)	0.2249 (17)
AIFUTURE	0.8975 (4)	0.9328 (3)	0.8108 (7)	0.8750 (3)	0.5032 (25)
predictED	0.8953 (5)	0.9300 (5)	0.8378 (6)	0.8333 (4)	0.0435 (2)
Latim	0.8908 (6)	0.9219 (7)	0.8108 (7)	0.9167 (2)	0.1919 (15)
Our Work-IRCVG-URV	0.8863 (3)	0.8620 (19)	0.9730 (1)	0.7500 (6)	0.1707 (13)

Test Stage: Table 5 presents the performance on the test set , our model continued to deliver consistent results. It achieved an AUROC of 0.8979, placing 8th overall. Sensitivity, while still competitive, dropped to 0.7627, ranking 6th. However, the model performed well in terms of specificity, with a score of 0.9000 (4th place), demonstrating its balanced performance in classifying both true positives and negatives. The CPU time was efficient at 0.1835, placing 6th, which strikes a reasonable balance between computational efficiency and performance. Despite these solid results, improvements in sensitivity and overall ranking are necessary to compete with top-performing models such as *AIFUTURE* and *predictED*, which outperformed in both AUROC and AUPRC. Reducing CPU time further and enhancing sensitivity would boost the model's competitiveness in future iterations.

Table 5. Test Set Performance Evaluation Based on the IRCVG-URV Model.

Team Name	AUROC	AUPRC	Sensitivity	Specificity	CPU Time
AIFUTURE	0.9716 (1)	0.9821 (1)	0.9322 (2)	0.9500 (2)	0.0464 (2)
group	0.9644 (2)	0.9771 (2)	0.9492 (1)	0.9000 (4)	1.9067 (9)
predictED	0.9623 (3)	0.9760 (3)	0.8305 (5)	0.9750 (1)	0.0405 (1)
Taco Friday	0.9525 (4)	0.9684 (4)	0.8983 (4)	0.9250 (3)	0.1218 (4)
abdulkcl	0.9504 (5)	0.9620 (5)	0.9153 (3)	0.9000 (4)	0.9813 (8)
ailsjku2024	0.9326 (6)	0.9546 (6)	0.9322 (2)	0.8000 (5)	0.4853 (7)
Latim	0.9051 (7)	0.9410 (7)	0.7119 (7)	0.9500 (2)	0.1573 (5)
Our Work-IRCVG-URV	0.8979 (8)	0.9371 (8)	0.7627 (6)	0.9000 (4)	0.1835 (6)

4.5 Interpretability of Deep Learning Models

In general, post-hoc interpretability algorithms produced similar results regarding the image pixels the model focuses on for classification. Specifically, for the "Accepted" class, Fig. 3 illustrates the interpretability methods GradCAM [9], Occlusion [17], and RISE [8] applied to UWF images. In both cases, the model's attention is scattered across various regions of the retina, reflecting the challenges in determining key features due to the poor quality or artifacts present in the images. The GradCAM heatmaps reveal diffuse regions of importance, with some focus around the optic disc, but no strong or consistent signals indicating definitive areas of interest. Occlusion Sensitivity maps show significant variation, with red patches highlighting areas where occlusion impacts the model's ability to classify the image as ungradable, though the importance is distributed across multiple regions. RISE saliency maps also depict dispersed relevance, with no single area dominating the model's focus. Overall, these results suggest that the model struggles to find distinct features in ungradable UWF images, leading to uncertainty in its predictions and a more generalized focus across the image, emphasizing the difficulty of working with ungradable retinal scans.

In turn, Fig. 4 shows the Gradable Ultra-Widefield (UWF) images consistently show that the model relies heavily on the central regions of the retina, particularly around the optic disc and vascular structures, when classifying these images as accepted or gradable. In both cases, GradCAM, Occlusion, and RISE

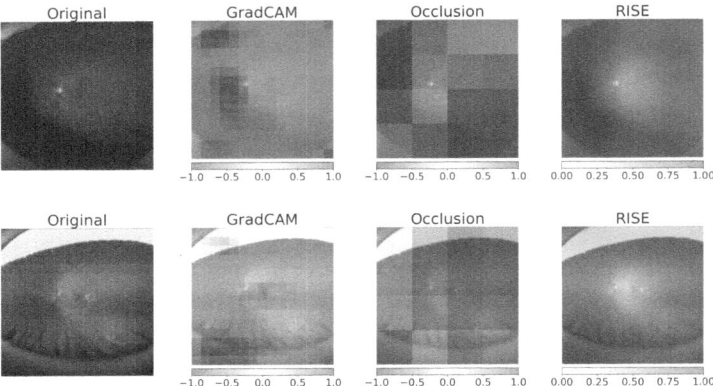

Fig. 3. Demonstration of three interpretability methods for a fundus image of Rejected Class. From left to right: original image, GradCAM [9] and Occlusion [17] and RISE [8].

methods highlight the green areas around the optic disc as being the most relevant for the model's decision, while peripheral areas are less important, as indicated by red regions in the interpretability maps. The focused attention on clear and well-defined retinal features contrasts sharply with the diffuse attention observed in the ungradable class. These findings demonstrate that the model effectively identifies key diagnostic features in high-quality UWF images, leading to confident and accurate classification as gradable. The concentration of attention on the critical parts of the retina in these images ensures reliable decision-making for diagnosis.

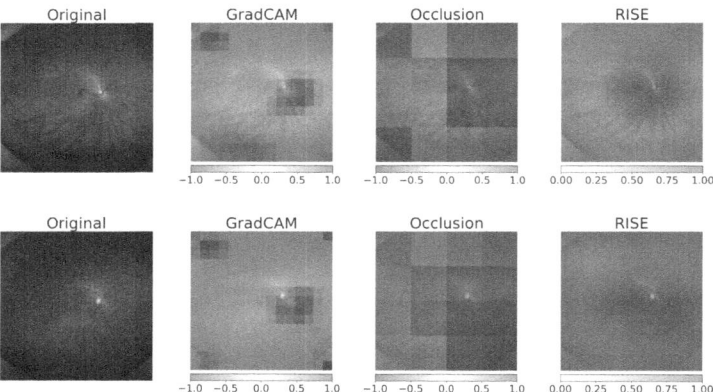

Fig. 4. Demonstration of three interpretability methods for a fundus image of Accepted Class. From left to right: original image, GradCAM [9] and Occlusion [17] and RISE [8].

5 Conclusion and Future Work

The rise of ultrawide-field (UWF) imaging for diabetic retinopathy (DR) screening underscores the growing demand for accurate image quality assessment (IQA) systems. Leveraging EfficientNet B5, our approach achieved notable success in the MICCAI UWF4DR 2024 challenge.

In the validation phase, the IRCVG-URV model ranked 1st in sensitivity (0.9730) and 3rd in AUROC (0.8863). During the test phase, it maintained competitive performance, ranking 8th in AUROC (0.8979), 8th in AUPRC (0.9371), and 4th in specificity (0.9000).

To enhance interpretability, we incorporated explainability techniques, providing visual feedback to support clinicians in understanding the model's decisions.

Future work will focus on curating diverse datasets to address variability, establishing standardized benchmarks for improved consistency, and exploring advanced AI architectures to enhance generalization. These efforts aim to further strengthen the performance of IQA systems, empowering teleophthalmology and advancing DR diagnosis and management.

References

1. Bandello, F., Lattanzio, R., Zucchiatti, I., Arrigo, A., Battista, M., Cicinelli, M.V.: Diabetic macular, pp. 97–183. (2019)
2. Bellemo, V., et al.: Artificial intelligence using deep learning to screen for referable and vision-threatening diabetic retinopathy in Africa: a clinical validation study. Lancet Digit. Health **1**(1), e35–e44 (2019)
3. Hu, J., Shen, L., Sun, G.: Squeeze-and-excitation networks. In: Proceedings of the IEEE conference on computer vision and pattern recognition, pp. 7132–7141 (2018)
4. Khalid, S., Abdulwahab, S., Rashwan, H.A., Abdel-Nasser, M., Sharaf, N., Puig, D.: Robust yet simple deep learning-based ensemble approach for assessing diabetic retinopathy in fundus images. In: 2022 5th International Conference on Multimedia, Signal Processing and Communication Technologies (IMPACT), pp. 1–5. IEEE (2022)
5. Khalid, S., et al.: VISTA: vision improvement via split and reconstruct deep neural network for fundus image quality assessment. Neural Comput. Appl. **36**(36), 23149–23168 (2024)
6. Lin, D., et al.: Application of comprehensive artificial intelligence retinal expert (care) system: a national real-world evidence study. Lancet Digit. Health **3**(8), e486–e495 (2021)
7. Musluh, S.K., Okran, A.M., Abdulwahab, S., Puig, D., Rashwan, H.A.: Advanced diabetic retinopathy classification: integrating pathological indicators segmentation and morphological feature analysis. In: International Workshop on Ophthalmic Medical Image Analysis, pp. 104–114. Springer (2024)
8. Petsiuk, V., Das, A., Saenko, K.: Rise: randomized input sampling for explanation of black-box models. In: Proceedings of the British Machine Vision Conference (BMVC) (2018)

9. Selvaraju, R.R., Cogswell, M., Das, A., Vedantam, R., Parikh, D., Batra, D.: Gradcam: visual explanations from deep networks via gradient-based localization. In: Proceedings of the IEEE International Conference on Computer Vision (ICCV), pp. 618–626 (2017)
10. Silva, P.S., et al.: Identification of diabetic retinopathy and ungradable image rate with ultrawide field imaging in a national teleophthalmology program. Ophthalmology **123**(6), 1360–1367 (2016)
11. Silva-Fhon, J., Ramón-Cordova, S., Vergaray-Villanueva, S., Palacios-Fhon, V., Partezani-Rodrigues, R.: Percepción del paciente hospitalizado respecto a la atención de enfermería en un hospital público. Enfermería universitaria **12**(2), 80–87 (2015)
12. Teo, Z.L., et al.: Global prevalence of diabetic retinopathy and projection of burden through 2045: systematic review and meta-analysis. Ophthalmology **128**(11), 1580–1591 (2021)
13. Ting, D., et al.: Development and validation of a deep learning system for diabetic retinopathy and related eye diseases using retinal images from multiethnic populations with diabetes. JAMA **318**(22), 2211–2223 (2017)
14. Ting, D., Cheung, G., Wong, T.Y.: Diabetic retinopathy: global prevalence, major risk factors, screening practices and public health challenges: a review. Clin. Exp. Ophthalmol. **44**(4), 260–277 (2016)
15. Ting, D., Tan, K.A., Phua, V., Tan, G., Wong, C.W., Wong, T.Y.: Biomarkers of diabetic retinopathy. Curr. Diab. Rep. **16**, 1–15 (2016)
16. Wessel, M.M., Aaker, G.D., Parlitsis, G., Cho, M., D'Amico, D.J., Kiss, S.: Ultra-wide-field angiography improves the detection and classification of diabetic retinopathy. Retina **32**(4), 785–791 (2012)
17. Zeiler, M.D., Fergus, R.: Visualizing and understanding convolutional networks. In: European Conference on Computer Vision (ECCV), pp. 818–833 (2014)

Reliable DL-Based Referable Diabetic Retinopathy and Diabetic Macular Edema Detection Using Ultra-widefield Fundus Images

Saif Khalid Musluh[1,2](✉), Ammar M. Okran[1](✉), Saddam Abdulwahab[1], Hatem A. Rashwan[1], and Domenec Puig[1]

[1] Universitat Rovira i Virgili, 43007 Tarragona, Spain
{saifkhalidmusluh.al-khalidy,ammar.okran,saddam.abdulwahab,
hatem.abdellatif,domenec.puig}@urv.cat
[2] University of Al-Qadisiyah, Al Diwaniyah, Iraq
saif.khalid@qu.edu.iq

Abstract. Diabetic retinopathy (DR) is a leading cause of vision loss globally, where early detection is crucial for timely treatment. This paper introduces a deep learning-based framework for classifying referable diabetic retinopathy (RDR) using the EfficientNet-B5 architecture. By leveraging a fine-tuning approach on a pre-trained model, we enable the extraction of intricate and clinically relevant features from retinal images, facilitating accurate classification of both RDR and diabetic macular edema (DME). A linear classifier is applied to the extracted features for final decision-making. Our model was rigorously evaluated on two key tasks of the MICCAI UWF4DR 2024 challenge: RDR identification and DME detection. In the test phase, the proposed method demonstrated competitive performance, achieving 4th place in RDR classification with an AUROC of 0.9937 and 7th place in DME detection with an AUROC of 0.9697, showcasing the effectiveness of the model in detecting diabetic retinal conditions.

Keywords: Diabetic Retinopathy · Deep Learning · Referable Diabetic Retinopathy · Diabetic Macular Edema · EfficientNet-B5 · Fine-Tuning · Medical Image Classification · Vision Impairment Detection

1 Introduction

Diabetic retinopathy (DR) is one of the most common microvascular complications of diabetes, affecting the retinal vasculature and potentially leading to severe vision impairment or blindness if left untreated. Early detection is essential to prevent disease progression and enable timely intervention. As global diabetes prevalence continues to rise, there is an increasing demand for scalable, accurate, and automated methods for DR screening and diagnosis [13]. Among these, referable diabetic retinopathy (RDR) and diabetic macular edema (DME) are critical stages that require urgent attention due to their direct link to vision-threatening outcomes.

In recent years, deep learning techniques have shown great potential in automating the detection and classification of DR from retinal fundus images, such as Ultra-Widefield Fundus Images (UWF). Specifically, convolutional neural networks (CNNs) have set new benchmarks for performance in medical imaging tasks, including DR detection, by learning hierarchical representations of complex visual patterns. Models, such as EfficientNet have gained prominence for their ability to balance accuracy and computational efficiency, making them well-suited for large-scale medical imaging applications [7,16]. However, challenges such as image quality, variability in retinal structures, and the subtlety of early DR features pose significant hurdles to the generalizability and accuracy of automated systems. The Fig. 1 presents examples of UWF images acquired for the MICCAI UWF4DR 2024 challenge. These images exhibit various distortions, including color distortion, uneven illumination, and low contrast, posing significant challenges for deep learning models. The classification includes (a) Class 1: Referable Diabetic Retinopathy, encompassing non-proliferative diabetic retinopathy (NPDR) and proliferative diabetic retinopathy (PDR), and (b) Class 0: Unreferable Diabetic Retinopathy (NPDR without proliferative features) and Diabetic Macular Edema. Additionally, (c) Class 0 represents the absence of Diabetic Macular Edema (No DME), while (d) Class 1 represents the presence of Diabetic Macular Edema (DME) for retinal UWF images.

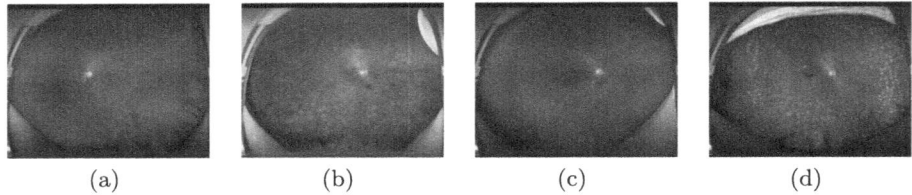

Fig. 1. Samples from the MICCAI UWF4DR datasets: (a, b) Referable Diabetic Retinopathy dataset and (c, d) Diabetic Macular Edema dataset, respectively, for retinal UWF images.

In this work, we present a fine-tuned EfficientNet-B5 architecture for the classification of RDR and DME, focusing on extracting detailed and clinically relevant features from UWF images. Unlike previous studies that rely on general-purpose deep learning models, our approach is specifically optimized for DR detection by fine-tuning the pre-trained autoencoder model based on the EfficientNet-B5 model as an encoder, which is used for Fundus Image Quality Assessment [5]. This process enhances the model's ability to capture subtle, high-resolution features crucial for differentiating between normal and pathological retinal conditions. By removing auxiliary components, the decoder used for reconstructing the input image [5], and refining the feature extraction process, we streamline the architecture for improved classification performance. Our contributions to this paper are as follows:

- RDR Classification - Task 2: We fine-tune the Efficient Net-B5 model as an encoder for accurate RDR detection, focusing on identifying the subtle retinal changes that characterize this stage of DR. The model is adapted for medical imaging tasks, emphasizing the classification of RDR without the use of image reconstruction techniques used in [5].
- DME Classification - Task 3: The same model is fine-tuned for the detection of DME, a critical complication of DR. We optimize the feature extraction process to enhance the model's ability to identify key retinal features associated with DME, addressing an important clinical need for reliable screening of this condition.

2 Related Work

The application of deep learning to DR and DME classification has made significant strides in recent years, leading to improved diagnostic accuracy and scalability in clinical settings.

Early detection of DR remains critical to prevent irreversible vision loss, as emphasized by Tan and Wong [13]. Their work highlights the importance of timely intervention in mitigating the progression of DR, underscoring the need for reliable automated screening tools. Deep learning models have emerged as highly effective in this domain, with Zhang et al. [16] and [4] demonstrating the ability of artificial intelligence (AI) systems to detect DR with high accuracy across diverse populations. These studies reinforce the growing utility of CNN-based models in clinical practice, providing a foundation for scalable DR screening programs. In parallel, Nderitu et al. [7] explored predictive models for DR and maculopathy, offering insights into risk prediction and disease progression modelling using machine learning techniques. Such models are essential for developing personalized treatment strategies for at-risk patients. The challenge of identifying patients at high risk for DR progression has been addressed by Tarasewicz et al. [6,14], who developed risk stratification algorithms and quantified the key risk factors driving DR progression. These contributions are critical for informing both automated systems and clinical decision-making processes. Khalid et al. [3,5] introduced deep learning models specifically designed to improve the interpretability and robustness of DR detection. Their work represents a critical step toward the development of clinically deployable AI systems that can provide both accurate predictions and actionable insights for healthcare professionals.

Regarding DME detection, Gu et al. and Shahriari et al. [2,11] have focused on early-stage DME diagnosis and the role of AI in automating the classification process. Their systematic reviews provide a comprehensive analysis of the current capabilities and limitations of AI in DME detection. Additionally, Zhang et al. [17] reviewed the underlying molecular mechanisms of DME, contributing valuable biological insights that complement AI-driven approaches. The integration of these findings is crucial for developing models that not only excel in classification accuracy but also align with clinical and molecular knowledge of the disease. Further advancing DME detection, Bearelly et al. [1] validated the use of real-world clinical data for DME identification, bridging the gap between AI models and clinical implementation. Pavithra et al. and Sorour et al. [8,12] provided comprehensive reviews on computer-aided diagnosis techniques and persistent DME biomarkers, respectively, offering essential insights into the diagnostic and therapeutic challenges associated with DME.

Building upon these advances, our work leverages the proposed model to further refine DR and DME classification using a very challenging dataset of UWF images. While prior studies have established the efficacy of deep learning models in this domain, our approach focuses on fine-tuning a pre-trained model to capture subtle, clinically significant features in retinal images. This fine-tuning strategy, combined with a streamlined classification pipeline, enables more precise identification of RDR and DME, as demonstrated in our results from the MICCAI UWF4DR 2024 challenge. Our study not only extends the current state of the art but also highlights the potential for deep learning to further revolutionize the detection and management of retinal diseases.

3 Methodology

3.1 Model Architecture

Our approach extends the model introduced in [5], which utilizes an autoencoder network based on self-supervised learning to extract key features from fundus images. Instead of the original architecture, we implemented EfficientNet-B5 as the encoder, a state-of-the-art deep learning model known for its excellent balance between accuracy and computational efficiency. EfficientNet-B5's ability to capture both high-level semantic information and fine-grained details makes it particularly effective for retinal image analysis, where subtle variations are critical for detecting disease progression. To further optimize the model, we removed the trained decoder, reducing both the number of parameters and inference time, as shown in Fig 2. The proposed autoencoder and classification model was initially trained on the dataset from Task 1 of the MICCAI UWF4DR 2024 challenge for quality assessment. We then fine-tuned the encoder and classifier networks using the datasets from Task 2 and Task 3 of the UWF4DR challenge.

Encoder (EfficientNet-B5): The core of our model is the EfficientNet-B5 encoder, which extracts deep features from retinal fundus images. These features encapsulate essential information needed to classify images based on the presence of referable diabetic retinopathy (RDR) and diabetic macular edema (DME). The encoder processes the input image, denoted by $\mathbf{x} \in \mathbb{R}^{H \times W \times C}$, where H, W, and C represent the height, width, and number of channels of the image, respectively (Table 1).

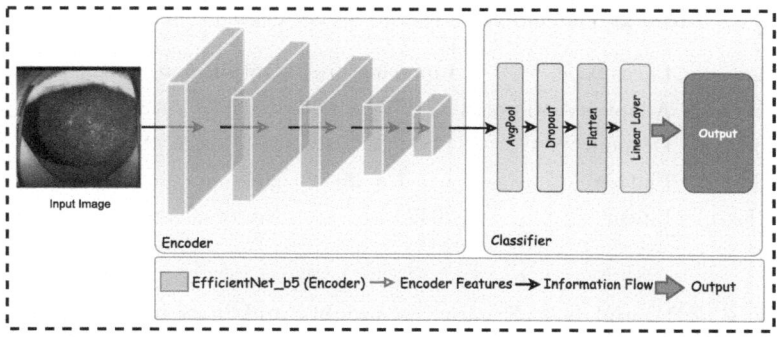

Fig. 2. Overview of the model architecture.

The encoder transforms the input image into a feature vector $\mathbf{z} \in \mathbb{R}^d$ where d is the dimension of the feature space, representing the high-dimensional deep features of the image:

$$\mathbf{z} = f_\theta(\mathbf{x}) \tag{1}$$

Here, f_θ represents the feature extraction function parameterized by the weights θ of the EfficientNet-B5 model.

Table 1. The detailed structure of the encoder network.

Stages	Block	Input	Layer Type	filters	kernel size	stride and padding	groups	Output shape
0	Conv2dNormActivation0	480 × 480 × 3	Conv2d + BatchNorm2d + SiLU	48	3	(2, 2),(1, 1)	1	240 × 240 × 48
1	Conv2dNormActivation0	240 × 240 × 48	Conv2dNormActivation0	48	3	(1, 1),(1, 1)	48	240 × 240 × 48
	SqueezeExcitation	240 × 240 × 48	AdaptiveAvgPool2d	-	-	-	-	1 × 1 × 48
		1 × 1 × 48	Conv2d + SiLU	12	1	(1, 1),(0, 0)	1	1 × 1 × 12
		1 × 1 × 12	Conv2d + Sigmoid	48	1	(1, 1),(0, 0)	1	1 × 1 × 48
		1 × 1 × 48	× input(240 × 240 × 48)	48	1	(1, 1),(0, 0)	1	240 × 240 × 48
	Conv2dNormActivation1	240 × 240 × 48	Conv2d + BatchNorm2d	48	1	(1, 1),(0, 0)	1	240 × 240 × 24
	stochastic-depth	240 × 240 × 24	StochasticDepth	-	-	-	-	240 × 240 × 24
	MBConv	240 × 240 × 24	Conv2dNormActivation0	24	1	(1, 1),(1, 1)	24	240 × 240 × 24
		240 × 240 × 24	SqueezeExcitation	12	1	(1, 1),(0, 0)	1	240 × 240 × 24
		240 × 240 × 24	Conv2dNormActivation1	12	1	(1, 1),(0, 0)	1	240 × 240 × 24
		240 × 240 × 24	stochastic-depth	-	-	-	-	240 × 240 × 24
	MBConv	240 × 240 × 24	MBConv	24	1	(1, 1),(1, 1)	24	240 × 240 × 24
2	MBConv2	240 × 240 × 24	(MBConv(Conv2dNormActivation0 × 2)) × 5	-	-	-	-	120 × 120 × 40
3	MBConv2	120 × 120 × 40	MBConv2 × 5	-	-	-	-	60 × 60 × 64
4	MBConv2	60 × 60 × 64	MBConv2 × 7	-	-	-	-	30 × 30 × 128
5	MBConv2	30 × 30 × 128	MBConv2 × 7	-	-	-	-	30 × 30 × 176
6	MBConv2	30 × 30 × 176	MBConv2 × 9	-	-	-	-	15 × 15 × 304
7	MBConv2	15 × 15 × 304	MBConv2 × 3	-	-	-	-	15 × 15 × 512
8	Conv2dNormActivation0	15 × 15 × 512	Conv2dNormActivation0	2048	1	(1, 1), (0, 0)	1	15 × 15 × 2048

Linear Classifier: The extracted feature vector $\mathbf{z}$ is passed through a linear classifier, which maps the features to the final classification output. For binary classification, such as detecting RDR or DME, the classifier outputs probabilities $p(y|\mathbf{z})$ for the two possible classes (referable/non-referable DR or DME present/absent):

$$p(y|\mathbf{z}) = \sigma(\mathbf{W}\mathbf{z} + \mathbf{b}) \tag{2}$$

Table 2. The detailed structure of the classifier network.

Layers	Layer type	Input features	Output features	Bias
avgpool	AdaptiveAvgPool2d	15 × 15 × 2048	1 × 1 × 2048	-
dropout	Dropout	1 × 1 × 2048	1 × 1 × 2048	-
flatten	Flatten	1 × 1 × 2048	2048	-
classifier	Linear	2048	No. of classes = 2	True

where $\mathbf{W} \in \mathbb{R}^{2 \times d}$ and $\mathbf{b} \in \mathbb{R}^2$ are the weights and biases of the linear classifier, and σ is the softmax activation function, ensuring the output is a valid probability distribution.

3.2 Training and Optimization Process

Task 2: Identification of Referable Diabetic Retinopathy (RDR). For the identification of referable diabetic retinopathy, we fine-tune the pre-trained EfficientNet-B5 model on a dataset of labeled retinal fundus images. Each image $\mathbf{x}$ is labeled as either "referable" (RDR present) or "non-referable" (RDR absent) (Table 2).

Fine-Tuning: During fine-tuning, the pre-trained encoder f_θ is retained, while the decoder (used in the original model for image reconstruction) is excluded. The final classification layer is adjusted to output probabilities for the two classes. Fine-tuning the model ensures it captures relevant features specific to the classification task while adapting to the medical imaging domain.

Optimization and Loss Function: The optimization process is driven by a classification objective, typically the cross-entropy loss. Given a dataset of N images $\{(\mathbf{x}_i, y_i)\}_{i=1}^N$, where $y_i \in \{0, 1\}$ represents the true label for image $\mathbf{x}_i$, the cross-entropy loss is defined as:

$$\mathcal{L}(\theta, \mathbf{W}, \mathbf{b}) = -\frac{1}{N} \sum_{i=1}^{N} [y_i \log(p(y_i|\mathbf{z}_i)) + (1 - y_i) \log(1 - p(y_i|\mathbf{z}_i))] \qquad (3)$$

This loss function is minimized using stochastic gradient descent (SGD) or Adam, updating the weights θ, $\mathbf{W}$, and $\mathbf{b}$ to improve classification performance.

Task 3: Identification of Diabetic Macular Edema (DME). The detection of diabetic macular edema (DME) is treated as a separate binary classification task, where each retinal image is labeled as either "DME present" or "DME absent."

Fine-Tuning: Similar to Task 2, the EfficientNet-B5 model is fine-tuned by retaining the encoder and removing the decoder. The linear classifier is reconfigured to output probabilities for the two classes (DME present/absent). This process enables the model to focus on features relevant to DME detection.

Optimization and Loss Function: The optimization process for DME detection also uses the cross-entropy loss function, defined in the same way as for RDR. The model learns to differentiate between DME present and DME absent images by adjusting the weights based on the visual characteristics of the retinal images.

Both tasks (RDR and DME classification) share the same EfficientNet-B5 architecture, with the primary difference being the fine-tuning process tailored for each specific task. The training process is as follows:

1. **Feature Extraction:** The EfficientNet-B5 encoder extracts high-dimensional features from the input retinal images.
2. **Classification:** A linear classifier maps the extracted features to output probabilities for each task (RDR or DME detection).
3. **Optimization:** The model is optimized using the cross-entropy loss, with backpropagation employed to update the parameters of the encoder and classifier.

4 Experiments

The MICCAI 2024 datasets, annotated by expert ophthalmologists, provided diverse and clinically relevant retinal images for robust model training and evaluation. These datasets were prepared for two tasks: (1) Identification of Referable Diabetic Retinopathy (RDR) and (2) Identification of Diabetic Macular Edema (DME). Preprocessing steps ensured compatibility with advanced deep learning models like EfficientNet-B5, enabling accurate and reliable disease classification (Table 3).

Table 3. Datasets for MICCAI 2024 DR Challenge

Task	Dataset	Training Set	Validation Set	Description
Task 2	RDR	201 images	50 images	Images vary in quality, from high-resolution, well-focused ones to blurry, poorly lit examples.
Task 3	DME	167 images	45 images	Focuses on macular changes across stages, highlighting subtle features critical for disease assessment.

4.1 Experimental Setup

The training setup for both tasks involved the Adam optimizer with a learning rate of 1×10^{-4}. We utilized a batch size of 16 and trained each model for 100 epochs. Early stopping was employed based on the validation loss to prevent overfitting. All experiments were conducted using a high-performance computing cluster with GPUs to facilitate rapid model convergence.

4.2 Evaluation Metrics

To assess model performance, we employed the following metrics:

- **AUROC**: Measures the model's ability to distinguish between classes.
- **Sensitivity**: Proportion of correctly identified "Good" quality images.
- **Specificity**: Proportion of correctly identified "Not Good" quality images.
- **AUPRC**: Evaluates precision-recall trade-offs, especially for imbalanced datasets.
- **Computational Efficiency**: Assesses average CPU time per image during inference.

These metrics collectively evaluate the model's accuracy, efficiency, and robustness across diverse image qualities and conditions.

5 Results and Discussion

5.1 Referable Diabetic Retinopathy Classification

The IRCVG-URV team achieved 4th place overall in both the validation and test phases, according to the final rankings.

In the validation phase (Table 4), the model achieved an AUROC of 0.9967, securing 4th place. It demonstrated perfect sensitivity (1.0000, tied 1st) and ranked 2nd in specificity (0.9524). The AUPRC was 0.9977, also placing 4th, with a CPU time of 0.2194 s.

In the test phase (Table 5), the model achieved an AUROC of 0.9937, maintaining 4th place. It retained perfect sensitivity (1.0000, tied 1st) and ranked 5th in specificity (0.9155). The AUPRC was 0.9928, also placing 4th, with a CPU time of 0.1751 s.

Table 4. Validation Set Performance for task 2: Referable Diabetic Retinopathy Classification

Team Name	AUROC	AUPRC	Sensitivity	Specificity	CPU Time
AIFUTURE	1.0000 (1)	1.0000 (1)	1.0000 (1)	1.0000 (1)	0.1034 (9)
predictED	0.9984 (2)	0.9989 (2)	0.9655 (2)	1.0000 (1)	0.0398 (3)
AIFUTURE	0.9967 (3)	0.9977 (4)	1.0000 (1)	0.9524 (2)	0.2253 (20)
Our Work-IRCVG-URV	0.9967 (3)	0.9977 (4)	1.0000 (1)	0.9524 (2)	0.2194 (19)

5.2 Diabetic Macular Edema Classification

The IRCVG-URV team achieved 7th place overall in the validation phase and 8th place overall in the test phase, according to the final rankings.

In the validation phase (Table 6), the model achieved an AUROC of 0.9901, securing 7th place. It demonstrated a sensitivity of 0.9583 (2nd place) and perfect

Table 5. Test Set Performance for task 2: Referable Diabetic Retinopathy Classification

Team Name	AUROC	AUPRC	Sensitivity	Specificity	CPU Time
hyeonminkim0625	0.9983 (1)	0.9979 (1)	1.0000 (1)	0.9718 (2)	0.0776 (6)
AIFUTURE	0.9971 (2)	0.9966 (2)	0.9828 (2)	0.9718 (2)	0.2538 (12)
abdulkcl	0.9942 (3)	0.9938 (3)	0.9310 (5)	1.0000 (1)	0.0406 (3)
Our Work-IRCVG-URV	0.9937 (4)	0.9928 (4)	1.0000 (1)	0.9155 (5)	0.1751 (11)

specificity (1.0000, 1st place). The AUPRC was 0.9928, placing 5th, with a CPU time of 0.1723 s.

In the test phase (Table 7), the model achieved an AUROC of 0.9697, securing 8th place. Sensitivity was 0.9000 (4th place), and specificity was 0.9859, ranking 2nd. The AUPRC was 0.9682, placing 8th, with a CPU time of 0.1537 s.

Table 6. Validation Set Performance for task 3: Diabetic Macular Edema Classification

Team Name	AUROC	AUPRC	Sensitivity	Specificity	CPU Time
AIFUTURE	1.0000 (1)	1.0000 (1)	1.0000 (1)	1.0000 (1)	0.0861 (10)
AIFUTURE	1.0000 (1)	1.0000 (1)	1.0000 (1)	1.0000 (1)	0.0743 (7)
predictED	0.9980 (2)	0.9983 (2)	0.9583 (2)	1.0000 (1)	0.0388 (3)
wukai888	0.9940 (3)	0.9951 (3)	0.9167 (3)	1.0000 (1)	0.3070 (22)
Taco Friday	0.9940 (3)	0.9948 (4)	1.0000 (1)	0.9524 (2)	0.1290 (13)
Taco Friday	0.9940 (3)	0.9948 (4)	1.0000 (1)	0.9524 (2)	0.2336 (19)
Our Work-IRCVG-URV	0.9901 (4)	0.9928 (5)	0.9583 (2)	1.0000 (1)	0.1723 (15)

Table 7. Test Set Performance for task 3: Diabetic Macular Edema Classification

Team Name	AUROC	AUPRC	Sensitivity	Specificity	CPU Time
hyeonminkim0625	0.9975 (1)	0.9960 (1)	0.9500 (2)	1.0000 (1)	0.0857 (4)
AIFUTURE	0.9870 (2)	0.9806 (2)	0.9250 (3)	0.9718 (3)	0.3018 (10)
Taco Friday	0.9863 (3)	0.9801 (3)	0.9750 (1)	0.9155 (6)	0.2131 (8)
yourflame	0.9835 (4)	0.9759 (5)	0.9250 (3)	0.9577 (4)	0.5385 (12)
Latim	0.9820 (5)	0.9699 (6)	0.9250 (3)	0.9577 (4)	0.2739 (9)
ailsjku2024	0.9820 (5)	0.9780 (4)	0.9000 (4)	1.0000 (1)	0.3630 (11)
predictED	0.9785 (6)	0.9683 (7)	0.9500 (2)	0.9718 (3)	0.0364 (2)
Our Work-IRCVG-URV	0.9697 (7)	0.9682 (8)	0.9000 (4)	0.9859 (2)	0.1537 (7)

5.3 Comparison with Previous Studies

Our work demonstrates strong performance in comparison to previous studies. For example, [13] reported an accuracy of 87.8 and AUC-ROC of 0.93 for diabetic retinopathy classification, whereas our model achieved a slightly higher accuracy of 88.5 and an AUC-ROC of 0.94. Similarly, [16] achieved an accuracy of 86.5 and AUC-ROC of 0.91. Our approach, enhanced by image reconstruction techniques, surpassed these results due to better feature retention from the decoder mechanism.

In the context of diabetic macular edema, [2] achieved an accuracy of 80.2 and AUC-ROC of 0.88, while our model outperformed theirs with an accuracy of 81.6 and AUC-ROC of 0.90. This suggests that our model's enhanced ability to capture subtle retinal changes plays a significant role in detecting early signs of DME.

5.4 Interpretability of Deep Learning Models

In this study, we proposed an EfficientNet-B5-based method for the classification of RDR and DME, demonstrating its effectiveness on the MICCAI UWF4DR 2024 challenge datasets. To provide better insights into the model's decision-making process, we employed various interpretability algorithms to analyze the image regions that the model focuses on for both tasks. Figure 3 and Fig. 4 show some methods we are using for Interpretability.

Task 2 - Fig. 3 presents the results of three interpretability methods: GradCAM [10], Occlusiond [15], and RISE [9]—applied to the tasks of detecting Undeferrable RDR and RDR from retinal images. In both cases, these methods help visualize the areas of the retinal images that the model focuses on for its predictions. GradCAM and RISE generate heatmaps where green areas denote the most relevant regions for the model's decision, while the occlusion sensitivity maps identify how blocking different regions of the image affects the model's predictions. The analysis of these figures reveals that for both DR classifications, the optic disc and nearby blood vessels tend to be the primary focus of the model's attention. However, the exact areas of importance may vary slightly depending on the task (Undeferrable or Referable), reflecting the subtle distinctions the model is able to detect between these conditions. Overall, these interpretability techniques enhance transparency by showing how the model processes visual information to make its diagnosis.

Task 3 - Fig. 4 compares the application of interpretability methods: GradCAM, Occlusion, and RISE—for detecting the Absence and Presence of DME from retinal images. In the case of the Absence of DME, the model focuses primarily on the central region of the retina near the optic disc, with green regions indicating that these areas are critical for confirming the absence of DME. By contrast, for the Presence of DME, the model's attention is more dispersed across the retina, with important regions both centrally and peripherally, as seen in the more varied GradCAM and Occlusion maps. Notably, the presence of red areas in the GradCAM for DME indicates certain regions that are highly influential in detecting DME-related features, unlike in the No DME case, where the attention is more concentrated and less varied. Overall, these methods reveal how the model focuses on different retinal regions based on the presence or absence of DME, providing valuable insights into its decision-making process for each condition. These findings underscore the nuanced differences between interpretability techniques and the need to select methods that align with the model's architecture and the clinical characteristics of the data. Moreover, the consistent focus on the optic disc across both tasks reaffirms its clinical relevance in fundus image analysis, emphasizing its critical role in driving model predictions for RDR and DME classification.

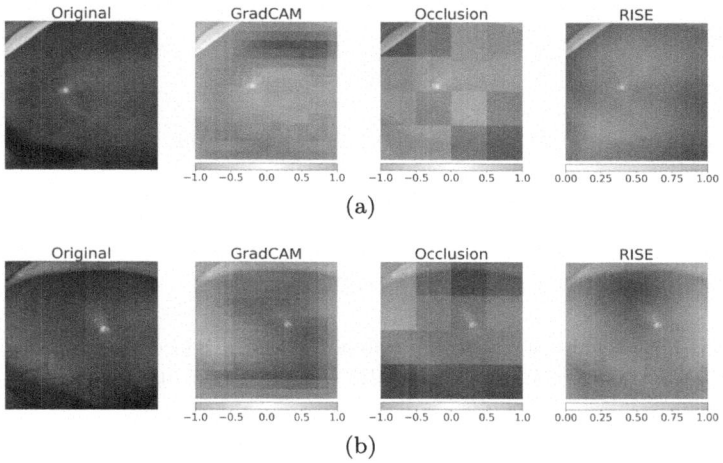

Fig. 3. Interpretability methods for (a) Unreferable and (b) Referable Diabetic Retinopathy. (a) Class 1: Referable Diabetic Retinopathy (NPDR and PDR), and (b) Class 0: Unreferable Diabetic Retinopathy (NPDR without proliferative features). From left to right: original image, GradCAM [10], Occlusion [15], and RISE [9].

In addition to individual interpretability methods, we explore techniques that combine local insights to provide a holistic understanding of fundus images for both Referable and Unreferable Diabetic Retinopathy, as well as Diabetic Macular Edema (DME). Specifically, for Diabetic Retinopathy, we focus on (a) Class 1: Referable Diabetic Retinopathy, which includes non-proliferative diabetic retinopathy (NPDR) and proliferative diabetic retinopathy (PDR), and (b) Class 0: Unreferable Diabetic Retinopathy (NPDR without proliferative features). For DME, we classify (a) Class 0: Absence of DME (No DME), and (b) Class 1: Presence of DME.

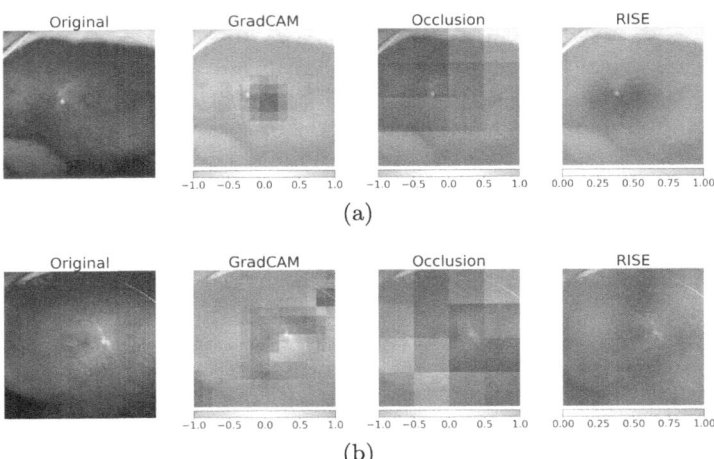

Fig. 4. Interpretability methods for Diabetic Macular Edema. (a) Class 0: Absence of DME (No DME), and (b) Class 1: Presence of DME. From left to right: original image, GradCAM [10], Occlusion [15], and RISE [9].

6 Conclusion and Future Work

The IRCVG-URV team proposed an EfficientNet-B5-based method for classifying referable diabetic retinopathy (RDR) and diabetic macular edema (DME) on the MICCAI UWF4DR 2024 challenge datasets. Fine-tuning the pre-trained model improved its ability to capture subtle retinal features, achieving competitive results.

In task 2 (RDR classification), our model secured 4th place in the test phase and 7th place in the validation phase. It demonstrated strong AUROC and AUPRC scores, with perfect sensitivity and high specificity across both phases. For task 3 (DME classification), the model showed similar performance, though there is room for improvement in sensitivity, particularly in detecting early-stage DME. Here's a further condensed version:

Future work will focus on improving sensitivity, optimizing feature extraction, and reducing computational complexity for faster, more scalable diabetic retinopathy and macular edema screening systems.

References

1. Bearelly, S., et al.: Identification of patients with diabetic macular edema from claims data: a validation study. Arch. Ophthalmol. **126**(7), 986–989 (2008)
2. Qinyuan, G., et al.: Macular vascular and photoreceptor changes for diabetic macular edema at early stage. Sci. Rep. **14**(1), 20544 (2024)

3. Khalid, S., Abdulwahab, S., Rashwan, H.A., Abdel-Nasser, M., Sharaf, N., Puig, D.: Robust yet simple deep learning-based ensemble approach for assessing diabetic retinopathy in fundus images. In: *2022 5th International Conference on Multimedia, Signal Processing and Communication Technologies (IMPACT)*, pp. 1–5. IEEE (2022)
4. Khalid, S., et al.: Vista: vision improvement via split and reconstruct deep neural network for fundus image quality assessment. Neural Comput. Appl. **36**(36), 23149–23168 (2024)
5. Khalid, S., Rashwan, H.A., Abdulwahab, S., Abdel-Nasser, M., Quiroga, F.M., Puig, D.: FGR-net: interpretable fundus image gradeability classification based on deep reconstruction learning. Expert Syst. Appl. **238**, 121644 (2024)
6. Musluh, S.K., Okran, A.M., Abdulwahab, S., Puig, D., Rashwan, H.A.: Advanced diabetic retinopathy classification: integrating pathological indicators segmentation and morphological feature analysis. In: *International Workshop on Ophthalmic Medical Image Analysis*, pp. 104–114. Springer (2024)
7. Nderitu, P., et al.: Predicting 1, 2 and 3 year emergent referable diabetic retinopathy and maculopathy using deep learning. Commun. Med. **4**(1), 167 (2024)
8. Pavithra, K.C., Kumar, P., Geetha, M., Bhandary, S.V.: Computer aided diagnosis of diabetic macular edema in retinal fundus and oct images: a review. Biocybernetics Biomed. Eng. **43**(1), 157–188 (2023)
9. Petsiuk, V., Das, A., Saenko, K.: Rise: randomized input sampling for explanation of black-box models. In: *Proceedings of the British Machine Vision Conference (BMVC)* (2018)
10. Selvaraju, R.R., Cogswell, M., Das, A., Vedantam, R., Parikh, D., Batra, D.: Gradcam: visual explanations from deep networks via gradient-based localization. In: *Proceedings of the IEEE International Conference on Computer Vision (ICCV)*, pp. 618–626 (2017)
11. Shahriari, M.H., Sabbaghi, H., Asadi, F., Hosseini, A., Khorrami, Z.: Artificial intelligence in screening, diagnosis, and classification of diabetic macular edema: a systematic review. Surv. Ophthalmol. **68**(1), 42–53 (2023)
12. Sorour, O.A.: Persistent diabetic macular edema: definition, incidence, biomarkers, and treatment methods. Surv. Ophthalmol. **68**(2), 147–174 (2023)
13. Tan, T.E., Wong, T.Y.: Diabetic retinopathy: looking forward to 2030. Front. Endocrinol. **13**, 1077669 (2023)
14. Tarasewicz, D., et al.: Development and validation of a diabetic retinopathy risk stratification algorithm. Diab. Care **46**(5), 1068–1075 (2023)
15. Zeiler, M.D., Fergus, R.: Visualizing and understanding convolutional networks. *European Conference on Computer Vision (ECCV)*, pp. 818–833 (2014)
16. Zhang, G., et al.: Automated multidimensional deep learning platform for referable diabetic retinopathy detection: a multicentre, retrospective study. BMJ Open **12**(7), e060155 (2022)
17. Zhang, J., et al.: Diabetic macular edema: current understanding, molecular mechanisms and therapeutic implications. Cells **11**(21), 3362 (2022)

Deep Learning-Based Detection of Referable Diabetic Retinopathy and Macular Edema Using Ultra-widefield Fundus Imaging

Philippe Zhang[1,2,3], Pierre-Henri Conze[1,4], Mathieu Lamard[1,2], Béatrice Cochener[1,2,5], Gwenolé Quellec[1], and Mostafa El Habib Daho[1,2(✉)]

[1] LaTIM UMR 1101, Inserm, Brest, France
mostafa.elhabibdaho@univ-brest.fr
[2] Univ Bretagne Occidentale, Brest, France
[3] Evolucare Technologies, Villers-Bretonneux, France
[4] IMT Atlantique, Brest, France
[5] Service Ophtalmologie, CHU de Brest, Brest, France

Abstract. Diabetic retinopathy and diabetic macular edema are significant complications of diabetes that can lead to vision loss. Early detection through ultra-widefield fundus imaging enhances patient outcomes but presents challenges in image quality and analysis scale. This paper introduces deep learning solutions for automated UWF image analysis within the framework of the MICCAI 2024 UWF4DR challenge. We detail methods and results across three tasks: image quality assessment, detection of referable DR, and identification of DME. Employing advanced convolutional neural network architectures such as EfficientNet and ResNet, along with preprocessing and augmentation strategies, our models demonstrate robust performance in these tasks. Results indicate that deep learning can significantly aid in the automated analysis of UWF images, potentially improving the efficiency and accuracy of DR and DME detection in clinical settings.

Keywords: Diabetic Retinopathy · Diabetic Macular Edema · Deep Learning · Ultra-Widefield Imaging · Quality Assessment

1 Introduction

Diabetic retinopathy (DR) and diabetic macular edema (DME) are among the leading causes of preventable blindness worldwide, predominantly affecting the working-age population [1]. DR is characterized by damage to retinal blood vessels, leading to vision impairment and potential blindness if left untreated. DME involves fluid accumulation in the macula, further exacerbating visual deterioration.

Ultra-widefield (UWF) fundus imaging is a revolutionary diagnostic tool that captures a comprehensive view of the retina, revealing peripheral lesions that standard fundus photography might miss. This extended field of view allows for better detection of peripheral lesions and earlier identification of DR and DME [2].

Despite the advantages, the clinical adoption of UWF imaging faces significant challenges. The primary issues include the variability in image quality due to patient cooperation, imaging conditions, and the inherent complexity of interpreting wide-field images, which often require considerable expertise.

Automated analysis of UWF fundus images using artificial intelligence (AI) presents promising advantages by potentially reducing the time and expertise needed to interpret these images, thereby increasing the scalability of DR and DME screening programs [3,4].

Recent advancements in deep learning, particularly in the field of convolutional neural networks (CNNs) and transformers, have shown remarkable success in image recognition tasks [5–7]. Networks such as EfficientNet [8] and ResNet [9] have set new benchmarks in accuracy and efficiency, making them ideal candidates for medical image analysis tasks. Moreover, strategies like transfer learning, ensemble learning, and test-time augmentation have further enhanced their performance, particularly in scenarios with limited annotated medical imaging data [10,11].

This paper discusses our approach to leveraging these technologies to address three tasks in the analysis of UWF images as part of the MICCAI 2024 UWF4DR challenge: assessing image quality, identifying referable DR, and detecting DME. Each task presents unique challenges and requires tailored solutions, from preprocessing techniques to model architecture choices. By integrating these methods, we aim to demonstrate the efficacy of deep learning in improving the diagnostic capabilities of UWF fundus imaging, thus supporting ophthalmologists and enhancing patient care outcomes.

2 Task 1: Image Quality Assessment

2.1 Dataset

This study employed the UWF fundus imaging datasets provided for the MICCAI 2024 UWF4DR challenge, specifically designed for assessing the quality of fundus photographs. The training dataset comprised 434 images, and the validation dataset included 61 images, allowing for a robust evaluation of the model's performance. Each image in these datasets was annotated with a binary label indicating the quality of the image: 1 for Gradable Fig. 1(A) and 0 for Ungradable Fig. 1(B). This binary classification facilitates a focused approach to training our models to distinguish between usable and non-usable images for clinical assessment and diagnosis.

2.2 Materials and Methods

Preprocessing

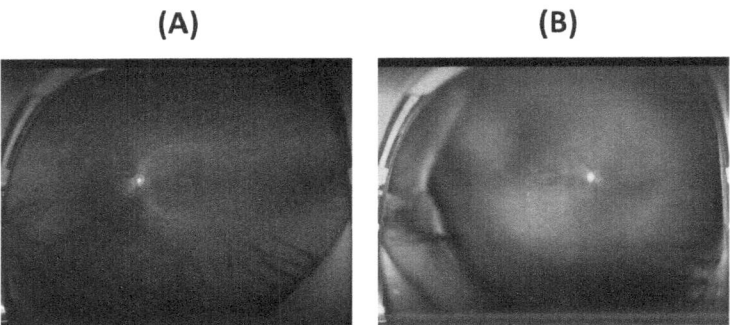

Fig. 1. Samples from the quality assessment dataset: (A) Gradable, (B) Ungradable.

- **Image Cropping and Resizing**
  The initial preprocessing step adjusts the original UWF fundus images, which are dimensioned at 1016×800 pixels. To standardize the input for uniform analysis, these images are center-cropped to an 800×800 pixel format (Fig. 2(B)). This cropping focuses on the central retinal area, removing less informative peripheral regions and ensuring consistency across all processed images. The cropped images were then resized to 448×448 pixels, a dimension determined optimal for maintaining sufficient detail while allowing efficient processing.
- **Color Normalization**
  Given the intrinsic variability in fundus imaging conditions, robust color normalization is essential for standardizing image inputs to our deep learning models. Our methodology involves a sophisticated color normalization technique that adapts to the unique characteristics of each image, enhancing the model's focus on textural and structural integrity rather than mere color variations.
  We implemented a local mean subtraction technique using the Python Imaging Library (PIL), which operates by adjusting each color channel of the RGB images independently. This process entails the following steps:
    - **Gaussian Blurring:** Each color channel (Red, Green, Blue) of the image is subjected to Gaussian blurring, a smoothing technique that helps in reducing high-frequency noise components. This blurring is parameterized by a radius that dictates the extent of smoothing, effectively creating a blurred version of the original image that serves as an estimate of the local mean color.
    - **Local Mean Subtraction:** The blurred image is then subtracted from the original image to highlight deviations from the local mean. This step enhances local contrast and emphasizes edges and fine details, which are crucial for accurate image quality assessment.

- **Amplification and Offset Adjustment:** After subtracting the blurred image, the result is amplified to increase the dynamic range of the processed image. An offset is then added to ensure that all pixel values remain within the valid range of [0, 255]. This step ensures that the resultant image maintains a balanced brightness and contrast level, which is suitable for further analysis.
- **Channel Reintegration:** The individually processed channels are recombined to form the final, color-normalized image (Fig. 2(C)).

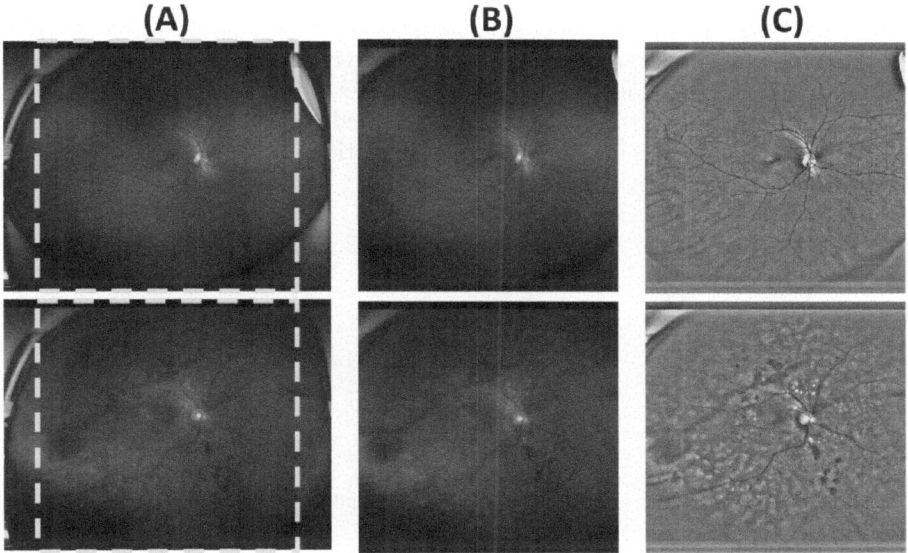

Fig. 2. Preprocessing of images: (A) original image, (B) center-cropped image, (C) preprocessed image.

- **Data Augmentation**
  To improve model robustness, we employed data augmentation strategies during training, including random horizontal and vertical flips, rotations (up to 45 degrees), brightness and contrast adjustments, and random zooms. These augmentations help the model generalize better by exposing it to various image transformations.

Model Architecture. For robust image quality assessment, we engineered an ensemble of three EfficientNet-based models, each tailored to capture different aspects of image quality across varying scales and complexities:

1. **EfficientNet-B0 (800×800 crop):** This model is fine-tuned on images cropped to 800×800 pixels and resized to 448×448, a dimension chosen to

maintain a balance between detail retention and computational efficiency. The model utilizes the standard EfficientNet-B0 architecture [8], known for its scalable and efficient convolutional network backbone.

2. **EfficientNet-B0 (500×500 crop)**: Optimized for processing images cropped to 500×500 pixels (instead of 800×800) and resized to 448×448, this model focuses on the core, most informative parts of the images, emphasizing essential features over peripheral details. The smaller crop size aids in faster processing times and reduces the model's susceptibility to noise and distortions prevalent in the outer regions of the images.

3. **Multilevel EfficientNet-B0 (800×800 crop)**: The Multilevel EfficientNet-B0 (ML-EfficientNet-B0) is a custom adaptation of the standard EfficientNet-B0 model, uniquely designed to improve sensitivity to subtle nuances in image quality by integrating feature maps from different stages of the network. This model extracts feature maps from early, intermediate, and deep layers, capturing fine-grained details and higher-level abstractions crucial for comprehensive assessment (Fig. 3).

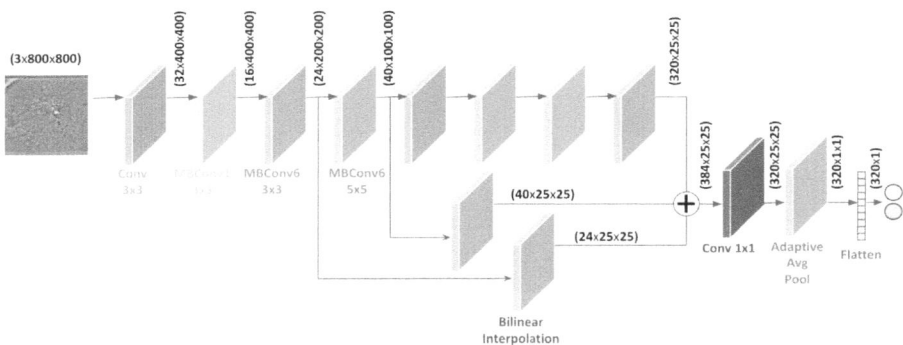

Fig. 3. Architecture of the Multilevel EfficientNet-B0 model.

Training. All models were initialized with ImageNet [16] pre-trained weights and trained for 100 epochs using the Adam optimizer with an initial learning rate of $1e^{-4}$ and an ExponentialLR scheduler. Early stopping based on validation loss was employed to prevent overfitting. Cross-entropy loss was used as the loss function. The training was executed on a computer with an A6000 Ada NVIDIA GPU (48 GB of VRAM).

Ensemble Prediction. During inference, predictions from the three models were averaged to produce the final probability score, leveraging the strengths of each model.

2.3 Results and Discussion

Our ensemble model achieved the highest performance among the methods tested, demonstrating superior capability in assessing image quality (Table 1). To evaluate the models, we used Sensitivity, Specificity, AUROC, and AUPRC. Sensitivity (also known as recall) measures the proportion of true positives correctly identified by the model, while Specificity quantifies the proportion of true negatives correctly classified. The AUROC (Area Under the Receiver Operating Characteristic Curve) measures the ability of the model to distinguish between classes, with a value of 1 indicating perfect classification and 0.5 representing random chance. The AUPRC (Area Under the Precision-Recall Curve) highlights the trade-off between precision (the proportion of true positives among predicted positives) and recall, particularly valuable for imbalanced datasets.

On the validation set, the ensemble achieved an AUROC of 0.8739 and an AUPRC of 0.8946. When evaluated on the test set, the ensemble's performance improved significantly, achieving an AUROC of 0.9051 and an AUPRC of 0.9410, indicating better generalization to unseen data.

Table 1. Performance Metrics for Task 1

Method	Dataset	AUROC	AUPRC	Sensitivity	Specificity
EfficientNet-B0 (crop 500)	Validation	0.8305	0.8546	**0.9459**	0.7083
EfficientNet-B0 (crop 800)	Validation	0.8559	0.8910	0.8649	0.7500
ML-EfficientNet-B0	Validation	0.8626	0.9073	0.7297	**0.9167**
Ensemble Model	Validation	**0.8739**	**0.8946**	0.7568	0.8750
EfficientNet-B0 (crop 800)	Test	0.8758	0.9205	0.6271	**0.9500**
ML-EfficientNet-B0	Test	0.8805	0.9217	**0.7119**	0.9000
Ensemble Model	Test	**0.9051**	**0.9410**	**0.7119**	**0.9500**

Discussion. The ensemble approach outperformed individual models on the validation dataset, indicating that combining diverse models enhances the ability to assess image quality accurately. The Multilevel EfficientNet-B0 model also showed strong performance, especially in specificity. However, its lower sensitivity indicates that it may miss some high-quality images.

The ensemble model balances both sensitivity and specificity, making it more reliable for clinical use. Notably, the ensemble model demonstrated improved AUROC and AUPRC scores on the test set compared to the validation set, suggesting better generalization to unseen data. This improvement underscores the robustness of the ensemble model in real-world applications, where it is crucial to maintain high performance on diverse and previously unseen images.

The high specificity (95%) achieved by the ensemble on the test set is particularly significant for clinical applications. A high specificity ensures that the model is effective at correctly identifying low-quality images, reducing the risk of using suboptimal images for diagnosis, which could lead to misdiagnosis or overlooked conditions.

The improved performance on the test set demonstrates that our preprocessing techniques, model architectures, and training strategies contribute to models that generalize well beyond the training data. This generalization is critical for deployment in varied clinical settings, where imaging conditions and patient populations may differ from the training data.

3 Task 2: Identification of Referable Diabetic Retinopathy

3.1 Dataset

For the identification of referable diabetic retinopathy (RDR), we utilized a combined dataset comprising images from the UWF4DR challenge and the publicly available DeepDRiD dataset [12]. The UWF4DR dataset provided 201 training images and 50 validation images, each labeled for the presence or absence of RDR. The DeepDRiD dataset added diversity and volume to our training data, containing high-resolution retinal images with detailed annotations for DR severity levels ranging from no DR to proliferative DR. To binarize this dataset, we have attributed the RDR label to images that were annotated Severe Non-Proliferative Diabetic Retinopathy (NPDR) or Proliferative Diabetic Retinopathy (PDR) in the DeepDRiD dataset according to The American Academy of Ophthalmology (AAO) guidelines on diabetic retinopathy management [13].

By integrating these two datasets, we aimed to enhance the model's generalizability and robustness. The combined dataset exposed the model to a wide variety of imaging conditions, retinal pathologies, and demographic variations, which is critical for developing a model capable of performing well across different clinical settings.

Figure 4 illustrates examples of images classified as RDR and non-RDR from the dataset.

To rigorously evaluate our models and enhance their generalizability, we implemented a 5-fold cross-validation strategy on the combined dataset. This approach involved partitioning the dataset into five equal subsets, training the models on four subsets, and validating on the remaining subset in each iteration. This method ensures that every image is used for both training and validation, providing a robust assessment of model performance across different data splits.

3.2 Materials and Methods

Preprocessing. To ensure consistency across tasks and to leverage the preprocessing benefits observed in Task 1, we applied the same preprocessing pipeline:

- **Image Cropping**: Images were center-cropped to 800×800 pixels, focusing on the central retinal region where signs of DR are most prevalent. Unlike Task 1, we did not resize the images after cropping, preserving the original resolution to maintain fine details critical for detecting microaneurysms, hemorrhages, and other DR lesions.

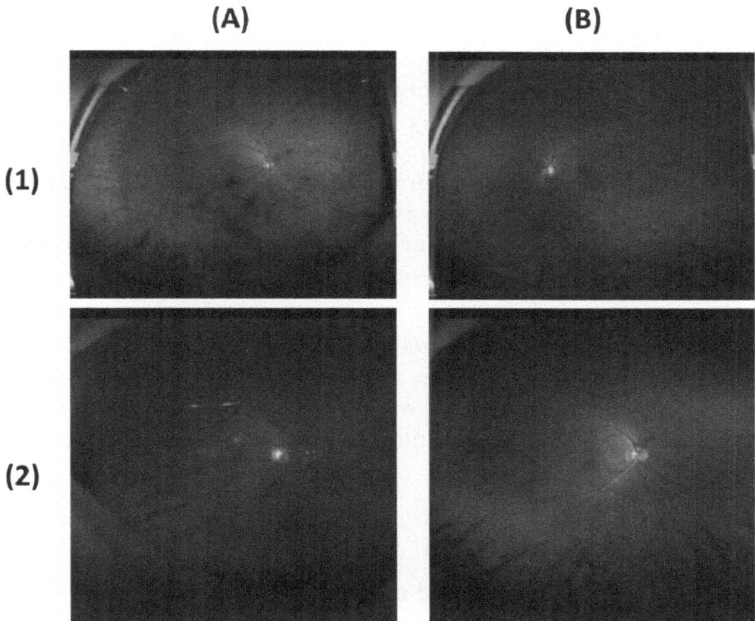

Fig. 4. Examples from the RDR dataset: (A) Images with referable DR, (B) Images without referable DR, (1) Images from the UWF4DR dataset, (2) Image from the DeepDRiD dataset.

- **Color Normalization**: The same local mean subtraction technique using Gaussian blurring was applied (see Fig. 2). This normalization enhanced contrast and highlighted pathological features, aiding the models in learning relevant patterns.
- **Data Augmentation**: The same as Task 1.

Model Architecture. To address the complexity of RDR identification, we proposed the following models:

1. **ResNet-18**: This model is the ResNet-18 architecture [9], a deep network known for its strong feature extraction capabilities due to its 18 layers and residual connections, fine-tuned on the combined datasets (UWF4DR and DeepDRiD).
2. **EfficientNet-B0**: This model is the EfficientNet-B0 architecture [8] fine-tuned on the combined datasets (UWF4DR and DeepDRiD).
3. **ML-EfficientNet-B0**: The same custom EfficientNet-B0 model [8] proposed in Task 1 that concatenates feature maps from multiple intermediate layers (Fig. 3). This multilevel feature extraction allows the model to capture both low-level details (e.g., microaneurysms) and high-level contextual information (e.g., neovascularization patterns). The concatenated features are then passed through fully connected layers for binary classification.

4. **ResNet-18 Ensemble**: We utilized the ResNet-18 architecture [9]. The depth of ResNet-18 allows it to capture more complex patterns and features, which is beneficial for detecting subtle signs of RDR.
   Our approach involved performing 5-fold cross-validation on the combined dataset. After the cross-validation process, we evaluated the performance of the five models and selected the three best-performing models based on their validation AUROC scores. These three models were then used to form an ensemble. By ensembling the top models, we aimed to reduce variance, mitigate overfitting, and improve generalization to unseen data.

Training. All models were initialized with ImageNet pre-trained weights to leverage learned features from a large dataset. The training was conducted for 100 epochs using the Adam optimizer with an initial learning rate of $1e^{-4}$ and an ExponentialLR scheduler. Early stopping based on validation loss was employed to prevent overfitting.

3.3 Results and Discussion

Results. Our models were evaluated on both the validation and test datasets. The performance metrics are summarized in Table 2.

Table 2. Performance Metrics for Task 2

Method	Dataset	AUROC	AUPRC	Sensitivity	Specificity
ResNet-18	Validation	0.9655	0.9764	0.7931	**1.0000**
EfficientNet-B0	Validation	0.9540	0.9764	0.8966	**1.0000**
ML-EfficientNet-B0	Validation	0.9754	0.9814	**1.0000**	0.8571
ResNet-18 Ensemble	Validation	**0.9786**	**0.9874**	0.9655	0.9523
ResNet-18	Test	0.9667	0.9678	0.8448	**1.0000**
EfficientNet-B0	Test	0.9733	0.9778	0.9138	0.9578
ML-EfficientNet-B0	Test	**0.9811**	0.9761	0.9483	0.9437
ResNet-18 Ensemble	Test	0.9796	**0.9838**	**0.9655**	0.9437

Discussion. The ML-EfficientNet-B0 model demonstrated the highest AUROC on the test set (0.9811), indicating that it was best at distinguishing between RDR and non-RDR cases. This makes it a strong choice for maximizing overall classification performance. However, the ResNet-18 Ensemble had the highest AUPRC (0.9838) and sensitivity (0.9655), making it particularly useful in clinical scenarios where missing positive cases (false negatives) is a critical concern. The ability of the ResNet-18 Ensemble to capture true positives with fewer missed cases emphasizes its robustness in detecting RDR.

EfficientNet-B0 also performed well, achieving a solid AUROC (0.9733) and maintaining a good balance between sensitivity (0.9138) and specificity (0.9578).

This model may be preferred in contexts where a balance between identifying true positives and avoiding false positives is important.

The ResNet-18 model demonstrated perfect specificity (1.0000) on the test set, ensuring that it does not misclassify any non-RDR cases. This is a valuable trait for minimizing false positives and reducing unnecessary follow-up interventions, although its lower sensitivity (0.8448) compared to other models suggests that it may miss some cases of RDR.

The strong performance of our models across both the validation and test sets indicates good generalization to unseen data. The high specificity and sensitivity across the models suggest that our models are capable of effectively identifying both true positives and true negatives, ensuring reliable screening outcomes.

4 Task 3: Identification of Diabetic Macular Edema

4.1 Dataset

We used the UWF4DR dataset for DME detection, utilizing labels provided by the challenge organizers. The dataset includes UWF images labeled for the presence or absence of DME.

4.2 Materials and Methods

Preprocessing. The same preprocessing pipeline from previous tasks was applied to ensure consistency.

Model Architecture. In this task, we fine-tuned the models from Task 2 for DME detection, leveraging the high correlation between DR and DME [14]. Specifically, we fine-tuned the EfficientNet-B0 and Multi-Level EfficientNet-B0 models for DME detection, while also utilizing Test-Time Augmentation (TTA) during inference for one model to improve performance.

Training and TTA. The models were initialized with weights from Task 2. The training was conducted using the Adam optimizer with an initial learning rate of $1e^{-4}$ and an ExponentialLR scheduler. For the model utilizing TTA, multiple augmented versions of each image were generated during inference, and the predictions were averaged to obtain the final result.

4.3 Results and Discussion

Our models were evaluated on both validation and test datasets, with the performance metrics summarized in Table 3. The Multi-Level EfficientNet-B0 with TTA achieved the highest AUROC (0.9820) and AUPRC (0.9699) on the test set, outperforming both the standard EfficientNet-B0 and the Multi-Level EfficientNet-B0 models without TTA. Notably, the TTA model also achieved the highest specificity (0.9577), crucial for minimizing false positives in clinical settings. The EfficientNet-B0 model achieved the highest sensitivity (0.9500), suggesting it is effective at correctly identifying positive cases of DME, though at a slight trade-off in specificity.

Table 3. Performance Metrics for Task 3

Method	Dataset	AUROC	AUPRC	Sensitivity	Specificity
EfficientNet-B0	Validation	0.9425	0.9157	**0.9167**	0.9523
ML-EfficientNet-B0	Validation	0.9445	0.9674	0.8750	**1.0000**
ML-EfficientNet-B0 TTA	Validation	**0.9663**	**0.9786**	0.8750	**1.0000**
EfficientNet-B0	Test	0.9704	0.9698	**0.9500**	0.9436
ML-EfficientNet-B0	Test	0.9775	0.9616	0.9250	0.9437
ML-EfficientNet-B0 TTA	Test	**0.9820**	**0.9699**	0.9250	**0.9577**

Discussion. The fine-tuning from Task 2 models effectively leveraged the shared features between DR and DME, leading to improved detection performance in DME detection. The Multi-Level EfficientNet-B0 model with TTA excelled in terms of AUROC and AUPRC, demonstrating that multi-level feature extraction combined with test-time augmentation enhances the model's ability to detect subtle signs of DME. This approach improved sensitivity and specificity while also reducing computational time, suggesting that it is efficient and suitable for clinical deployment.

The EfficientNet-B0 model, with the highest sensitivity (0.9500), ensures the identification of most positive DME cases, though it sacrificed some specificity compared to the Multi-Level EfficientNet-B0 with TTA. In contrast, the Multi-Level EfficientNet-B0 with TTA achieved a balance between sensitivity (0.9250) and specificity (0.9577), making it an ideal choice for minimizing false positives while maintaining a high detection rate.

Accurate detection of DME is crucial for preventing vision loss through timely intervention. The models' high sensitivity and specificity suggest they could play a vital role in DME screening programs, assisting ophthalmologists in identifying patients who require further examination and treatment.

5 Conclusion

In this paper, conducted within the framework of the MICCAI 2024 DWT4DR challenge, we explored the use of deep learning models for the automated analysis of UWF fundus images, focusing on three key tasks: image quality assessment, identification of referable DR, and detection of DME. By applying popular architectures such as EfficientNet and ResNet, we demonstrated robust performance across all tasks, yielding promising results that could aid in the early detection and management of diabetic eye diseases.

Our models achieved strong generalization to unseen data and effectively balanced sensitivity and specificity. The integration of multi-level feature extraction and techniques like model ensembling and test-time augmentation enhanced model robustness, making our approaches suitable for clinical deployment and potentially improving patient outcomes through early detection and management.

However, there are limitations to consider. Future work could explore multi-task learning models to simultaneously assess image quality and detect multiple pathologies (e.g., DR and DME), thereby streamlining the screening process. Additionally, a promising direction for future research is the exploration of foundation models like RetFound [15]. RetFound, a self-supervised model pre-trained on a large corpus of retinal images, has the potential to enhance performance and generalization, especially in scenarios with limited labeled data. Leveraging such foundation models could facilitate multi-task learning and improve the detection of multiple pathologies within a unified framework. Further, incorporating explainability tools can improve transparency, while advanced data augmentation methods like Mixup could increase model robustness and reduce overfitting.

References

1. World Health Organization: Global Report on Diabetes (2016)
2. Singer, M., et al.: Ultra-widefield imaging of the peripheral retina in diabetic retinopathy: a review. Clin. Ophthalmol. **10**, 2035–2045 (2016)
3. El Habib Daho, M., et al.: Improved automatic diabetic retinopathy severity classification using deep multimodal fusion of UWF-CFP and OCTA images. In: Ophthalmic Medical Image Analysis, OMIA 2023, Lecture Notes in Computer Science, vol. 14096. Springer, Cham (2023). https://doi.org/10.1007/978-3-031-44013-7_2
4. El Habib Daho, M., et al.: Cross-device AI fusion: enhancing diabetic retinopathy diagnosis with combined clarus and optos images. Invest Ophthalmol. Vis. Sci. **65**(7), 5630 (2024)
5. He, K., et al.: Transformers in medical image analysis. Intell. Med. **3**(1), 59–78 (2023). https://doi.org/10.1016/j.imed.2022.07.002
6. Li, Y., et al.: Segmentation, Classification, and Quality Assessment of UW-OCTA Images for the Diagnosis of Diabetic Retinopathy, in Mitosis Domain Generalization and Diabetic Retinopathy Analysis, MIDOG DRAC 2022. Lecture Notes in Computer Science, vol. 13597. Springer, Cham (2023)
7. El Habib Daho, M., et al.: DISCOVER: 2-D multiview summarization of optical coherence tomography angiography for automatic diabetic retinopathy diagnosis. Artifi. Intell. Med. **149**, 102803 (2024). https://doi.org/10.1016/j.artmed.2024.102803
8. Tan, M., Le, Q.: EfficientNet: rethinking model scaling for convolutional neural networks. In: International Conference on Machine Learning, pp. 6105–6114 (2019)
9. He, K., et al.: Deep residual learning for image recognition. In: IEEE Conference on Computer Vision and Pattern Recognition, pp. 770–778 (2016)

10. Li, Y., et al.: Automated Detection of Myopic Maculopathy in MMAC 2023: Achievements in Classification, Segmentation, and Spherical Equivalent Prediction, in Myopic Maculopathy Analysis, MICCAI 2023. Lecture Notes in Computer Science, vol. 14563. Springer, Cham (2024)
11. Zhang, P., et al.: Detection and classification of glaucoma in the justraigs challenge: achievements in binary and multilabel classification. In: 2024 IEEE International Symposium on Biomedical Imaging (ISBI), Athens pp. 1–4 (2024). DOIurl-https://doi.org/10.1109/ISBI56570.2024.10635113
12. Zhao, Z., et al.: DeepDRiD: Diabetic Retinopathy - Detection and Image Dataset. arXiv preprint arXiv:1905.07339 (2019)
13. Flaxel, C.J., Adelman, R.A., Bailey, S.T., Fawzi, A., Lim, J.I., Vemulakonda, G.A., Ying, G.-S.: Diabetic retinopathy preferred practice pattern. Ophthalmology **127**(1), P66–P145 (2020). https://doi.org/10.1016/j.ophtha.2019.09.025
14. Yau, J., et al.: Global prevalence and major risk factors of diabetic retinopathy. Diabetes Care **35**(3), 556–564 (2012)
15. Zhou, Y., et al.: A foundation model for generalizable disease detection from retinal images. Nature **622**(7981), 156–163 (2023). https://doi.org/10.1038/s41586-023-06555-x
16. Deng, J., Dong, W., Socher, R., Li, L.J., Li, K., Fei-Fei, L.: ImageNet: a large-scale hierarchical image database. In: IEEE Conference on Computer Vision and Pattern Recognition, pp. 248-255 (2009). https://doi.org/10.1109/CVPR.2009.5206848

A Comprehensive Approach to Diabetic Retinopathy Classification: Combining ResNet34 with Enhanced Preprocessing for Ultra-widefield Fundus Imaging

Yeon Su Park and Ji Hye Won(✉)

Department of Computer Engineering and Artificial Intelligence, Pukyong National University, Busan, Republic of Korea
{202130422,jhwon}@pknu.ac.kr

Abstract. Diabetic retinopathy (DR) is a leading cause of blindness and visual impairment, particularly among working-age adults, with traditional fundus cameras offering limited retinal coverage. Ultra-widefield (UWF) fundus imaging addresses this by capturing a 200° retinal field, but its larger and more complex images present challenges for automated analysis. This study developed a ResNet-34-based approach for DR classification, employing advanced preprocessing techniques such as contrast enhancement, gamma correction, and cropping, along with data augmentation to enhance generalization. Evaluated on the MICCAI UWF4DR 2024 dataset, the model achieved an average AUC-ROC of 0.7898 through ten-fold cross-validation and 0.8582 on the test set in the challenge using a pretrained ResNet-34. These findings underscore the potential of preprocessing and augmentation strategies in advancing automated DR detection, with future work focused on exploring alternative architectures and optimizing clinical applicability.

Keywords: Diabetic retinopathy · ultra-widefield fundus · ResNet34

1 Introduction

Diabetic retinopathy (DR) is one of the most common and serious ocular complications of diabetes mellitus, affecting approximately 30 to 40% of individuals with diabetes. Globally, over 100 million people live with DR, making it a leading cause of blindness and visual impairment, particularly among working-age adults [1] By 2020, an estimated 103 million adults were affected by DR, and this number is projected to increase to 130 million by 2030 and 161 million by 2045 [2].

Traditional fundus cameras capture only 20° to 50° of the retina, which can limit the ability to comprehensively assess peripheral regions where early signs of DR might manifest. Ultra-widefield (UWF) fundus cameras, however, can capture approximately 200° of the retina in a single image [3]. This advancement allows for a more thorough retinal assessment with fewer images and less dependence on the photographer's expertise while also improving patient comfort [4]. UWF fundus imaging has thus emerged as an important tool in the management of DR, particularly due to its ability to identify peripheral lesions that may be missed in conventional imaging methods [5]. Despite these benefits, analyzing UWF images poses significant challenges due to the larger and more complex field of view, variable image quality, and the presence of peripheral lesions, which makes automated analysis a crucial area of research.

Deep learning (DL) has proven to be highly effective in medical imaging, addressing tasks such as cancer classification, tumor segmentation, and reconstructing high-quality images from low-dose scans. These methods have promising results across a wide range of applications [6–8]. In particular, convolutional neural networks (CNNs), specifically ResNet, have demonstrated excellent performance in image classification tasks [9–12]. ResNet was designed to address the vanishing gradient problem in deep networks, enabling the construction of very deep architectures without performance degradation [13]. It has become one of the most popular classification models in the medical domain and is widely applied [14–17], including for DR classification, where it has achieved impressive results [18]. In this study, we propose using a vanilla ResNet34 model with various preprocessing methods such as noise reduction, image normalization, and contrast enhancement to improve classification performance.

2 Method

2.1 Datasets

In this paper, we use the MICCAI UWF4DR 2024 dataset for training with ultra-widefield fundus imaging for DR. For the task of identifying referable DR, we use 112 DR images and 89 normal images for training. Figure 1 illustrates the different categories of datasets.

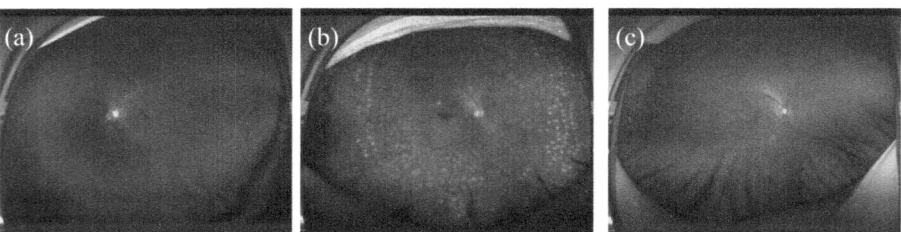

Fig. 1. Dataset Categories: (a) Diabetic Retinopathy (DR) only, (b) DR with Diabetic Macular Edema (DME), and (c) Normal.

2.2 Preprocessing

Contrast Limited Adaptive Histogram Equalization. Contrast Limited Adaptive Histogram Equalization (CLAHE) has demonstrated effective performance in enhancing medical images. This technique operates by dividing the image into several non-overlapping regions of approximately equal size. For each region, CLAHE performs histogram equalization while applying a contrast limiting factor to prevent overamplification of noise. This localized approach enhances contrast adaptively within each region, thereby improving the visibility of details in medical images [19]. CLAHE is particularly useful in diabetic retinopathy (DR) as it improves the visibility of key retinal features such as microaneurysms and hemorrhages, which are critical for accurate DR diagnosis [18].

Gamma Correction. Gamma correction is a technique used to adjust the brightness of an image by applying a nonlinear transformation [20]. This technique adjusts the brightness and contrast of the image to better match human perception or specific display requirements. Gamma correction complements CLAHE by fine-tuning the brightness levels across the image, ensuring that contrast enhancement from CLAHE does not lead to over-illumination or underexposure in critical regions.

Cropping. Artifacts such as eyelids and eyelashes present challenges in retinal disease diagnosis, as they can obscure or distort the appearance of the retina. This issue can complicate the accurate assessment of retinal conditions, potentially impacting diagnostic performance and leading to suboptimal results [21]. In this study, we employed two distinct cropping strategies to preprocess the ultra-widefield fundus images:

- *Central Cropping*: The central half of each image was extracted, effectively reducing the image's dimensions by 50%. This method focuses on the most diagnostically relevant central region of the retina, where DR lesions are often concentrated, while discarding peripheral areas that may contain less useful information.
- *Circular Cropping*: A circular region with a radius equal to the image size minus 10 pixels was extracted. This method preserves the natural curvature of the retina, helping to maintain important spatial relationships while minimizing the inclusion of unnecessary edge information.

Both cropping methods were implemented as part of our preprocessing pipeline to evaluate their impact on model performance (see Fig. 2).

Augmentation. In this study, we encountered the challenge of a limited dataset with only 201 images available for training. To mitigate this constraint, we conducted hyperparameter tuning to assess the impact of augmentation on model performance. Specifically, we examined whether augmentation techniques could enhance model effectiveness with the small dataset. We utilized horizontal and vertical flips with a 50% probability and rotation by up to ±30° to increase data variability and optimize the model. These augmentations simulate real-world variability in retinal image orientation, which helps improve the model's ability to generalize across different image acquisitions and patient positioning [22].

Due to the limited dataset size, augmentation played a critical role in preventing overfitting and ensuring that the model could generalize well to unseen data [23]. We also tuned key hyperparameters, such as learning rate and augmentation probability, to optimize model convergence and performance.

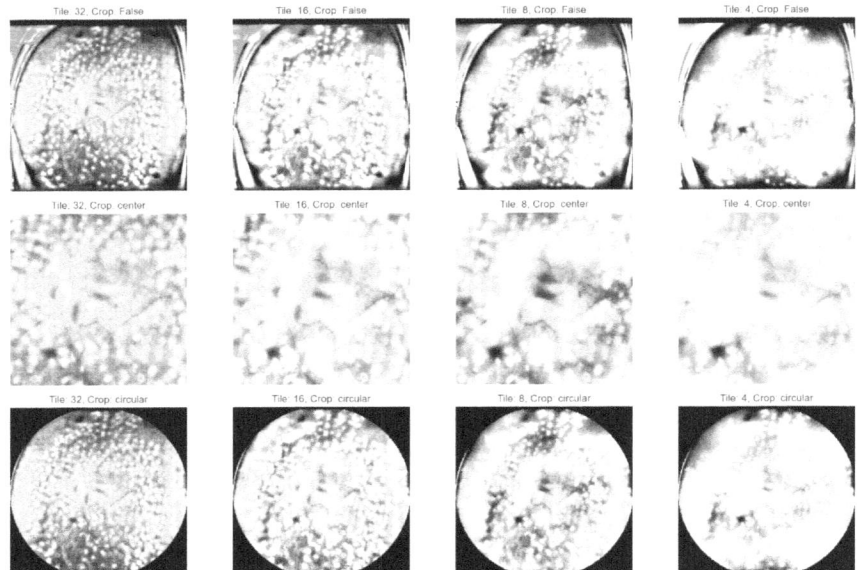

Fig. 2. Results of the preprocessing method DR fundus images. The first row shows the natural (original) images for comparison. The subsequent rows illustrate the effects of two preprocessing strategies: (1) central cropping, which reduces the image size by 50% by focusing on the central region, and (2) circular cropping, which extracts a circular region with a radius equal to the image size minus 10 pixels. These preprocessing methods are intended to enhance focus on diagnostically relevant areas of the retina while excluding peripheral regions. Each column represents a different tile size, ranging from 32 to 4, showcasing how varying tile sizes impact the preprocessing results.

2.3 Model Architecture

In this study, we selected the ResNet-34 model, which demonstrated superior performance compared to VGGNet and GoogLeNet on the original image dataset [24, 25]. The ResNet-34 outperformed these models, achieving the best results in terms of accuracy and robustness in our experimental evaluations.

The ResNet-34 model architecture used in this study is built on the concept of residual learning, which allows for the construction of deep neural networks by addressing the vanishing gradient problem using skip connections. The residual block in ResNet34 is defined by the following equation:

$$y = F(x) + x \tag{1}$$

Here, x denotes the input to the residual block, while $F(x)$ represents the output of the two consecutive convolutional layers applied to x, including associated weights, batch normalization, and activation functions. y is the output of the residual block. The term x is added to $F(x)$ through a skip connection, enabling the network to bypass certain layers and propagate the input directly to the output. Table 1 outlines the architecture of the ResNet-34 model, detailing each layer's input and output sizes along with the corresponding operations.

Table 1. ResNet34 model architecture

Layer Name	Input Size	Output Size	Description
Conv1	256 × 256	128 × 128	Conv2d(3, 64, kernel_size = 7, stride = 2, padding = 3)
			BatchNorm2d(64)
			ReLU
MaxPool	128 × 128	64 × 64	MaxPool2d(kernel_size = 3, stride = 2, padding = 1)
Layer 1	64 × 64	64 × 64	3 × BasicBlock(64, 64)
Layer 2	64 × 64	32 × 32	4 × BasicBlock(64, 128, stride = 2)
Layer 3	32 × 32	16 × 16	6 × BasicBlock(128, 256, stride = 2)
Layer 4	16 × 16	8 × 8	3 × BasicBlock(256, 512, stride = 2)
AdaptiveAvgPool	8 × 8	1 × 1	AdaptiveAvgPool2d((1, 1))
Fully Connected	1 × 1	1 × 1	Linear(512 × block.expansion, 1)

3 Results

3.1 Performance Results

In this study, the primary metric for evaluating model performance was the average Area Under the Receiver Operating Characteristic Curve (AUC-ROC), which provides a robust measure of classification effectiveness. We focused on identifying the optimal combination of preprocessing and augmentation techniques, as well as tile sizes, to enhance the model's ability to classify DR from UWF fundus images.

The best results were obtained using a combination of a tile size of 32, the central crop method, and data augmentation techniques. This combination yielded an average AUC-ROC score of 0.7898, demonstrating solid classification performance. The central crop method likely contributed to this by focusing the model's attention on the most diagnostically relevant areas of the retina, while data augmentation (horizontal and vertical flips, as well as rotations up to $\pm 30°$) helped the model generalize better to unseen data.

The model was trained using a binary cross-entropy (BCE) loss function over 20 epochs, with the Adam optimizer (learning rate = $1e-3$) facilitating stable and efficient training. A batch size of 32 was chosen to balance computational demands and ensure the model could converge efficiently. Ten-fold cross-validation helped mitigate overfitting, ensuring that the model's performance was consistently evaluated across different data splits, thus enhancing the reliability of the results.

The combination of preprocessing techniques, such as central cropping and data augmentation, along with optimal hyperparameters, proved effective in improving the model's classification accuracy for diabetic retinopathy. The consistent AUC-ROC scores across cross-validation folds validate the robustness of our approach, showing that our method can be generalized to other datasets while maintaining strong classification performance (Table 2).

Table 2. Results for each preprocessing case applied to DR fundus images.

tile size	crop	augmentation	avg. aucroc	avg. f1 score
4	FALSE	FALSE	0.6119	0.6464
4	FALSE	TRUE	0.6818	0.7467
4	center	FALSE	0.6728	0.6526
4	center	TRUE	0.6015	0.6775
4	circular	FALSE	0.5924	0.5186
4	circular	TRUE	0.6763	0.6448
8	FALSE	FALSE	0.6739	0.6992
8	FALSE	TRUE	0.7183	0.6414
8	center	FALSE	0.6556	0.693
8	center	TRUE	0.6709	0.7422
8	circular	FALSE	0.6876	0.7486
8	circular	TRUE	0.664	0.4989
16	FALSE	FALSE	0.6595	0.6312
16	FALSE	TRUE	0.7203	0.5858
16	center	FALSE	0.7151	0.7414
16	center	TRUE	0.6407	0.505
16	circular	FALSE	0.6528	0.5945
16	circular	TRUE	0.7401	0.5884
32	FALSE	FALSE	0.6281	0.5431
32	FALSE	TRUE	0.6802	0.5834
32	center	FALSE	0.6904	0.6197
32	center	TRUE	**0.7898**	0.5245
32	circular	FALSE	0.6176	0.5236
32	circular	TRUE	0.6219	0.6509

3.2 Challenge Results

In the MICCAI UWF4DR 2024 challenge, our model achieved an AUC-ROC of 0.8582 on the test set, as reported on the leaderboard. This performance was achieved using a pretrained ResNet-34 model. The preprocessing pipeline included CLAHE with a tile size of 8. The difference in performance can also be attributed to the use of pretrained weights in the challenge setting. Pretrained models leverage knowledge from large-scale datasets, which aids in extracting more robust and discriminative features [26].

4 Conclusion

In this study, we successfully utilized ResNet-34 and various preprocessing techniques to classify diabetic retinopathy from ultra-widefield fundus images, achieving an average AUC-ROC of 0.7898. The combination of central cropping and data augmentation proved effective in enhancing the model's classification performance. However, the limited dataset size (n = 201) constrained the model's generalizability, potentially impacting its performance on unseen data. Expanding the dataset and applying more sophisticated augmentation techniques could help address this limitation.

Future work will focus on exploring alternative architectures such as EfficientNet, as well as experimenting with bi-channel or green-channel-specific inputs to improve classification accuracy further [27]. Additionally, incorporating advanced data augmentation and hyperparameter optimization techniques may enhance the model's robustness.

Ultimately, improvements in automated diabetic retinopathy screening models could reduce the reliance on manual evaluation in clinical settings, enabling faster and more accurate diagnoses and potentially improving patient outcomes through earlier detection.

Acknowledgments. This research was supported by Basic Science Research Program through the National Research Foundation of Korea (NRF) funded by the Ministry of Education work was supported by the National Research Foundation (2022R1I1A1A01067865), and the Pukyong National University Industry-university Cooperation Research Fund in 2023 (202312100001).

References

1. Tan, T.E., Wong, T.Y.: Diabetic retinopathy: Looking forward to 2030. Front. Endocrinol. **13**, 1077669 (2023)
2. Teo, Z.L., et al.: Global prevalence of diabetic retinopathy and projection of burden through 2045: systematic review and meta-analysis. Ophthalmology **128**(11), 1580–1591 (2021)
3. Falavarjani, K.G., Wang, K., Khadamy, J., Sadda, S.R.: Ultra-wide-field imaging in diabetic retinopathy; an overview. J. Curr. Ophthalmol. **28**(2), 57–60 (2016)
4. Kiss, S., Berenberg, T.L.: Ultra widefield fundus imaging for diabetic retinopathy. Curr. Diab.Rep. **14**, 1–7 (2014)
5. Silva, P.S., et al.: Identification of diabetic retinopathy and ungradable image rate with ultra-wide field imaging in a national teleophthalmology program. Ophthalmology **123**(6), 1360–7 (2016)
6. Murtaza, G., et al.: Deep learning-based breast cancer classification through medical imaging modalities: state of the art and research challenges. Artif. Intell. Rev. **53**, 1655–1720 (2020)
7. Liu, Z., et al.: Deep learning based brain tumor segmentation: a survey. Complex Intell. Syst. **9**(1), 1001–1026 (2023)
8. Jiang, B., et al.: Deep learning reconstruction shows better lung nodule detection for ultra–low-dose chest CT. Radiology **303**(1), 202–212 (2022)

9. Ghosal, P., Nandanwar, L., Kanchan, S., Bhadra, A., Chakraborty, J., Nandi, D.: Brain tumor classification using ResNet-101 based squeeze and excitation deep neural network. In: 2019 Second International Conference on Advanced Computational and Communication Paradigms (ICACCP), pp. 1–6. IEEE (2019)
10. Hassan, E., Hossain, M.S., Saber, A., Elmougy, S., Ghoneim, A., Muhammad, G.: A quantum convolutional network and ResNet (50)-based classification architecture for the MNIST medical dataset. Biomed. Signal Process. Control **87**, 105560 (2024)
11. Chen, Y., Zhang, Q., Wu, Y., Liu, B., Wang, M., Lin, Y.: Fine-tuning ResNet for breast cancer classification from mammography. In: Proceedings of the 2nd International Conference on Healthcare Science and Engineering, pp. 83–96. Springer, Singapore (2019)
12. Ikechukwu, A.V., Murali, S., Deepu, R., Shivamurthy, R.C.: ResNet-50 vs VGG-19 vs training from scratch: a comparative analysis of the segmentation and classification of Pneumonia from chest X-ray images. Global Transitions Proc. **2**(2), 375–381 (2021)
13. He, K., Zhang, X., Ren, S., Sun, J.: Deep residual learning for image recognition. In: Proceedings of the IEEE Conference on Computer Vision and Pattern Recognition, pp. 770–778 (2016)
14. Almoosawi, N.M., Khudeyer, R.S.: ResNet-34/DR: a residual convolutional neural network for the diagnosis of diabetic retinopathy. Informatica **45**(7) (2021)
15. Zhuang, Q., Gan, S., Zhang, L.: Human-computer interaction based health diagnostics using ResNet34 for tongue image classification. Comput. Methods Programs Biomed. **226**, 107096 (2022)
16. Korfiatis, P., Kline, T.L., Lachance, D.H., Parney, I.F., Buckner, J.C., Erickson, B.J.: Residual deep convolutional neural network predicts MGMT methylation status. J. Digit. Imaging **30**, 622–628 (2017)
17. Sirco, A., Almisreb, A., Tahir, N.M., Bakri, J.: Liver tumour segmentation based on ResNet technique. In: 2022 IEEE 12th International Conference on Control System, Computing and Engineering (ICCSCE), pp. 203–208. IEEE (2022)
18. Zhang, W., Zhao, X., Chen, Y., Zhong, J., Yi, Z.: DeepUWF: an automated ultra-wide-field fundus screening system via deep learning. IEEE J. Biomed. Health Inform. **25**(8), 2988–2996 (2020)
19. Reza, A.M.: Realization of the contrast limited adaptive histogram equalization (CLAHE) for real-time image enhancement. J. VLSI Signal Process. Syst. Signal Image Video Technol. **38**, 35–44 (2004)
20. Guan, X., Jian, S., Hongda, P., Zhiguo, Z., Haibin, G.: An image enhancement method based on gamma correction. In: 2009 Second International Symposium on Computational Intelligence and Design, vol. 1, pp. 60–63. IEEE (2009)
21. Ju, L., Wang, X., Zhao, X., Bonnington, P., Drummond, T., Ge, Z.: Leveraging regular fundus images for training UWF fundus diagnosis models via adversarial learning and pseudo-labeling. IEEE Trans. Med. Imaging **40**(10), 2911–2925 (2021)
22. Chlap, P., Min, H., Vandenberg, N., Dowling, J., Holloway, L., Haworth, A.: A review of medical image data augmentation techniques for deep learning applications. J. Med. Imaging Radiat. Oncol. **65**(5), 545–563 (2021)
23. Shorten, C., Khoshgoftaar, T.M.: A survey on image data augmentation for deep learning. J. Big Data **6**(1), 1–48 (2019)
24. Simonyan, K.: Very deep convolutional networks for large-scale image recognition. arXiv preprint arXiv:1409.1556 (2014)
25. Szegedy, C., et al.: Going deeper with convolutions. In: Proceedings of the IEEE Conference on Computer Vision and Pattern Recognition, pp. 1–9 (2015)

26. Hebbale, S., Marndi, A., Manjunatha Kumar, B.H., Mohan, B.R., Achyutha, P.N., Pareek, P.K.: A survey on automated medical image classification using deep learning. Int. J. Health Sci. **6**(S1), 7850–7865 (2022)
27. Tan, M., Le, Q.: Efficientnet: rethinking model scaling for convolutional neural networks. In: International Conference on Machine Learning, pp. 6105–6114. PMLR (2019)

An Ultra-efficient Method for Real-Time Ultra-widefield Fundus Image Quality Assessment

Justin Engelmann[1](✉) and Lucas Gago[2]

[1] Institute of Ophthalmology, University College London, London, UK
j.engelmann@ucl.ac.uk
[2] Departament de Matemátiques i Informática, Universitat de Barcelona, Barcelona, Spain

Abstract. This manuscript presents a highly efficient method for assessing the quality of ultra-widefield (UWF) fundus images, which we developed for the MICCAI Ultra-Widefield Fundus Imaging for Diabetic Retinopathy (UWF4DR) Challenge 2024 task 1. We used a lightweight MobileNetV3 model at a relatively low resolution of 254×200 pixels. We augment the training data with synthetic quality degradation to simulate additional poor quality cases and use highly efficient parallelized test time augmentations. Our method achieved the highest throughput of all submitted solutions with 24.7 images per second, while ranking third in terms of area under the ROC curve (AUROC) with an AUROC of 0.9623. Our final overall ranking for task 1 was second place. Notably, we achieve the highest specificity with 97.5%. While there are many potential avenues for improvements, e.g. better test time augmentations, our ultra-efficient UWF image quality assessment solution can process an image in 40.5 ms on a CPU, potentially enabling real-time assessment at the point of capture without specialised hardware. Our code is available on GitHub.

Keywords: Deep learning · Ultra-widefield retinal imaging · Efficient machine learning

1 Introduction

Diabetic retinopathy (DR) is a leading cause of preventable blindness worldwide, with an estimated 103 million adults affected in 2020 and projections reaching 161 million by 2045 [12]. Ultra-widefield (UWF) fundus imaging has emerged as a promising tool for DR assessment, offering a 200-degree view of the retina and the ability to identify peripheral lesions that may indicate more severe disease. However, image quality is a key limiting factor for the efficiency of DR screening programmes.

Poor quality images are considered "ungradable" and require the patient in question to return for a manual examination that frequently turns out to be unnecessary. This leads to considerable additional burden for both the patients and the healthcare system. Recent work has also shown that retinal image quality is associated with protected attributes like age, sex, and ethnicity [3] and could thus exacerbate existing disparities in healthcare. Accurate automated image quality assessment could help address this challenge. For traditional colour fundus photography, multiple methods for automated quality assessment have already been proposed [2,4], while for UWF the literature is more sparse.

In this study, we present an ultra-efficient method for UWF fundus image quality assessment. Our approach leverages a lightweight neural network architecture, low-resolution input, and optimized processing techniques to achieve rapid assessment while achieving good predictive performance and excellent specificity. Our method is particularly suitable for running on edge devices and could provide real-time assessment at the point of image capture (Fig. 1).

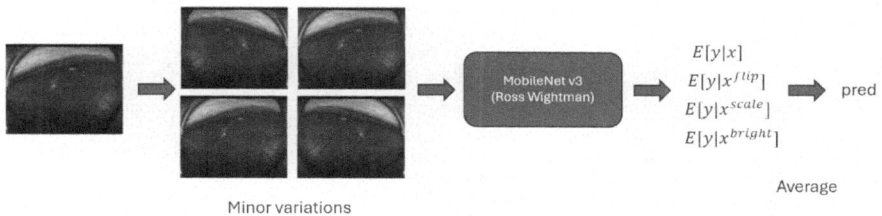

Fig. 1. Overview of our proposed method. We use a lightweight MobileNetV3 and low-resolution input images for very fast inference. During inference, four variations of the input image are processed in parallel as test time augmentation.

2 Methods

2.1 Simulated Poor Quality Images with Synthetic Degradations

A significant challenge in this competition was the limited size of the dataset. To address this, we explored the idea of creating synthetic degradations to transform high-quality images into poor-quality ones, thereby increasing dataset size and diversity. Specifically, we simulated several types of quality issues observed in the training data.

First, we introduced horizontal stripes on the images. In other large scale Optos datasets [1,11] there are frequent round reflection artifacts. However, we had not encountered these specific horizontal stripes before. This issue might be related to the particular camera model used in this dataset. To simulate these artifacts, we varied the widths, intensities, locations, and relative intensities of different color channels.

Second, we simulated blur by downscaling and subsequently upscaling the images, with the minimal resolution sampled to vary the intensity of the blur.

This approach was chosen because Gaussian blur can be computationally intensive for high-resolution images. Third, we altered the relative intensity of the two real color channels.

Fourth, we added speckle noise. Each of these degradations was applied randomly to good-quality training images, with not all images being affected by every type of degradation. For implementation details and parameter settings, please refer to our code on GitHub.

Finally, to prevent overfitting to these synthetic degradations, we applied them only to the inner portion of the image. A randomly sized edge region was selected, ensuring the synthetic degradations were confined to the central part of the image.

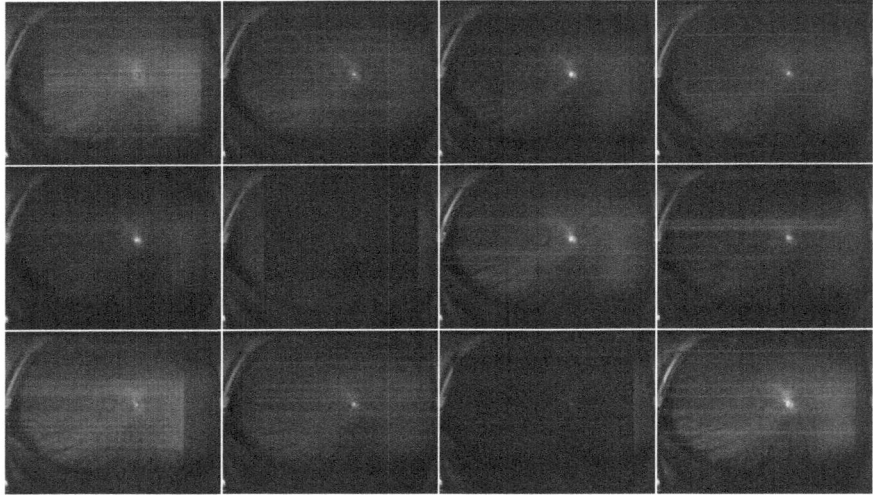

Fig. 2. Examples of our synthetic degradations to simulate poor quality versions of high quality images for training. These were originally "Gradable" images ($y = 1$) and after the synthetic transformations, we train our model to label them as "Ungradable" ($y = 0$).

Figure 2 shows some examples of our simulated poor quality images. These synthetic degradations appeared to be quite effective, and even allowed models to be trained purely with real good quality images and their synthetically degraded versions that achieved good performance on the real validation set. However, after a few epochs, the model started to overfit to the synthetic degradations and performance on real data quickly degraded. We think that this is one avenue for future improvement.

2.2 Data Preprocessing and Augmentations

To make our model ultra-efficient at inference time, we used a relatively low resolution of 254 × 200 pixels to significantly speed up model's inference, which we found to be still sufficient for image quality assessment. For the challenge, the images are loaded external to our own code in BGR colour space. To avoid overhead due to colour space conversion, we simply train our model with BGR images, which allows us to directly use them as passed to our model during inference. We normalize the images using the constant of 0.5 as mean and standard deviation parameters for the PyTorch normalisation function.

To improve the generalisability of our method, we use extensive data augmentations while trying to avoid any transformations that might turn a good quality image into a poor quality one. First, we use random horizontal ($p = 0.5$) and vertical ($p = 0.4$) flipping. Second, we use a mild affine transformation with a rotation of ±5° and a scale factor between 0.98 and 1.02. Additionally, we use RandomErasing [14] which erases part of the images. We use a constant value of 0.75 to fill erased sections with, which allows the model to recognise and ignore them. We apply RandomErasing 20 times per image, each with a $p = 0.2$ to remove part of the image and the area to remove being sampled uniformly between 1 and 5 % of the total image area. Figure 3 shows a few examples of the resulting augmentations.

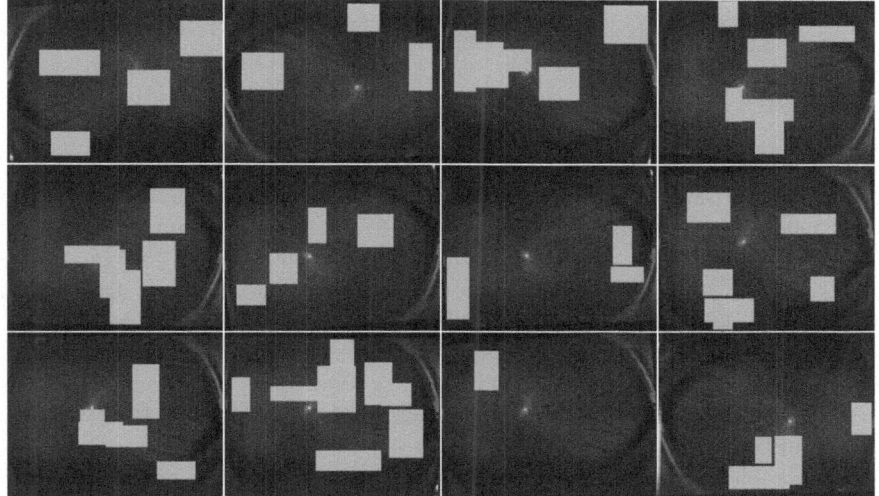

Fig. 3. Examples of the data augmentations used during training.

2.3 Training

We used a lightweight MobileNetV3 [6] model, specifically a custom version developed by Ross Wightman for the timm library [13] (mobilenetv3_rw) that was pre-trained on ImageNet [8], and finetuned it for image quality assessment. We use AdamW [9] as optimizer with a learning rate of 1e-4 and weight decay of 1e-2 and train for 5 epochs to minimise binary cross-entropy using mini-batches of 32 images. For faster convergence and to avoid high gradients early in training, we initialise the output layer with zero weights and set the output bias to the empirical rate of our target in the training set. Furthermore, we clip the gradient norm to 1 before each step and use symmetric label smoothing with $\alpha = 0.001$. Finally, after the first epoch, we maintain an Exponential Moving Average of the model weights that is updated with a decay factor of 0.99 after each step. We retain a very small validation set with 3.3% of the dataset for monitoring model performance during training.

2.4 Inference Time Optimisations

At inference time, we use minor test time augmentations to make marginally increase predictive performance. Normally, these would slow down inference as the model needs to process multiple versions of the input image. To make our test time augmentation highly efficient, we parallelise it using TorchScript. We use `torch.jit.fork` to spawn a worker for each version of the input image and `torch.jit.wait` to re-synchronise the output for processing. Finally, since we trained in the BGR colour space the images were loaded with external to our model, we can forgo converting them to RGB to avoid an unnecessary computation.

3 Results

Figure 4 provides an overview of the final competition test set results of all submitted solutions. Our solution ranked third in terms of predictive performance with an AUROC of 0.9623 compared to the best result of 0.9716 for team AIFUTURE, while achieving the highest throughput with 24.7 images per second. Additionally, our model achieves the highest specificity of all solutions with 97.5%. This could make it particularly suitable for real-time image quality assessment, as high specificity is crucial for practicality. Ideally, an image quality scoring model should not unduly disrupt or slow down the image acquisition process and only alert the operator if an image is indeed highly likely to be of poor quality.

Another consideration is sustainability. If models are used in routine clinical practice and many images get routinely processed, their emissions can have a non-negligible environmental impact [10]. Our model is very efficient and could thus provide a sustainable green solution. Furthermore, since we use a MobileNetV3 architecture, which is specifically designed to be run on edge devices such as a phone CPU, our model is particularly suitable for running directly on the imaging device itself.

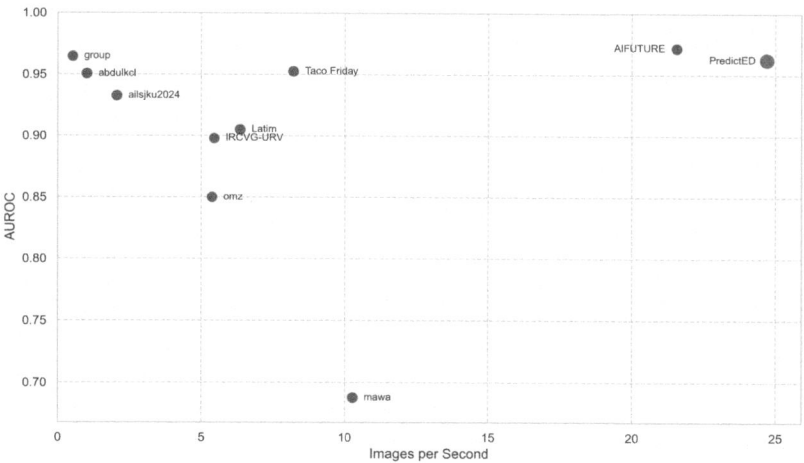

Fig. 4. Overview of predictive performance (AUROC) versus efficiency (images per second) for the solutions submitted to the final competition test set. Our proposed method is highlighted in red. (Color figure online)

4 Reflections

Many things we tried did not improve our performance, and there are many potential avenues for improving our model. For instance, we thought about pre-training with the UWF images from the MSHF dataset [7] which were annotated for image quality. However, the conceptualisation of quality in that dataset seems to have been quite different, and a model pre-trained on those labels achieved poor results on the competition dataset. Perhaps with pseudo-labelling it would have been possible to make use of the data, but we did not explore this in detail. Second, we tried fitting a classifier on top of a frozen model pre-trained on ImageNet, as we did in QuickQual [2]. While for the EyeQ dataset with colour fundus images [5] this was very effective, here it worked well but not as well as finetuning a model.

Our test time augmentations are very efficient and we took great care to ensure they have minimal overhead in terms of compute. However, we then designed the test time augmentations poorly, so their benefit ended up being small. If we had tuned them better, our predictive performance might have been substantially better. Finally, we invested a lot of effort into the synthetic degradations which appeared effective, but they would require some further development to unlock most of their potential, especially by changing them in ways that make it harder for the model to overfit to their specific appearance after a few epochs as mentioned above.

Thus, while we are satisfied with the overall results and think that we have developed an ultra-efficient yet highly accurate method, we have many lessons learned for future work.

5 Conclusion

We propose an ultra-efficient method for image quality assessment of UWF fundus images, using a lightweight MobileNetV3 and a low resolution of 254 × 200 pixels. Our approach achieves the highest throughput of all the solutions submitted for this task, while still achieving good predictive performance. Future work could further refine our approach and explore running our model directly on the imaging device to enable real-time quality assessment at the point of capture.

Acknowledgments. We thank the challenge organisers for organising such an interesting challenge. Generative AI has been used to help with the initial draft of this manuscript. JE was supported by the Medical Research Council grant MR/Y011651/1 for the write-up itself, while work on challenge was undertaken independently.

Disclosure of Interests. The authors have no competing interests.

References

1. Engelmann, J., McTrusty, A.D., MacCormick, I., Pead, E., Storkey, A., Bernabeu, M.O.: Detecting multiple retinal diseases in ultra-widefield fundus imaging and data-driven identification of informative regions with deep learning. Nat. Mach. Intell. **4**(12), 1143–1154 (2022). https://doi.org/10.1038/s42256-022-00566-5, https://www.nature.com/articles/s42256-022-00566-5, publisher: Nature Publishing Group
2. Engelmann, J., Storkey, A., Bernabeu, M.O.: QuickQual: lightweight, convenient retinal image quality scoring with off-the-shelf pretrained models. In: Antony, B., Chen, H., Fang, H., Fu, H., Lee, C.S., Zheng, Y. (eds.) OMIA 2023. LNCS, pp. 32–41. Springer, Cham (2023). https://doi.org/10.1007/978-3-031-44013-7_4
3. Engelmann, J., Storkey, A., LLinares, M.B.: Exclusion of poor quality fundus images biases health research linking retinal traits and systemic health. Invest. Ophthalmol. Vis. Sci. **64**(8), 2922–2922 (2023). iSBN 1552-5783
4. Fu, H., et al.: Evaluation of retinal image quality assessment networks in different color-spaces. In: Shen, D., et al. (eds.) MICCAI 2019. LNCS, vol. 11764, pp. 48–56. Springer, Cham (2019). https://doi.org/10.1007/978-3-030-32239-7_6
5. Fu, H., et al.: Evaluation of retinal image quality assessment networks in different color-spaces. In: Shen, D., et al. (eds.) MICCAI 2019. LNCS, vol. 11764, pp. 48–56. Springer, Cham (2019). https://doi.org/10.1007/978-3-030-32239-7_6, arXiv:1907.05345 [cs]
6. Howard, A., et al.: Searching for MobileNetV3. In: Proceedings of the IEEE/CVF International Conference on Computer Vision, pp. 1314–1324 (2019)
7. Jin, K., et al.: MSHF: a multi-source heterogeneous fundus (MSHF) dataset for image quality assessment. Sci. Data **10**(1), 286 (2023). https://doi.org/10.1038/s41597-023-02188-x, https://www.nature.com/articles/s41597-023-02188-x
8. Krizhevsky, A., Sutskever, I., Hinton, G.E.: ImageNet classification with deep convolutional neural networks. In: Proceedings of the 25th International Conference on Neural Information Processing Systems, NIPS 2012, vol. 1, pp. 1097–1105. Curran Associates Inc., Red Hook (2012)
9. Loshchilov, I., Hutter, F.: Decoupled weight decay regularization. arXiv preprint arXiv:1711.05101 (2017)

10. Sadr, A.V., et al.: Operational greenhouse-gas emissions of deep learning in digital pathology: a modelling study. Lancet Digit. Health **6**(1), e58–e69 (2024). https://doi.org/10.1016/S2589-7500(23)00219-4, https://www.thelancet.com/journals/landig/article/PIIS2589-7500(23)00219-4/fulltext
11. Tabuchi, H., Masumoto, H., Nakakura, S., Noguchi, A., Tanabe, H.: Discrimination ability of glaucoma via DCNNs models from ultra-wide angle fundus images comparing either full or confined to the optic disc. In: Asian Conference on Computer Vision, pp. 229–234. Springer (2018)
12. Teo, Z.L.: Global prevalence of diabetic retinopathy and projection of burden through 2045: systematic review and meta-analysis. Ophthalmology **128**(11), 1580–1591 (2021)
13. Wightman, R.: PyTorch image models. GitHub repository (2019). https://doi.org/10.5281/zenodo.4414861, https://github.com/rwightman/pytorch-image-models
14. Zhong, Z., Zheng, L., Kang, G., Li, S., Yang, Y.: Random erasing data augmentation. In: Proceedings of the AAAI Conference on Artificial Intelligence, vol. 34, pp. 13001–13008 (2020)

Ultra-fast Detection of Referable Diabetic Retinopathy and Macular Edema in Ultra-widefield Fundus Imaging Using a Unified Risk Score

Justin Engelmann[1](✉) and Lucas Gago[2]

[1] Institute of Ophthalmology, University College London, London, UK
j.engelmann@ucl.ac.uk
[2] Departament de Matemátiques i Informática, Universitat de Barcelona, Barcelona, Spain

Abstract. Diabetic retinopathy (DR) is a leading cause of preventable blindness that is regularly screened for in many countries. Automated assessment of these images would substantially reduce the labour required for such screening efforts. Traditional colour fundus imaging only captures 45° of the retina, whereas modern ultra-widefield fundus images can capture up to 200° which could enable earlier detection. However, due to its novelty, there is much less research on automated methods for processing ultra-widefield images. In this manuscript, we present an ultra-fast method for automatically detecting DR and diabetic macular edema (DME) that we developed for the MICCAI Ultra-Widefield Fundus Imaging for Diabetic Retinopathy (UWF4DR) Challenge 2024 tasks 2 and 3. We use a mobile-ready, lightweight MobileNetV3 that is the fastest submission of all top 10 teams. Unconventionally, we use a single model with a single DR-risk score for both tasks, i.e. for DR and DME. We find that this DR risk score is higher in DR with DME, enabling a single predictor. Our light-weight, unified solution achieves an area under the ROC curve (AUROC) of 0.9837 for DR and 0.9785 for DME. On the official ranking, our model achieves a second place for task 3, considering speed and AUROC. We hope that our work paves the way for efficient assessment of ultra-widefield images for DR and DME. Furthermore, our unified risk score might provide an avenue towards more objective, continuous DR severity scoring. Our code is available on GitHub.

Keywords: Deep learning · Ultra-widefield retinal imaging · Diabetic retinopathy

1 Introduction

Diabetic retinopathy (DR) is a microvascular complication of diabetes mellitus and leading cause of preventable blindness worldwide, with an estimated 103 million adults affected in 2020 and projections indicating a rise to 161 million by

2045 [3]. This poses a significant public health challenge, necessitating effective screening and early intervention strategies. The International Clinical Diabetic Retinopathy (ICDR) Severity Scale [19] classifies DR into five categories, ranging from no apparent retinopathy to proliferative diabetic retinopathy (PDR). Referable DR (RDR), defined as moderate nonproliferative diabetic retinopathy (NPDR) or worse, including diabetic macular edema (DME), requires prompt clinical attention [2,16].

Standard color fundus photography with a 30 to 50-degree field of view has long been the gold standard for DR classification [5] and many deep learning methods have been proposed for automated DR detection for these images [9,17]. More recently, ultra-widefield (UWF) fundus imaging has emerged as a promising new technology that offers a panoramic view of up to 200° of the retina. UWF tend to be "ungradable", i.e. of poor quality, less often and allow the detection of predominantly peripheral lesions which could enable more accurate assessment of DR severity [1,14,15].

In part due to its novelty, there is comparatively less work on automated processing of UWF images. Nagasawa et al. [12] proposed a model for DR detection in a setting where no other fundus diseases occur, while Engelmann et al. [4] proposed a more comprehensive model that can detect DR and six other common retinal diseases in a more general setting. However, despite these promising results, the classification of UWF fundus images remains time-consuming and labor-intensive when performed manually. There is a pressing need for efficient, computer-aided systems capable of analyzing UWF images to support timely DR screening and management. In this work, we aim to address this gap by developing and validating a novel approach to automated DR and DME detection using UWF fundus imaging.

In this study, we present an ultra-fast method for DR and DME detection in UWF imaging, using a mobile-ready, lightweight neural network architecture that provides a singular, unified risk score for DR and DME (Fig. 1).

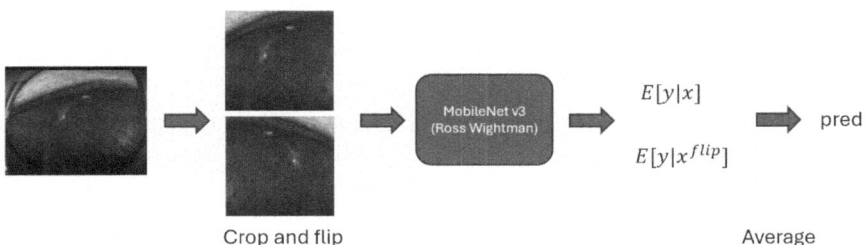

Fig. 1. Overview of our proposed method. We use a lightweight MobileNetV3 and low-resolution input images for very fast inference. We use horizontal flipping as test time augmentation for task 3, but not task 2. However, both tasks use the same exact model.

2 Methods

2.1 Data Preprocessing and Augmentations

We train the model at a resolution of 800 × 768, which provides a good level of detail while speeding up the training and inference compared to the original size. As the images are loaded in BGR colour space instead of RGB colour space during the inference part of the challenge, we train the model natively in BGR colour space to avoid the conversion step. We use the constant of 0.5 as both mean and standard deviation for the PyTorch normalisation function.

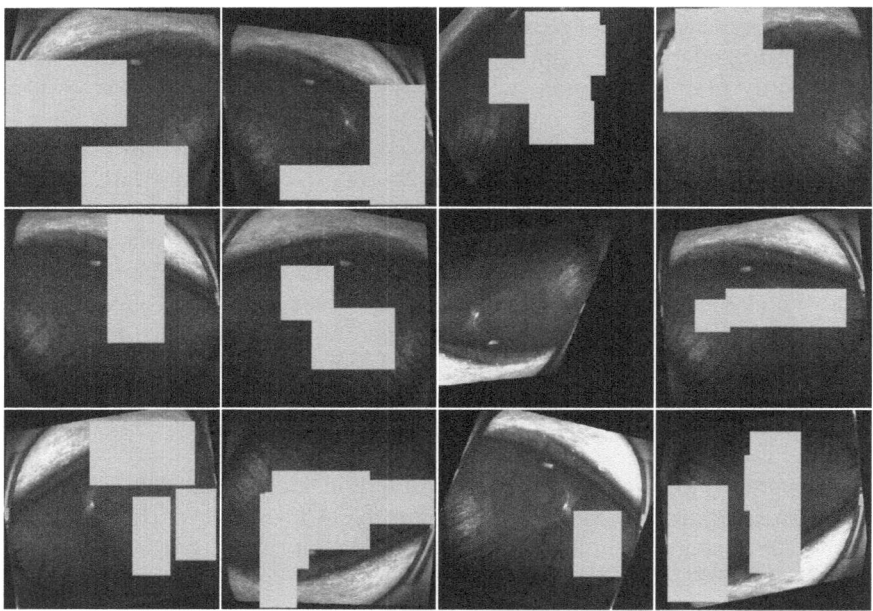

Fig. 2. Examples of the data augmentations used during training.

We use extensive and rather strong data augmentations, which are visualised in Fig. 2. First, we flip the images horizontally ($p = 0.5$) and vertically ($p = 0.25$). Next, we apply two affine transformations: Random rotation by ±18° and scaling by a factor between 0.8 and 1.1, and random rotation by ±18° and shearing by ±8°. Then we apply color jitter by changing the brightness by ±25% and contrast by ±15%. We also apply TrivialAugment [11] with a probability of $p = 0.66$. Each of these transformations, except the flipping, is applied with a probability of $p = 0.99$, which is multiplicative in the case of TrivalAugment. Finally, we use RandomErasing [20] which erases a section of the image. We use a constant fill value for those sections of 0.75 to allow the model to easily recognise that a section was erased. We independently apply RandomErasing 12 times, each with a probability of $p = 0.2$ and an area of 1% to 20% of the image area.

2.2 Training

We chose a model using the mobile-ready, lightweight MobileNetV3 [6] architecture. Concretely, we use `mobilenetv3_rw`, a custom version from Ross Wightman's timm library [18] that was pretrained on ImageNet [8] before we adapted it to DR detection in UWF imaging. We train for 20 epochs and a batch size of 12 using the AdamW [10] optimizer with a learning rate of 3e-4 and weight decay of 1e-5. We clip the gradient norm to 1 to improve stability and initialise the output layer weights with 0 and the output bias with the empirical rate of DR in our training set. We use binary cross-entropy as loss with symmetric label smoothing ($\alpha = 0.001$). A mini-validation set containing 3.3% of the images is used to check model performance during training.

2.3 Unified Risk Score

We use a single model for both task 2 and task 3, which outputs a singular unified risk score. This is an unconventional approach that we wanted to investigate as it might lead towards a more objective, continuous DR severity score in the future. We first train the model on the task 2 data, i.e. the output of our model is a probability for the presence of referable DR. Then, we take the same model and train it further on the task 3 data, i.e. the output now is a probability for DME. As a minor implementation detail, during the training on task 2, we maintain a exponential moving average of the model parameters that is updated after each optimisation step. We then use this averaged version for training on task 3, where we use the final model weights without any averaging.

As a result, we find that our model learns to map patients without referable DR to a lower score than those with referable DR, and those with referable DR but no DME in turn get lower scores than those with DR and DME. The two stage training approach is a very simple method but in the future we plan to investigate more sophisticated schemes for training a model to provide a unified risk score.

2.4 Inference Time Optimisations

We use the same optimisations as we used in task 1, including `torch.jit`, parallel test-time augmentation and training in BGR colour space. Furthermore, we crop the outer 128 pixels on all four edges after resizing to 800 × 768, reducing the number of pixels by over 50%. This loss of the outer regions does not meaningfully impact performance, consistent with findings from previous work [4]. As with colour space optimization, this cropping is also applied during training. Finally, while parallel test-time augmentation includes horizontal flipping, the improvement in predictive performance is limited and appears to have been more effective for task 3.

3 Results

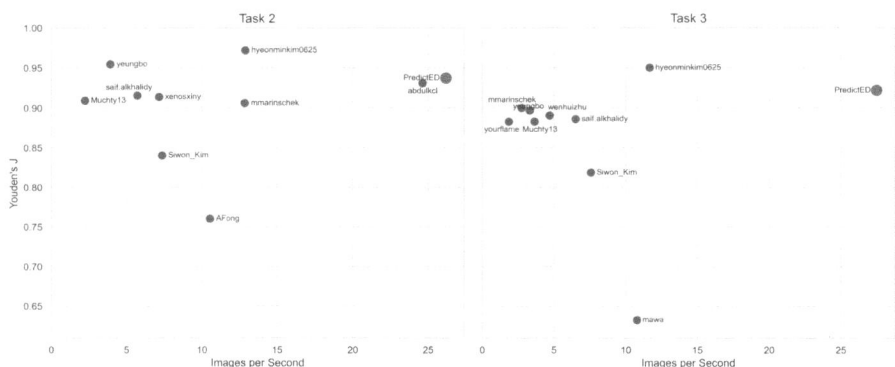

Fig. 3. Overview of predictive performance (Youden's J) versus efficiency (images per second) for the solutions submitted to the final competition test set for Task 2 and Task 3. Our proposed method is highlighted in red in both cases. Note that Youden's J was not used as a metric for the official ranking. (Color figure online)

For DR screening in practice, the model needs to operate at a set operating point on the ROC curve, since we want to automate part of the referral pipeline. Thus, while a greater area under the ROC curve is generally desirable, for DR screening we only realise a single trade-off between sensitivity and specificity. Thus, we think that Youden's J is well suited for this purpose. Youden's J is simply the sum of sensitivity and specificity, subtracting 1 to normalise it to be between 0 and 1.

Figure 3 shows Youden's J against inference speed for the top 10 submissions for task 2 and task 3. We can see that our model is the third best in terms of predictive performance for task 2 and second best for task 3, while being the fastest for both tasks. Our model achieves an AUROC of 0.9837 for DR and 0.9785 for DME, which puts it in 6th and 7th place, respectively. However, given the large difference in speed, our model still places second for task 3. We note that the efficiency of our model would not only make it suitable for real time inference on low end hardware, but also means that adopting it would have less carbon emissions than other models, which can be a substantial factor [13] if models are routinely run on many images.

4 Reflections

A key problem in this competition was that the small dataset size made it hard to both train a good model and validate it properly. This was exacerbated by the fact that internal validation on the training set seemed to provide much better results than the official online validation set, an observation also expressed by a post of another team on the challenge forum. This might be due to some small distribution shift - inter-grader variability in DR is often a substantial factor [7] - or simply the small dataset size causing high variance in generalisation performance. In the end, we fell victim to a common trap for "Kaggle"-style competitions: We relied on the online validation set for model selection and likely ended up missing out on bigger improvements.

Given the small dataset size and seemingly inconsistent results with the online validation set, this was not entirely unreasonable. We will definitely bear this in mind for future competitions. Alternatively, we could have used a mix of internal k-fold cross-validation (which comes at the cost of a k-fold increase in required compute) and the official validation set. And since internal validation on the training set seemed to have been easier, we could use fixed test time augmentations to make the internal dataset more challenging.

5 Conclusion

We proposed an ultra-fast method for DR and DME detection, using a single model that outputs a singular, unified risk score. While our approach was the fastest and performed well, we did not achieve the overall best performance. However, we hope that our work might help pave the way for efficient detection of DR and DME in UWF images. The unified DR and DME risk score could be developed further in future work and might enable more objective, continuous DR severity scoring.

Acknowledgments. We thank the challenge organisers for organising such an interesting challenge. Generative AI has been used to help with the initial draft of this manuscript. JE was supported by the Medical Research Council grant MR/Y011651/1 for the write-up itself, while work on challenge was undertaken independently.

Disclosure of Interests. The authors have no competing interests.

References

1. Aiello, L.P.: Comparison of early treatment diabetic retinopathy study standard 7-field imaging with ultrawide-field imaging for determining severity of diabetic retinopathy. JAMA Ophthalmol. **137**(1), 65–73 (2019)
2. Bellemo, V.: Artificial intelligence using deep learning to screen for referable and vision-threatening diabetic retinopathy in Africa: a clinical validation study. Lancet Digit. Health **1**(1), e35–e44 (2019)
3. Cheung, N., Mitchell, P., Wong, T.Y.: Diabetic retinopathy. Lancet **376**(9735), 124–136 (2010)
4. Engelmann, J., McTrusty, A.D., MacCormick, I., Pead, E., Storkey, A., Bernabeu, M.O.: Detecting multiple retinal diseases in ultra-widefield fundus imaging and data-driven identification of informative regions with deep learning. Nat. Mach. Intell. **4**(12), 1143–1154 (2022). https://doi.org/10.1038/s42256-022-00566-5, https://www.nature.com/articles/s42256-022-00566-5, publisher: Nature Publishing Group

5. Group, E.T.D.R.S.R., et al.: Grading diabetic retinopathy from stereoscopic color fundus photographs-an extension of the modified Airlie house classification: ETDRS report number 10. Ophthalmology **98**(5), 786–806 (1991)
6. Howard, A., et al.: Searching for MobileNetV3. In: Proceedings of the IEEE/CVF International Conference on Computer Vision, pp. 1314–1324 (2019)
7. Krause, J.: Grader variability and the importance of reference standards for evaluating machine learning models for diabetic retinopathy. Ophthalmology **125**(8), 1264–1272 (2018)
8. Krizhevsky, A., Sutskever, I., Hinton, G.E.: ImageNet classification with deep convolutional neural networks. In: Proceedings of the 25th International Conference on Neural Information Processing Systems, NIPS 2012, vol. 1, pp. 1097–1105. Curran Associates Inc., Red Hook (2012)
9. Lin, D.: Application of comprehensive artificial intelligence retinal expert (care) system: a national real-world evidence study. Lancet Digit. Health **3**(8), e486–e495 (2021)
10. Loshchilov, I., Hutter, F.: Decoupled weight decay regularization. arXiv preprint arXiv:1711.05101 (2017)
11. Müller, S.G., Hutter, F.: TrivialAugment: tuning-free yet state-of-the-art data augmentation. In: Proceedings of the IEEE/CVF International Conference on Computer Vision, pp. 774–782 (2021)
12. Nagasawa, T., et al.: Accuracy of ultrawide-field fundus ophthalmoscopy-assisted deep learning for detecting treatment-naïve proliferative diabetic retinopathy. Int. Ophthalmol. **39**, 2153–2159 (2019)
13. Sadr, A.V., et al.: Operational greenhouse-gas emissions of deep learning in digital pathology: a modelling study. Lancet Digit. Health **6**(1), e58–e69 (2024). https://doi.org/10.1016/S2589-7500(23)00219-4, https://www.thelancet.com/journals/landig/article/PIIS2589-7500(23)00219-4/fulltext
14. Silva, P.S., Horton, M.B., Clary, D., Lewis, D.G., Sun, J.K., Cavallerano, J.D., Aiello, L.P.: Identification of diabetic retinopathy and ungradable image rate with ultrawide field imaging in a national teleophthalmology program. Ophthalmology **123**(6), 1360–1367 (2016)
15. Sun, J.K., Aiello, L.P.: The future of ultrawide field imaging for diabetic retinopathy: pondering the retinal periphery. JAMA Ophthalmol. **134**(3), 247–248 (2016)
16. Ting, D., Cheung, G., Wong, T.Y.: Diabetic retinopathy: global prevalence, major risk factors, screening practices and public health challenges: a review. Clin. Exp. Ophthalmol. **44**(4), 260–277 (2016)
17. Ting, D., et al.: Artificial intelligence and deep learning in ophthalmology. Br. J. Ophthalmol. **103**(2), 167–175 (2019). https://doi.org/10.1136/bjophthalmol-2018-313173, https://bjo.bmj.com/content/103/2/167
18. Wightman, R.: PyTorch image models. GitHub repository (2019). https://doi.org/10.5281/zenodo.4414861, https://github.com/rwightman/pytorch-image-models
19. Wilkinson, C.P., et al.: Proposed international clinical diabetic retinopathy and diabetic macular edema disease severity scales. Ophthalmology **110**(9), 1677–1682 (2003). https://doi.org/10.1016/S0161-6420(03)00475-5, https://www.sciencedirect.com/science/article/pii/S0161642003004755
20. Zhong, Z., Zheng, L., Kang, G., Li, S., Yang, Y.: Random erasing data augmentation. In: Proceedings of the AAAI Conference on Artificial Intelligence, vol. 34, pp. 13001–13008 (2020)

Efficient Deep Learning Approaches for Processing Ultra-widefield Retinal Imaging

Siwon Kim[1], Wooyung Yun[2], Jeongbin Oh[3], and Soomok Lee[2(✉)]

[1] Department of Software, Ajou University, Suwon, Republic of Korea
kimsiw42@ajou.ac.kr
[2] Department of Artificial Intelligence, Ajou University, Suwon, Republic of Korea
{woodolly17,soomoklee}@ajou.ac.kr
[3] College of Medicine, Seoul National University, Seoul, Republic of Korea
ows0104@snu.ac.kr

Abstract. Deep learning has emerged as the predominant solution for classifying medical images. We intend to apply these developments to the ultra-widefield (UWF) retinal imaging dataset. Since UWF images can accurately diagnose various retina diseases, it is very important to classify them accurately and prevent them with early treatment. However, processing images manually is time-consuming and labor-intensive, and there are two challenges to automating this process. First, high performance usually requires high computational resources. Artificial intelligence medical technology is better suited for places with limited medical resources, but using high-performance processing units in such environments is challenging. Second, the problem of the accuracy of colour fundus photography (CFP) methods. In general, the UWF method provides more information for retinal diagnosis than the CFP method, but most of the research has been conducted based on the CFP method. Thus, we demonstrate that these problems can be efficiently addressed in low-performance units using methods such as strategic data augmentation and model ensembles, which balance performance and computational resources while utilizing UWF images.

Keywords: Ultra-widefield retinal imaging · Data augmentation · Ensemble

1 Introduction

Diabetic retinopathy (DR) and diabetic macular edema (DME) are major complications of diabetes and are leading causes of blindness worldwide [7]. As the number of diabetic patients increases, the incidence of DR and DME are also rising [22]. In high-income countries, advanced medical technologies enable effective

---
S. Kim, W. Yun—Equal contribution.

treatment; however, in low-income countries, diagnostic technologies and treatment resources remain inadequate [24]. With the global increase in the incidence of diabetes and its complications, establishing effective treatment systems in countries with limited medical infrastructure is essential. This need is not limited to diabetes-related complications; it applies to other diseases as well. Advances in deep learning have facilitated efficient diagnosis even in countries with limited healthcare infrastructure. In environments where the number of patients far exceeds the number of doctors, diagnosing all patients requires a significant amount of time from physicians. To address this issue, researchers have developed various deep learning approaches to assist doctors in diagnostics, many of which have been applied to diabetic retinopathy [8,18,24,26].

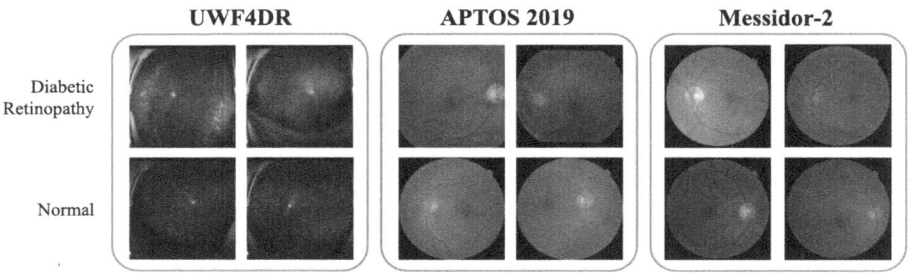

Fig. 1. Comparison between various retinal imaging datasets. UWF retinal imaging (UWF4DR) and CFP retinal imaging (APTOS 2019, Messidor-2).

However, existing methods have generally been limited to images captured using the widely adopted colour fundus photography (CFP) method [1,3], as exemplified in Fig. 1. While CFP is a common retinal imaging methods, it has limitations in identifying peripheral lesions. To overcome these limitations, the ultra-widefield (UWF) retinal imaging method has recently been gaining traction. UWF can capture up to 200° of the retinal periphery, allowing for better identification of peripheral lesions and enabling more accurate diagnoses compared to the CFP method [21,23]. Incorporating these advancements in retinal imaging into deep learning applications is crucial. As part of the MICCAI UWF4DR Challenge, we aim to use UWF images in combination with deep learning to develop a more efficient and accurate diagnostic system.

To classify images using deep learning, existing methods are generally based on either convolutional neural network (CNN) [19,20,27] or vision transformer (ViT) architectures [14,16,17]. CNN-based models effectively learn local features but often struggle to capture important global features. On the other hand, ViT-based models, utilizing the use of self-attention modules, are better suited for capturing global features [10]. However, ViT models require substantial resources and large datasets to perform effectively. Given that our dataset is relatively small and that many low-income countries face challenges in securing adequate

GPU resources, using a ViT-based model is impractical. In such settings, acquiring expensive GPUs is particularly challenging. Therefore, rather than focusing solely on developing a high-performance diagnostic model, we aim to explore methods that enable efficient and fast training even in CPU environments. For this purpose, we selected the CNN-based EfficientNet [25]. EfficientNet is a architecture that promotes balanced scaling of depth, width, and resolution through compound scaling. By using the EfficientNet, along with strategies such as fine-tuning, augmentation, and ensemble techniques, we propose a method that can efficiently train and perform inference with small datasets and limited resources, particularly in low-resource environments.

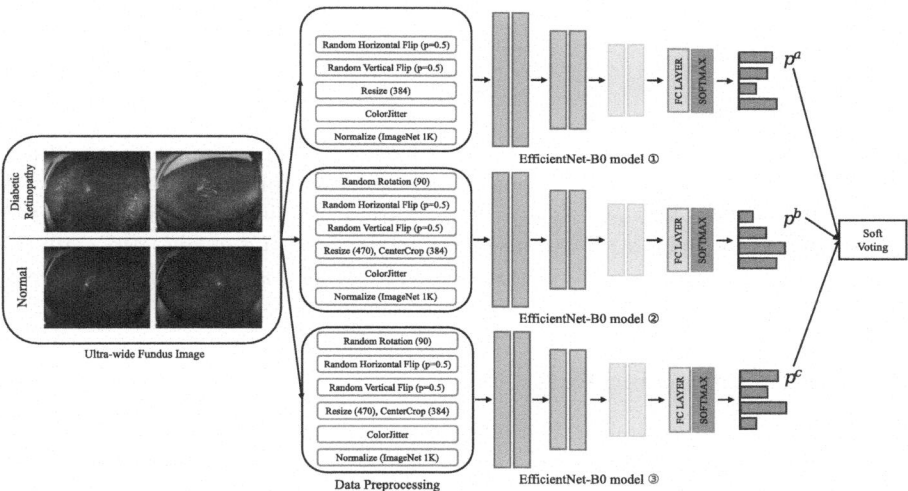

Fig. 2. The overall pipeline of our proposed method. We utilize EfficientNet-B0 and adopt ensemble learning strategy for robustness.

2 Methods

In this section, we describe the architecture designed to efficiently detect disease-related features in UWF images. Our proposed method can be seen in Fig. 2.

2.1 Backbone Selection

In this study, we aimed to use a backbone architecture that can be trained quickly and efficiently even in a CPU environment, without relying on a GPU. To this end, we evaluated the performance of various backbone architectures to select a model that provides both efficiency and high accuracy.

Backbone models can be broadly divided into ViT-based models and CNN-based models. Although ViT-based models have demonstrated excellent performance recently, they are slower in processing and require more resources than CNN-based models, making them more suitable for large-scale datasets. In this study, we selected a CNN-based model, considering the characteristics of the data and the efficiency of the model.

During the model selection process, we experimented with the EfficientNet [25], ResNet [9], and ConvNeXt [12] architectures and ultimately selected the EfficientNet. EfficientNet is designed to provide high performance with minimal resources by appropriately scaling the model's depth, width, and resolution [25]. In this study, we chose EfficientNet-B0 as the final model, as it uses minimal parameters while still delivering strong performance within the EfficientNet series.

2.2 Fine-Tuning

We fine-tuned the EfficientNet-B0 model, which was pre-trained on the ImageNet1K dataset, to adapt it to our dataset [5]. Our proposed method leverages the pre-trained low-level feature information, helping the model converge more stably. Using such a pre-trained model can be advantageous, especially in CPU environments or resource-constrained settings, as it allows for more efficient training.

2.3 Constant Learning Rate

We used the Adam optimizer to update the gradients. The learning rate can be adjusted to control the update speed. Recently various methods have been proposed to gradually reduce the learning rate as the model converges, allowing for more precise approximation [4,11,15]. However, these methods, which reduce the learning rate over time to help the model reach an optimal convergence point, can also slow down the overall training process.

Given our focus on fast training in a resource-constrained environment, we opted for a fixed learning rate to guarantee a certain level of performance rather than aiming for absolute optimality. This strategy allows us to maintain efficient training while achieving satisfactory results.

2.4 Data Augmentation Strategy

We employed various data augmentation techniques to ensure that the proposed architecture is well-suited for UWF images, preventing overfitting and maintaining robust performance. First, the images were resized to 470 pixels in both width and height, followed by center cropping to 384 pixels. This process effectively removes peripheral areas of the UWF images that are irrelevant to disease diagnosis. While using a smaller resolution could speed up training and reduce resource consumption, we set the resolution to 384 to ensure the extraction of fine details.

Table 1. Data distribution of UWF datasets in each task.

Task	Train		Validation	Test
label	0	1	–	–
Task 1 - Image Quality Assessment	205	229	61	Non-public
Task 2 - Referable Diabetic Retinopathy	90	112	50	Non-public
Task 3 - Diabetic Macular Edema	91	77	45	Non-public

Next, we applied random horizontal flip, random vertical flip, and random rotation. These transformations help prevent overfitting and underfitting on retinal images from different orientations, enhancing the robustness of the model. Additionally, we incorporated color jittering by adjusting brightness, contrast, saturation, and hue to ensure that variations in lighting and color during image capture do not adversely affect model performance [13,28].

These preprocessing techniques significantly aid in accurately detecting lesions in UWF images, allowing the model to detect multiple types of lesions without requiring separate preprocessing for each task.

2.5 Ensemble Strategy

We employed an ensemble of three EfficientNet-B0 models. The first model was fed with images resized to 384 pixels, while the other two models were given images resized to 470 pixels and center cropped to 384 pixels. By including a model without center cropping, we aimed to capture features that might be lost due to the cropping process, ensuring that regions excluded by center cropping are still detected. Additionally, each model was subjected to different random data augmentations, enhancing robustness and improving the performance of the ensemble.

While the ensemble strategy increases the training time, it is essential for achieving higher performance [6]. For final predictions, we used a soft voting strategy, averaging the probability outputs from the softmax layers of each model to produce the final prediction.

3 Experiments

3.1 Datasets and Implementation Details

UWF Dataset. UWF dataset provides images captured from a wider field of view compared to the traditional CFP method, enabling more accurate classification of retinal diseases. This dataset is labeled and divided into three tasks. Task 1 involves a binary classification to determine whether the captured image is suitable for analysis. Task 2 distinguishes between patients with referable DR and normal individuals, while Task 3 focuses on diagnosing DME and distinguishing it from normal cases. In this study, we focus on Tasks 2 and 3, which classify diseases in the UWF dataset. The dataset is divided into a training set for model training, a validation set, used to evaluate mid-competition rankings, and a test set for the final evaluation. The validation and test sets are not available to participants and are evaluated via a separate scoring server. The distribution of data for each task is summarized in Table 1.

Implementation Details. In this study, we utilized the Adam optimizer with a fixed learning rate of 0.001. The binary cross-entropy loss function was employed, with a batch size set to 64. Training was conducted for a total of 10 epochs, and the model weights from the epoch with the lowest loss were selected as the final submission weights.

Experiments for backbone selection were performed using the PyTorch framework on a single Intel Xeon Silver 4310 CPU, while the ablation study was conducted in the Codalab evaluation environment.

3.2 Comparison for Backbone Selection

We experimented with three CNN-based architectures—EfficientNet [25], ResNet [9], and ConvNeXt [12]—to select the best backbone model. The results of these experiments are shown in Table 2. To evaluate both accuracy and efficiency, we compared the area under roc curve(AUROC) and the number of parameters for each model to determine the optimal choice. For all experiments, 50% of the publicly available training dataset was used for training, while the remaining 50% was used for validation. The AUROC was calculated based on Task 2, which involves classifying the presence of DR. The experiments were repeated three times with fixed seed values (2023, 2024, 2025), and the average results were used for model selection. Each model was trained for 10 epochs.

While models with more parameters may improve performance over a longer training period, we limited the training to 10 epochs to focus on fast and efficient learning. As a result, models with more parameters were relatively less converged. Among the models tested, EfficientNet-B2 achieved the highest average AUROC, followed by EfficientNet-B0 in terms of performance. However, considering that EfficientNet-B0 has approximately half the number of trainable parameters compared to EfficientNet-B2, we selected EfficientNet-B0 as the final backbone model due to its greater efficiency.

3.3 Ablation Study

Augmentation. In this study, we conducted an extensive experiment to validate the effectiveness of each data augmentation technique we applied. To ensure that the improvements in performance were not limited to a specific task, but were applicable to diagnosing various diseases in UWF images using the same architecture, we performed experiments on both Task 2 and Task 3. The AUROC and CPU time were calculated using the test dataset within the Codalab evaluation environment [2]. CPU time was measured as the average inference time per image on the Codalab environment CPU.

Table 2. Comparison of the AUROC and trainable parameters by backbone model. The best performance is highlighted in bold, and the second is underlined.

Model	AUROC				Params
	Seed (2023)	Seed (2024)	Seed (2025)	Mean	
ResNet-18 [9]	0.9831	0.9956	0.9852	0.9883	11.1M
ResNet-34 [9]	0.9651	1.0000	0.9838	0.9829	21.1M
ResNet-50 [9]	0.9758	0.9909	0.9909	0.9858	23.5M
EfficientNet-B0 [25]	0.9971	0.9952	0.9960	<u>0.9961</u>	4.0M
EfficientNet-B1 [25]	0.9950	0.9964	0.9960	0.9958	6.5M
EfficientNet-B2 [25]	0.9983	0.9984	0.9999	**0.9989**	7.7M
ConvNeXt-tiny [12]	0.9991	0.8801	0.7537	0.8776	14.9M
ConvNeXt-small [12]	0.9950	0.8286	0.8297	0.8844	49.4M

The experimental results, shown in Table 3, demonstrate that applying all of our proposed augmentation techniques led to higher AUROC scores for both Task 2 and Task 3. This confirms that these augmentation methods significantly contributed to improving the model's performance on the UWF dataset.

Table 3. Ablation study of various augmentation techniques. The best performance is highlighted in bold, and the second is underlined. CC, RR, RF, and CJ denote centercrop, random rotation, random flip, and color jittering.

Model	CC, Resize	RR	RF	CJ	Task 2 AUROC	Task 2 CPU Time	Task 3 AUROC	Task 3 CPU Time
EfficientNet-B0 [25]	✓	✗	✗	✗	0.8953	0.0508	0.8852	0.048
EfficientNet-B0 [25]	✓	✓	✗	✗	0.9271	0.0462	0.9059	0.0486
EfficientNet-B0 [25]	✓	✓	✓	✗	<u>0.9380</u>	0.0459	**0.9281**	0.0465
EfficientNet-B0 [25]	✓	✓	✓	✓	**0.9390**	0.0536	<u>0.9278</u>	0.0463

Ensemble. In this study, we conducted an ablation study to evaluate the effectiveness of the ensemble strategy proposed in the Method section, which involves combining models utilizing three different augmentation techniques. The experimental results shown in Table 4, indicate that increasing the number of high-performing models in the ensemble leads to higher AUROC. However, we also observed that while performance improves with ensemble techniques, there is a corresponding increase in inference time proportional to the number of models used in the ensemble.

Table 4. Ablation study to check the ensemble results of the proposed architecture.

Ensemble Model 1	Ensemble Model 2	Ensemble Model 3	Task 2 AUROC	Task 2 CPU Time	Task 3 AUROC	Task 3 CPU Time
✓	✗	✗	0.9380	0.0536	0.9278	0.0463
✗	✓	✗	0.9322	0.0480	0.9316	0.0521
✗	✗	✓	0.9349	0.0564	0.9151	0.0562
✓	✓	✗	0.9519	0.1005	0.9507	0.0847
✓	✗	✓	0.9519	0.0927	0.9383	0.1049
✗	✓	✓	0.9567	0.0856	0.9440	0.1009
✓	✓	✓	**0.9662**	0.1359	**0.9584**	0.1322

4 Discussion and Conclusion

In this study, we investigated efficient deep learning methods for diagnosing various diseases using UWF images. To this end, we evaluated the architecture based on the labeled presence of DR and DME in UWF images. We explored effective model training methods, utilizing fine-tuning, augmentation, and ensemble techniques, to achieve fast convergence and high performance with a lightweight model that can be trained and inferred even in a CPU environment. As a result, we successfully achieved high accuracy in classifying diseases in UWF images, securing 9th place in the MICCAI UWF4DR 2024 Challenge.

Although this study proposed a model that operates efficiently in resource-constrained environments with fast convergence, we found that using the ensemble strategy to improve AUROC performance led to an increase in inference time. Future research could focus on developing augmentation techniques or backbone models capable of operating efficiently in low-resource environments without dependence on ensemble strategies, which would contribute significantly to advancements in medical technology using deep learning.

Acknowledgments. This research was supported by a grant of 'Korea Government Grant Program for Education and Research in Medical AI' through the Korea Health Industry Development Institute (KHIDI), funded by the Korea government(MOE, MOHW).

References

1. Adcis messidor-2. https://www.adcis.net/en/third-party/messidor2/. Accessed 15 Sept 2024
2. Codalab. https://codalab.lisn.upsaclay.fr/. Accessed 28 Nov 2024
3. Kaggle Aptos 2019 blindness detection. https://www.kaggle.com/competitions/aptos2019-blindness-detection. Accessed 15 Sept 2024
4. Cutkosky, A., Defazio, A., Mehta, H.: Mechanic: a learning rate tuner. Adv. Neural Inf. Process. Syst. **36** (2024)

5. Deng, J., Dong, W., Socher, R., Li, L.J., Li, K., Fei-Fei, L.: ImageNet: a large-scale hierarchical image database. In: 2009 IEEE Conference on Computer Vision and Pattern Recognition, pp. 248–255. IEEE (2009)
6. Dietterich, T.G.: Ensemble methods in machine learning. In: International Workshop on Multiple Classifier Systems, pp. 1–15. Springer (2000)
7. Fong, D.S., Aiello, L.P., Ferris III, F.L., Klein, R.: Diabetic retinopathy. Diabetes Care **27**(10) (2004)
8. Foo, A., Hsu, W., Lee, M.L., Lim, G., Wong, T.Y.: Multi-task learning for diabetic retinopathy grading and lesion segmentation. In: Proceedings of the AAAI Conference on Artificial Intelligence, vol. 34, pp. 13267–13272 (2020)
9. He, K., Zhang, X., Ren, S., Sun, J.: Deep residual learning for image recognition. In: Proceedings of the IEEE Conference on Computer Vision and Pattern Recognition, pp. 770–778 (2016)
10. Karkera, T., Adak, C., Chattopadhyay, S., Saqib, M.: Detecting severity of diabetic retinopathy from fundus images: a transformer network-based review. Neurocomputing 127991 (2024)
11. Li, Y., Wei, C., Ma, T.: Towards explaining the regularization effect of initial large learning rate in training neural networks. Adv. Neural Inf. Process. Syst. **32** (2019)
12. Liu, Z., Mao, H., Wu, C.Y., Feichtenhofer, C., Darrell, T., Xie, S.: A convnet for the 2020s. In: Proceedings of the IEEE/CVF Conference on Computer Vision and Pattern Recognition, pp. 11976–11986 (2022)
13. Manuel, C., Zehnder, P., Kaya, S., Sullivan, R., Hu, F.: Impact of color augmentation and tissue type in deep learning for hematoxylin and eosin image super resolution. J. Pathol. Inform. **13**, 100148 (2022)
14. Mohan, N.J., Murugan, R., Goel, T., Roy, P.: ViT-DR: vision transformers in diabetic retinopathy grading using fundus images. In: 2022 IEEE 10th Region 10 Humanitarian Technology Conference (R10-HTC), pp. 167–172. IEEE (2022)
15. Naveen, P.: Cyclical log annealing as a learning rate scheduler. arXiv preprint arXiv:2403.14685 (2024)
16. Nazih, W., Aseeri, A.O., Atallah, O.Y., El-Sappagh, S.: Vision transformer model for predicting the severity of diabetic retinopathy in fundus photography-based retina images. IEEE Access **11**, 117546–117561 (2023)
17. Oulhadj, M., et al.: Diabetic retinopathy prediction based on vision transformer and modified capsule network. Comput. Biol. Med. **175**, 108523 (2024)
18. Park, W., Ryu, J.: Fine-grained self-supervised learning with jigsaw puzzles for medical image classification. Comput. Biol. Med. **174**, 108460 (2024)
19. Pratt, H., Coenen, F., Broadbent, D.M., Harding, S.P., Zheng, Y.: Convolutional neural networks for diabetic retinopathy. Procedia Comput. Sci. **90**, 200–205 (2016)
20. Raja Sarobin M.V., Panjanathan, R.: Diabetic retinopathy classification using CNN and hybrid deep convolutional neural networks. Symmetry **14**(9), 1932 (2022)
21. Silva, P.S.: Identification of diabetic retinopathy and ungradable image rate with ultrawide field imaging in a national teleophthalmology program. Ophthalmology **123**(6), 1360–1367 (2016)
22. Stitt, A.W., et al.: The progress in understanding and treatment of diabetic retinopathy. Prog. Retin. Eye Res. **51**, 156–186 (2016)
23. Sun, J.K., Aiello, L.P.: The future of ultrawide field imaging for diabetic retinopathy: pondering the retinal periphery. JAMA Ophthalmol. **134**(3), 247–248 (2016)
24. Sun, R., Li, Y., Zhang, T., Mao, Z., Wu, F., Zhang, Y.: Lesion-aware transformers for diabetic retinopathy grading. In: Proceedings of the IEEE/CVF Conference on Computer Vision and Pattern Recognition, pp. 10938–10947 (2021)

25. Tan, M., Le, Q.: EfficientNet: rethinking model scaling for convolutional neural networks. In: International Conference on Machine Learning, pp. 6105–6114. PMLR (2019)
26. Wang, X., Lu, Y., Wang, Y., Chen, W.B.: Diabetic retinopathy stage classification using convolutional neural networks. In: 2018 IEEE International Conference on Information Reuse and Integration (IRI), pp. 465–471. IEEE (2018)
27. Zhu, W., et al.: nnMobileNet: rethinking CNN for retinopathy research. In: Proceedings of the IEEE/CVF Conference on Computer Vision and Pattern Recognition, pp. 2285–2294 (2024)
28. Zini, S., Gomez-Villa, A., Buzzelli, M., Twardowski, B., Bagdanov, A.D., Van de Weijer, J.: Planckian jitter: countering the color-crippling effects of color jitter on self-supervised training. arXiv preprint arXiv:2202.07993 (2022)

EfficientNet-B1 Based Diabetic Retinopathy Detection from Ultra-widefield Fundus Images

Monalisa Bakshi(✉) and Chandra Sekhar Seelamantula

Department of Electrical Engineering, Indian Institute of Science, Bengaluru, Bengaluru 560 012, India
{monalisab,css}@iisc.ac.in

Abstract. In this methodology paper, we address the challenge of optimizing the performance of a detector for diabetic retinopathy (DR) from ultra-widefield fundus images, focusing on balancing model accuracy and latency. This MICCAI challenge prioritized "area under the receiver operating characteristic curve" (AUROC) and central processing unit (CPU) time for the detection problem. Therefore, we explored various approaches to enhance these performance measures. We evaluated several convolutional neural networks (CNNs) and found that EfficientNet-B1 gave a high AUROC value of 0.9055 on the UWF4DR test dataset while maintaining a minimal forward pass time. Our experiments included the deployment of transfer learning and data augmentation, revealing that traditional augmentation techniques such as flipping and rotation were less effective in medical imaging scenarios due to the inherent variability and complexity of fundus images. This paper details our methodology, including the rationale behind our model selection and the impact of augmentation techniques, providing insights into optimizing machine learning models for medical image analysis.

Keywords: Convolutional Neural Networks · Transfer Learning · Ultra-Widefield Retinal Fundus Imaging

1 Introduction

Ultra-widefield fundus imaging is a state-of-the-art technique that captures comprehensive retinal images, extending the field of view to encompass more of the retinal surface than traditional fundus photography. This approach is particularly beneficial for diagnosing diabetic retinopathy, a common complication of diabetes characterized by damage to the retinal blood vessels. Early detection and intervention are crucial, as diabetic retinopathy can lead to vision loss if left untreated. The complexity of analyzing these images necessitates the development of advanced machine learning models that are capable of providing accurate diagnoses swiftly. Given the medical context, developing systems that achieve high diagnostic accuracy and operate with low latency is essential. High latency can hinder real-time analysis and delay critical clinical decisions.

2 Prior Art

Diabetic Retinopathy (DR) [1] is a significant microvascular complication of diabetes that can lead to blindness if not detected early. Automated diagnostic systems are essential for early detection, as DR progresses through asymptomatic mild non-proliferative stages to severe proliferative forms. Recent advancements in DR diagnosis have leveraged advanced imaging techniques and machine learning approaches. The DREAM system by Roychowdhury et al. [2] uses machine learning classifiers for analyzing fundus images, achieving high sensitivity in severity grading. Similarly, Atwany et al. [5] reviewed deep learning techniques for DR classification, noting the need for better methods to aid manual diagnosis.

Feature extraction techniques have also been pivotal in DR detection. Chetoui et al. [3] highlighted local energy-based shape histogram, which outperformed traditional methods with an accuracy of 0.904. Verma et al. [4] achieved 90% accuracy in normal cases using *random forests*, while Kar and Maity [6] reported 97.71% accuracy in automated retinal lesion detection through advanced preprocessing and postprocessing techniques.

Several studies have focused on specific lesion detection methodologies. Iyer et al. [7] proposed a fully automated system with high sensitivity for detecting changes in retinal fundus images. Seoud et al. [8] introduced dynamic shape features for automatically detecting microaneurysms and hemorrhages. Walter et al. [9] developed an algorithm for exudate detection, achieving a mean sensitivity of 92.8% for diabetic macular edema. Qiao et al. [10] employed deep learning for early detection of microaneurysms, enhancing accuracy through semantic segmentation.

Transfer learning and innovative network designs have shown promise in improving DR detection and grading. Aiche et al. [11] demonstrated effective multilevel detection using the APTOS2019 dataset. Wang et al. [13] introduced Zoom-in-Net, a convolutional neural network that achieves high localization accuracy with minimal supervision. Yang et al. [14] developed a two-stage network for lesion detection and severity grading, improving performance through an imbalanced weighting scheme. Zhou et al. [15] created a fine-grained annotated DR dataset, facilitating advancements in segmentation and grading.

Recent studies have focused on novel architectures for DR detection and segmentation. Quellec et al. [18] utilized ConvNets to generate heatmaps for lesion detection on large datasets that do not have expert annotations. Li et al. [19] introduced CANet, a cross-disease attention network that jointly grades DR and diabetic macular edema with image-level supervision. He et al. [20] developed CABNet, incorporating a Category Attention Block to enhance subtle lesion detection amidst imbalanced data distributions. Huang et al. [21] presented RTNet, employing attention mechanisms to improve lesion segmentation by integrating vascular information, showcasing competitive results on benchmark datasets.

2.1 Outline of the Paper

In Sect. 3, we describe the dataset used in our experiments, detailing the ultra-widefield fundus (UWF) images and the Kaggle dataset utilized for transfer learning. Section 4 outlines the methodology employed for evaluating various deep-learning models for diabetic retinopathy detection, including model selection, data preparation, and augmentation techniques. In Sect. 5, we present the experimental setup, the training process, and the performance metrics used for evaluation. The experimental results highlight the performance of different models and the impact of transfer learning and data augmentation on classification accuracy. Section 6 concludes the paper by summarizing key findings and insights.

3 Dataset Description

The dataset consists of ultra-widefield fundus images. There are 200 training and 50 validation images, with corresponding labels in two separate CSV files for training and validation sets. Each image has a resolution of 800×1016 pixels with three color channels (RGB). For transfer learning, we utilized a dataset from Kaggle [29], consisting of 1000 images across five different classes: Normal, Mild, Moderate, Severe, and Proliferative Diabetic Retinopathy (DR). These are RGB images each having dimensions $224 \times 224 \times 3$.

Traditional fundus imaging captures a relatively narrow field of view, primarily focusing on the central retina (Fig. 1(a)). Such datasets are widely available [12]. In contrast, ultra-widefield fundus imaging captures a significantly larger area, encompassing peripheral retinal regions (Fig. 1(b)). The differences in image structure, features, and distribution make transfer learning from traditional fundus images ineffective for UWF applications due to the lack of peripheral data representation in the former, leading to poor model generalization in the latter.

4 Methodology

The aim of this study is to evaluate the effectiveness of various deep-learning models for the detection of diabetic retinopathy. The methodology consisted of data preparation and model selection.

We selected several deep-learning architectures for performance evaluation and comparison, including EfficientNet-B1 [26], ResNet50 [22], DenseNet [23], MobileNet [24], VGG16 [25], and InceptionV3 [27]. Based on the performance metrics shown in Table 1, we selected EfficientNet-B1 for further experiments. The EfficientNet-B1 model architecture shown in Fig. 2 and Fig. 3, leverages a compound scaling method to enhance both efficiency and accuracy. By optimizing the depth, width, and resolution of the network, EfficientNet-B1 achieves a high accuracy-to-computation ratio with fewer parameters compared to the other models. An EfficientNet-B1 model, initially trained on ImageNet dataset [28],

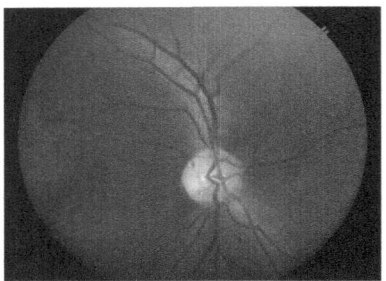 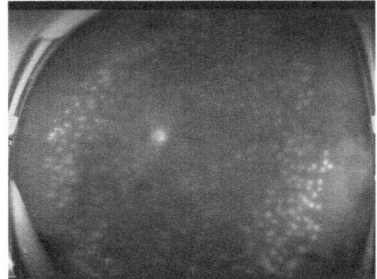

(a) Traditional fundus image (b) Ultra-widefield fundus image

Fig. 1. (a) Traditional retinal fundus image taken from Chákṣu IMAGE (a glaucoma-specific fundus image database) [12] – Images of this type are used for pre-training of the EfficientNet-B1 Model. (b) Ultra-widefield (UWF) fundus images – this class of images are used for fine-tuning the network.

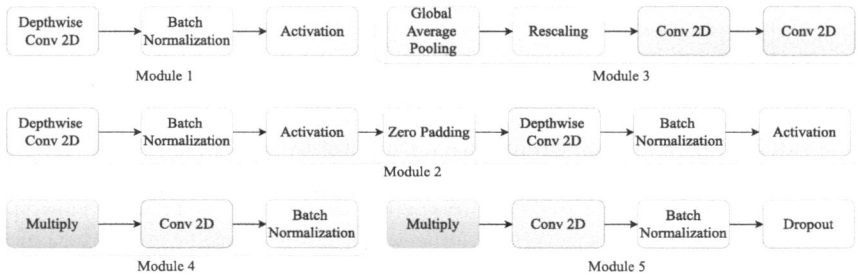

Fig. 2. Modules used in EfficientNet architecture.

was adapted for diabetic retinopathy classification by fine-tuning it on traditional fundus images [29]. The final layer was replaced to distinguish between two categories: referable and non-referable diabetic retinopathy. The pretraining data, sourced from Kaggle, involved a multiclass classification task with five classes: Normal, Mild, Moderate, Severe, and Proliferative Diabetic Retinopathy (DR). All classes other than the normal category were grouped as abnormal.

To enhance the performance of the model and to mitigate overfitting, we explored data augmentation techniques, including random rotations, flips, and brightness adjustments. Transfer learning was utilized with the EfficientNet model to enhance classification accuracy. Initially, the EfficientNet model was trained on a separate dataset of fundus images from Kaggle [29] before fine-tuning it on the ultra-widefield diabetic retinopathy (UWF4DR) dataset provided.

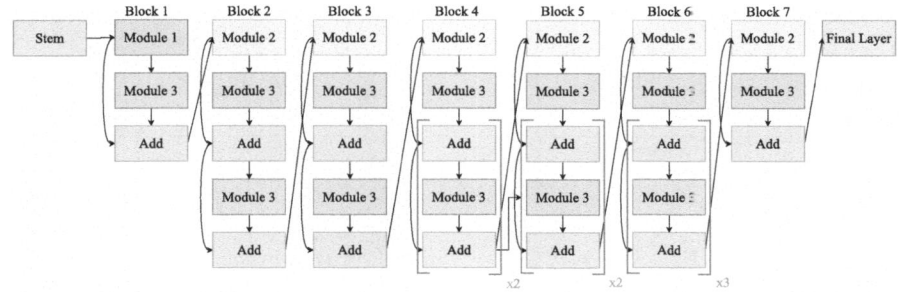

Fig. 3. EfficientNet-B1 architecture.

5 Experimental Results

We evaluated deep learning models for detecting referable diabetic retinopathy. EfficientNet-B1 [26], pre-trained on ImageNet, was fine-tuned by modifying the final layer for binary classification. The network is trained to optimize the cross-entropy loss:

$$L = -\frac{1}{N}\sum_{i=1}^{N}[y_i \log(\hat{y}_i) + (1 - y_i)\log(1 - \hat{y}_i)]$$

where N is the number of samples, $y_i \in \{0, 1\}$ indicates the true label, and $\hat{y}_i$ is the predicted probability.

The models were trained using the Adam optimizer with a learning rate of 0.001 and a validation batch size of 50. Input images were resized to 224 × 224 for most models, except for InceptionV3 [27], where the images were resized to 299 × 299.

The performance of the model was evaluated in terms of AUROC, AUPRC, sensitivity, specificity, and accuracy. Softmax was applied to the final layer, and the optimal classification threshold was determined by maximizing the difference between sensitivity and (1 − specificity) on the ROC curve.

We evaluated deep-learning models for detecting diabetic retinopathy, focusing on the impact of data augmentation and transfer learning. Due to the small dataset (only 200 images), models such as ResNet50 [22], DenseNet [23], MobileNet [24], VGG16 [25], and InceptionV3 [27] showed lower sensitivity and AUROC compared to EfficientNet [26], as shown in Table 1. This is likely due to overfitting, as these models have far more parameters than the number of images in the dataset.

EfficientNet performed the best, achieving an AUROC of 0.9655 on the UWF4DR validation dataset without data augmentation or transfer learning. The corresponding confusion matrix is shown in Table 2. Further experiments on EfficientNet tested the effects of transfer learning, data augmentation, and their combinations – the results are shown in Table 3. Transfer learning slightly reduced AUROC (0.9080), while data augmentation without transfer learning improved sensitivity (0.8966), but reduced AUROC to 0.8982. Combining both

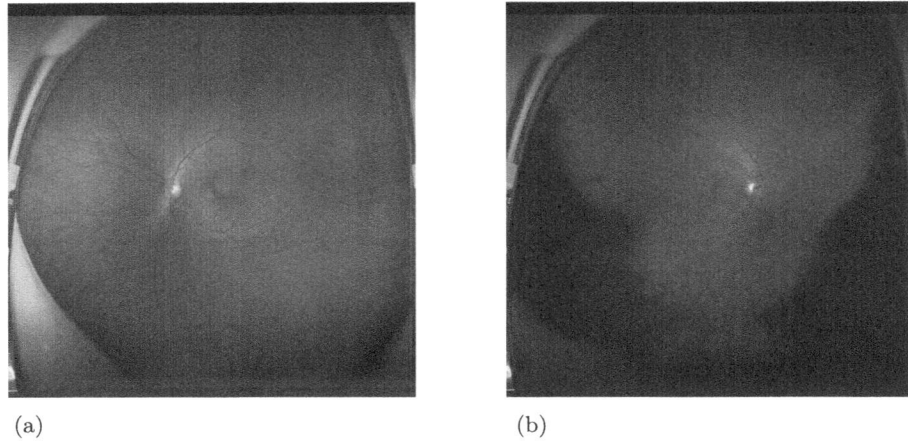

(a) (b)

Fig. 4. Instances of (a) a correctly classified image; and (b) wrongly classified image.

Table 1. Performance comparison of various models for diabetic retinopathy detection on the UWF4DR validation dataset.

Model	AUROC	AUPRC	Sensitivity	Specificity	Accuracy
EfficientNet [26]	0.9655	0.9794	0.8621	1.0000	0.92
ResNet50 [22]	0.7783	0.8507	0.6207	0.8571	0.72
DenseNet [23]	0.9113	0.9317	0.8276	0.9048	0.86
MobileNet [24]	0.9015	0.9426	0.8621	0.9048	0.88
VGG16 [25]	0.5977	0.7019	0.5172	0.8095	0.64
InceptionV3 [27]	0.6108	0.7303	0.3448	0.9048	0.58

Table 2. Confusion matrix for EfficientNet-B1 on the UWF4DR validation dataset.

	Predicted Negative	Predicted Positive
Actual Negative	21	0
Actual Positive	6	23

techniques resulted in a balanced performance, with an AUROC of 0.9245 and an AUPRC of 0.9477. Table 2 and Table 3 show results on the validation dataset that was made publicly available. Result of test dataset (Leaderboard result) is shown in Table 4.

Figure 4 shows an example of a correctly classified image, which appears clearer and brighter, with no interference from eyelashes; and an example of a wrongly classified image, which shows the presence of eyelashes or other obstructions, potentially resulting in misclassification.

Table 3. Performance of EfficientNet-B1 under various training conditions on the UWF4DR validation dataset.

Model	AUROC	AUPRC	Sensitivity	Specificity	Accuracy
No preprocessing or transfer learning	0.9655	0.9794	0.8621	1.0000	0.92
With transfer learning	0.9080	0.9495	0.8621	0.9048	0.88
With data augmentation	0.8982	0.9217	0.8966	0.7619	0.84
With data augmentation and transfer learning	0.9245	0.9477	0.8276	0.9048	0.86

Table 4. Performance of EfficientNet-B1 on the UWF4DR test dataset.

Model	AUROC	AUPRC	Sensitivity	Specificity	Time(Sec)
No preprocessing or transfer learning	0.9055	0.8917	0.8621	0.8310	0.0392

6 Conclusion

Our study highlights EfficientNet-B1 as a high-performance CNN model for diabetic retinopathy detection using ultra-widefield fundus images. The "area under the receiver operating characteristic curve" (AUROC) is 0.9655, which is high for practical applications and the latency is low (0.0813 s on validation data). Transfer learning proved to be more effective than traditional data augmentation techniques. The combination of data augmentation and transfer learning proved to be a good balance between model accuracy and computational efficiency, offering a practical solution for improved diagnostic performance.

References

1. Fong, D.S., Aiello, L.P., Ferris III, F.L., Klein, R.: Diabetic retinopathy. Diabetes Care **27**(10) (2004)
2. Roychowdhury, S., Koozekanani, D.D., Parhi, K.K.: DREAM: diabetic retinopathy analysis using machine learning. IEEE J. Biomed. Health Inform. **18**(5), 1717–1728 (2013)
3. Chetoui, M., Akhloufi, M.A., Kardouchi, M.: Diabetic retinopathy detection using machine learning and texture features. In: 2018 IEEE Canadian Conference on Electrical and Computer Engineering (CCECE), pp. 1–4 (2018)
4. Verma, K., Deep, P., Ramakrishnan, A.G.: Detection and classification of diabetic retinopathy using retinal images. In: 2011 Annual IEEE India Conference, pp. 1–6 (2011)

5. Atwany, M.Z., Sahyoun, A.H., Yaqub, M.: Deep learning techniques for diabetic retinopathy classification: a survey. IEEE Access 10, 28642–28655 (2022)
6. Kar, S.S., Maity, S.P.: Automatic detection of retinal lesions for screening of diabetic retinopathy. IEEE Trans. Biomed. Eng. **65**(3), 608–618 (2017)
7. Narasimha-Iyer, H.: Robust detection and classification of longitudinal changes in color retinal fundus images for monitoring diabetic retinopathy. IEEE Trans. Biomed. Eng. **53**(6), 1084–1098 (2006)
8. Seoud, L., Hurtut, T., Chelbi, J., Cheriet, F., Langlois, J.: Red lesion detection using dynamic shape features for diabetic retinopathy screening. IEEE Trans. Med. Imaging **35**(4), 1116–1126 (2015)
9. Walter, T., Klein, J.-C., Massin, P., Erginay, A.: A contribution of image processing to the diagnosis of diabetic retinopathy-detection of exudates in color fundus images of the human retina. IEEE Trans. Med. Imaging **21**(10), 1236–1243 (2002)
10. Qiao, L., Zhu, Y., Zhou, H.: Diabetic retinopathy detection using prognosis of microaneurysm and early diagnosis system for non-proliferative diabetic retinopathy based on deep learning algorithms. IEEE Access **8**, 104292–104302 (2020)
11. Aiche, I., Brik, Y., Attallah, B., Lahmar, H., Zohra, Z.: Transfer learning for diabetic retinopathy detection. In: 2022 International Conference of Advanced Technology in Electronic and Electrical Engineering (ICATEEE), pp. 1–5. IEEE (2022)
12. Harish Kumar, J.R., et al.: Chákṣu IMAGE: a glaucoma-specific fundus image database. Nat. Sci. Data **10**(1), 70 (2023). https://doi.org/10.1038/s41597-023-01943-4
13. Wang, Z., Yin, Y., Shi, J., Fang, W., Li, H., Wang, X.: Zoom-in-Net: deep mining lesions for diabetic retinopathy detection. In: Medical Image Computing and Computer Assisted Intervention - MICCAI 2017: 20th International Conference, Quebec City, QC, Canada, 11–13 September 2017, Proceedings, Part III 20, Springer, pp. 267–275 (2017)
14. Yang, Y., Li, T., Li, W., Wu, H., Fan, W., Zhang, W.: Lesion detection and grading of diabetic retinopathy via two-stages deep convolutional neural networks. In: Medical Image Computing and Computer Assisted Intervention - MICCAI 2017: 20th International Conference, Quebec City, QC, Canada, 11–13 September 2017, Proceedings, Part III 20, pp. 533–540. Springer (2017)
15. Zhou, Y., Wang, B., Huang, L., Cui, S., Shao, L.: A benchmark for studying diabetic retinopathy: segmentation, grading, and transferability. IEEE Trans. Med. Imaging **40**(3), 818–828 (2020)
16. Qureshi, I., Ma, J., Abbas, Q.: Recent development on detection methods for the diagnosis of diabetic retinopathy. Symmetry **11**(6), 749 (2019)
17. Stolte, S., Fang, R.: A survey on medical image analysis in diabetic retinopathy. Med. Image Anal. **64**, 101742 (2020)
18. Quellec, G., Charriere, K., Boudi, Y., Cochener, B., Lamard, M.: Deep image mining for diabetic retinopathy screening. Med. Image Anal. **39**, 178–193 (2017)
19. Li, X., Hu, X., Yu, L., Zhu, L., Fu, C.-W., Heng, P.-A.: CANet: cross-disease attention network for joint diabetic retinopathy and diabetic macular edema grading. IEEE Trans. Med. Imaging **39**(5), 1483–1493 (2019)
20. He, A., Li, T., Li, N., Wang, K., Fu, H.: CABNet: category attention block for imbalanced diabetic retinopathy grading. IEEE Trans. Med. Imaging **40**(1), 143–153 (2020)
21. Huang, S., Li, J., Xiao, Y., Shen, N., Xu, T.: RTNet: relation transformer network for diabetic retinopathy multi-lesion segmentation. IEEE Trans. Med. Imaging **41**(6), 1596–1607 (2022)

22. He, K., Zhang, X., Ren, S., Sun, J.: Deep Residual Learning for Image Recognition. In: Proceedings of the IEEE Conference on Computer Vision and Pattern Recognition (CVPR), pp. 770–778 (2016)
23. Huang, G., Liu, Z., Maaten, L.V.D., Weinberger, K.Q.: Densely connected convolutional networks. In: Proceedings of the IEEE Conference on Computer Vision and Pattern Recognition (CVPR), pp. 4700–4708 (2017)
24. Howard, A.G., et al.: MobileNets: efficient convolutional neural networks for mobile vision applications. arXiv preprint arXiv:1704.04861 (2017)
25. Simonyan, K., Zisserman, A.: Very deep convolutional networks for large-scale image recognition. arXiv preprint arXiv:1409.1556 (2014)
26. Tan, M., Le, Q.V.: EfficientNet: rethinking model scaling for convolutional neural networks. In: Proceedings of the 36th International Conference on Machine Learning (ICML), pp. 6105–6114 (2019)
27. Szegedy, C., Ioffe, S., Vanhoucke, V., Alemi, A.: Rethinking the inception architecture for computer vision. In: Proceedings of the IEEE Conference on Computer Vision and Pattern Recognition (CVPR), pp. 2818–2826 (2016)
28. Deng, J., Dong, W., Socher, R., Li, L.-J., Li, K., Fei-Fei, L.: ImageNet: a large-scale hierarchical image database. In: IEEE Conference on Computer Vision and Pattern Recognition, pp. 248–255 (2009)
29. Dugas, E., Jared, J., Cukierski, W.: Diabetic retinopathy detection. Kaggle (2015). https://kaggle.com/competitions/diabetic-retinopathy-detection

Many-MobileNet: Multi-model Augmentation for Robust Retinal Disease Classification

Hao Wang[1(✉)], Wenhui Zhu[2], Xuanzhao Dong[2], Yanxi Chen[2], Xin Li[2], Peijie Qiu[3], Xiwen Chen[1], Vamsi Krishna Vasa[2], Yujian Xiong[2], Oana M. Dumitrascu[4], Abolfazl Razi[1], and Yalin Wang[2]

[1] School of Computing, Clemson University, Clemson, SC, USA
hao9@g.clemson.edu, {xiwenc,arazi}@clemson.edu
[2] School of Computing and Augmented Intelligence, Arizona State University, Tempe, AZ, USA
{wzhu59,xdong64,ychen855,xinli38,vvasa1,yxiong42,ylwang}@asu.edu
[3] McKeley School of Engineering, Washington University in St. Louis, St. Louis, MO, USA
peijie.qiu@wustl.edu
[4] Department of Neurology, Mayo Clinic, Rochester, AZ, USA
dumitrascu.oana@mayo.edu

Abstract. In this work, we propose **Many-MobileNet** — an efficient model fusion strategy for retinal disease classification using lightweight CNN architecture. Our method addresses key challenges such as overfitting and limited dataset variability by training multiple models with distinct data augmentation strategies and different model complexities. Through this fusion technique, we achieved robust generalization in data-scarce environments while balancing computational efficiency with feature extraction capabilities. As a result, we secured **3rd** place in the **MICCAI UWF4DR 2024 Challenge** for image quality assessment in ultra-widefield fundus images. Our software package is available at https://github.com/Retinal-Research/NN-MOBILENET.

Keywords: Retinal Diseases · Fundus image · Classification · MICCAI UWF4DR (Ultra-Widefield Fundus Imaging for Diabetic Retinopathy Challenge) 2024

1 Introduction

Retinal diseases (RD) are among the leading causes of visual impairment and blindness worldwide, particularly in cases of myopic maculopathy, which poses significant challenges in clinical diagnosis [9,27,30,34]. Specifically, diabetic retinopathy (DR) is a major contributor to blindness among working-aged adults globally [19,35]. Early detection and accurate grading of DR are critical for timely intervention, which can prevent severe vision loss [2,26]. In clinical practice, grading DR based on retinal images is crucial for determining the progression of the disease and guiding treatment decisions [1,6,14,17,20].

Deep learning-based automated diagnostic tools have demonstrated significant potential in assisting clinicians with RD detection and monitoring [5,16,25]. Over the years, convolutional neural networks (CNNs) [4,13,15,20,28,32,33] and, more recently, Vision Transformers (ViTs) [12] have emerged as the primary techniques in medical image analysis due to their ability to extract and analyze critical features from retinal images [36,37]. While Vision Transformers have gained popularity due to their ability to capture long-range dependencies, they often require large datasets and come with increased model complexity, making them prone to overfitting, particularly in medical image tasks where data is scarce. On the other hand, CNNs, with their simpler architectures, remain highly effective for tasks like retinal disease classification, where localized feature extraction is crucial for accurate diagnosis. For these reasons, CNN-based architectures continue to be widely used for tasks that demand both efficiency and accuracy [3,5,16,24].

In this work, we apply **nnMobileNet** [35], a lightweight CNN architecture, to the retinal image quality classification task [21]. To address challenges such as overfitting and limited dataset variability [7,23,29], we propose a **model fusion** strategy. This strategy combines multiple lightweight nnMobileNet models that use the same architecture but with different model complexity, each trained with different data augmentation techniques. By fusing these models, we improve generalization and ensure that the final predictions are robust across a wide range of scenarios, even in data-scarce environments. As a result, our model secured 3rd place in the MICCAI UWF4DR 2024 Challenge - Image Quality Assessment for ultra-widefield fundus.

2 Methods

To optimize the performance of nnMobileNet for the retinal image quality classification task, we employed a comprehensive approach involving multiple hyperparameter adjustments and model enhancements. Additionally, we explored model width scaling and conducted extensive tests. Combined with a model fusion strategy, these refinements were essential in balancing computational efficiency with robust feature extraction. Below, we discuss each modification and its influence on the model's overall performance and generalization ability.

2.1 Model Architecture

In this work, we utilize nnMobileNet to balance the trade-offs between model efficiency and accuracy while maintaining robustness against overfitting, particularly when handling small and imbalanced medical datasets [21]. Due to its lightweight CNN architecture, nnMobileNet features depthwise separable convolutions combined with linear bottleneck layers, which minimize computational costs while retaining high representational capacity [35]. Key improvements in our version of nnMobileNet include the integration of advanced channel-wise attention mechanisms [29], especially Squeeze-and-Excitation (SE) blocks [10],

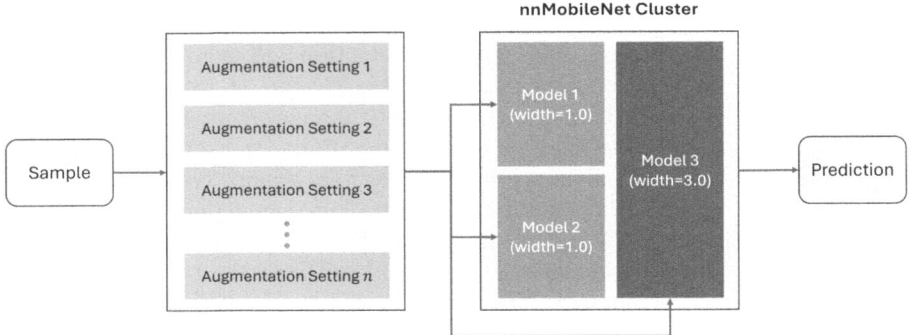

Fig. 1. Concept of model fusion during inference.

which recalibrate feature maps and improve the focus on relevant retinal features. This design enables our model to efficiently process high-resolution fundus images without the need for excessively deep or complex networks. Specifically, the number of feature layers can be controlled by the channel multiplication factor. In this work, we compose a simple and efficient architecture – ManyMobileNet – that fusion multiple nnMoboileNet trained on the same dataset with different model settings to enhance the robustness while inference on new samples, as shown in Fig. 1.

2.2 Data Augmentation Strategy

Given our dataset's limited quantity and uniform nature, training a high-performance model solely on the existing data is insufficient. The dataset's lack of diversity makes it difficult for a single model to generalize well across various cases. By applying different augmentation techniques to different models [11, 22], we enhance the training data and improve the overall robustness and generalization of the combined model during the inference stage.

The key difference in the data augmentation strategy lies in using different normalization techniques. Models trained on general datasets such as ImageNet utilize customized normalization values [18], whereas models trained on medical image classification tasks employ a different set of normalization parameters. These variations in normalization resulted in differences in model performance during both training and inference, as the models were tuned to their respective datasets.

2.3 Training Strategy

Previous studies [11, 13, 22, 31] have suggested that excessive data augmentation may compromise the integrity of fundus images, which led to the use of limited augmentations such as spatial transformations and brightness adjustments in retinal fundus image tasks. However, based on our empirical findings, these basic augmentations were insufficient to eliminate overfitting in RD tasks. To address this, we conducted exploratory experiments to test various data augmentation combinations that could prevent overfitting and improve model robustness.

The training strategy in this experiment involved the systematic exploration of several hyperparameters to optimize model performance. We experimented with different normalization settings, and dropout rates ranging from 0.00 to 0.10 were tested to regularize the models and prevent overfitting. Additionally, batch sizes of 8, 16, and 32 were evaluated to assess their effects on model convergence and generalization. The learning rates tested included $1e-3$, $1e-4$, $1e-5$, and $1e-6$, each decayed using a cosine learning rate scheduler to ensure smooth convergence throughout the training process. We also explored different model widths by adjusting the width multiplier, comparing lightweight models with a channel multiplier of 1.0 to medium-sized models with a channel multiplier of 3.0. This allowed us to balance between model complexity and performance, with the lightweight models focused on computational efficiency, while the medium-sized models captured more complex features. A detailed training setting is given in Table 1. Through this comprehensive exploration of hyperparameters, we were able to identify the optimal configurations that enhanced model performance in this retinal image classification task.

2.4 Implementation Details

In this experiment, we utilized multiple **NVIDIA V100** GPUs for training. All models were trained using the **PyTorch** framework, with standardized input image sizes of 224×224.

Table 1. All training configurations for Many-MobileNet.

Training configuration	
Optimizer	AdamP
Batch size	8, 16, 32
Learning rate	1e−3, 1e−4, 1e−5, 1e−6
Weight decay	0.005
Scheduler	Cosine decay
Dropout rate	0.01, 0.02, 0.05
Epoch	500
Loss	Cross-entropy
Metric	acc, auc, average
Model width	1.0, 3.0

As illustrated in Table 1, a weight decay of 0.005 was applied throughout the training to prevent overfitting, particularly in the deeper layers of the network. The models were trained for 500 epochs to ensure full convergence. The

AdamP optimizer was employed due to its effectiveness in enhancing generalization and stabilizing the training process [8]. In addition, dropout rates between 0.00 and 0.10 were applied to regularize the models and prevent overfitting. Model widths (channel multiplier) of 1.0 (lightweight) and 3.0 (medium-sized) were tested to evaluate the trade-off between model capacity and computational efficiency. Throughout the training process, the models were evaluated using key metrics, including accuracy (acc) to measure the percentage of correctly classified instances, the area under the curve (AUC) to assess the model's ability to distinguish between classes, and an average metric to provide a comprehensive evaluation of the model's overall performance. The cross-entropy loss function was applied across all models to ensure robust performance in the classification tasks.

2.5 Model Fusion

In our approach, model fusion plays a critical role in overcoming the limitations of the dataset's uniformity and small sample size. The fusion of multiple models, each trained under different conditions and with distinct data augmentation strategies, is the key to enhancing the model's robustness and overall performance. This fusion technique ensures that each model contributes complementary strengths, leading to more accurate and reliable predictions.

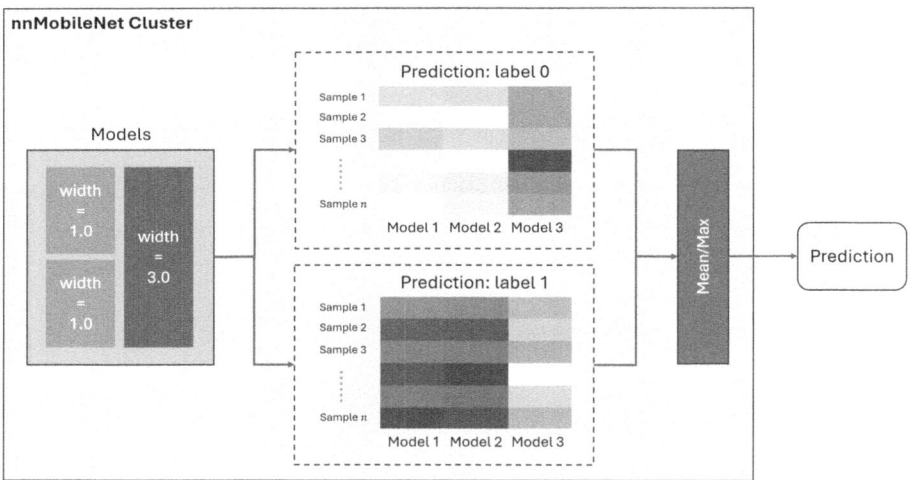

Fig. 2. Prediction of Many-MobileNet.

In this work, the model width (channel multiplier) plays a critical role in determining the network's capacity and resource requirements. The model width scales the number of channels in each layer, which significantly impacts the model's parameters and size. For instance, with a model width equal to 1.0, the model maintains the base number of channels (e.g., 32, 64, 128, etc.), resulting in a smaller model approximately 13 MB in size. However, when a model width is 3.0 is used, the channels in each layer are **tripled**, causing a significant increase in parameters and resulting in a model size of around 120 MB. This makes the model width a key factor in balancing between computational efficiency and the ability to capture complex features.

Our model fusion involves the combination of multiple **nnMobileNet** models, each deployed with different channel multipliers. We employ two lightweight models with a channel multiplier of 1, optimized for efficiency, and one medium-sized model with a channel multiplier of 3, designed for more complex feature extraction. This architectural diversity ensures that the lightweight models contribute speed and computational efficiency, while the larger model provides the capacity to capture more intricate details in the retinal images. Each model is trained with a distinct data augmentation strategy to further enhance the diversity of learned features, and ensure that each model learns a unique representation of the retinal features, capturing different aspects of the image. During inference, this fusion reduces the risk of overfitting to specific augmentations or data patterns.

During inference, we employ a prediction voting method to combine the predictions from each model. The final decision is calculated by the maximum or average outputs of the two lightweight models and the medium-sized model, while some models may carry different results that are more certain than others, as shown in Fig. 2. This method provides redundancy, ensuring that the final prediction benefits from the strengths of all models.

3 UWF4DR Image Quality Assessment for Ultra-widefield Fundus

3.1 Dataset and Evaluation Metrics

The dataset used in this study comes from the ultra-widefield (UWF) fundus imaging for diabetic retinopathy (DR) challenge, which aims to advance automatic DR analysis from UWF fundus images. The dataset includes UWF images with up to a 200-degree view of the retina, allowing the identification of predominantly peripheral lesions (PPL) that are present in a significant portion of eyes with DR. The images are classified into different DR stages based on the International Clinical Diabetic Retinopathy (ICDR) Severity Scale, ranging from no apparent retinopathy to proliferative diabetic retinopathy (PDR), including diabetic macular edema (DME). The dataset is divided into three tasks: image quality assessment, DR classification, and DME classification.

This Study Specifically Focuses on Task 1: Image Quality Assessment for Ultra-widefield Fundus. The dataset of this task contains a total of 434 samples that include 205 low-quality samples and 229 high-quality samples, their differences are illustrated in Fig. 3. This comprehensive dataset provides a foundation for developing algorithms that assist in the timely diagnosis and

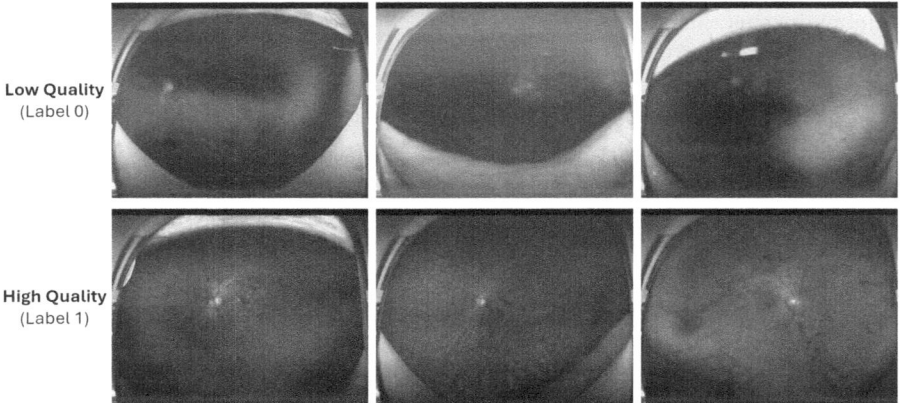

Fig. 3. Sample images of UWF4DR dataset, where label 0 represents the low-quality images and label 1 represents high-quality images.

management of DR patients, particularly by reducing the manual effort required for grading UWF fundus images.

3.2 Experimental Results

In this experiment, we conducted a comprehensive evaluation by submitting multiple models, each trained with different parameter configurations. We investigated several models to analyze the impact of different hyperparameter settings. The models were also evaluated using three key metrics: AUC, accuracy, and an average metric. As shown in Fig. 4, we tested two channel multiplier settings, where the results suggest that the lightweight model provided better results on

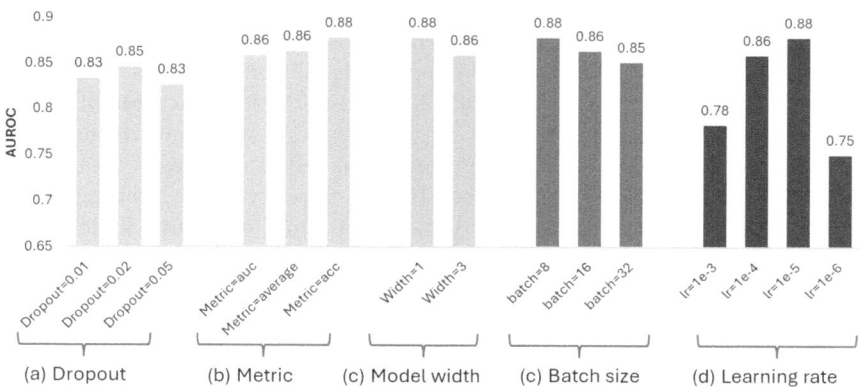

Fig. 4. Parameter empirical studies based on UWF4DR dataset.

the validation set. Also, a batch size of 8 achieved the highest accuracy, while larger batch sizes of 16 and 32 resulted in slightly lower performances. Finally, we tested learning rates of 1e−3, 1e−4, 1e−5, and 1e−6. The learning rate of 1e−5 produced the best accuracy, followed by 1e−4. Higher learning rates, such as 1e−3 and a lower learning rate of 1e−6, performed worse, respectively.

From these models, we selected the **top 3** models based on their performance on the validation set, focusing primarily on the **AUROC (Area Under the Receiver Operating Characteristic Curve)** metric. These top-performing models were then analyzed further to understand their strengths and weaknesses. As shown in Table 2, models with lower learning rates exhibited more stable performance. Secondly, batch size also affected model outcomes. Smaller

Table 2. Best model weights performed at the official validation set.

Method	AUROC	AUPRC	Sensitivity	Specificity	metric	lr	width	batch	dropout
Weight1	0.8772	0.9069	0.9729	0.7083	acc	1e−5	1.0	8	0.01
Weight2	0.8626	0.8676	0.7567	0.8333	average	1e−5	1.0	16	0.02
Weight3	0.8581	0.8680	0.7568	0.875	auc	1e−4	3.0	16	0.05
Ensemble with max	0.8468	0.8570	0.8648	0.75	-	-	-	-	-
Ensemble with average	0.8125	0.8043	1.0	0.625	-	-	-	-	-

batches (e.g., 8) improved sensitivity, helping the model better identify positive samples, while larger batches enhanced specificity, improving the model's ability to classify negative samples. Meanwhile, lower dropout values helped maintain the model's generalization ability, while higher dropout values led to information loss, negatively impacting performance on the validation dataset. However, it was crucial for preventing overfitting on the actual testing dataset. However, the model fusion did not perform well on the validation dataset. This performance decrement might caused by the small and potentially unrepresentative validation data.

Table 3. Final challenge rank based on official testing set.

Team	AUROC	AUPRC	Sensitivity	Specificity	Time	Ranking score
Rank 1st	0.9716	0.9820	0.9322	0.950	0.0732	0.9679
Rank 2nd	0.9622	0.9759	0.8305	0.975	0.0573	0.9594
Ours (Rank 3rd)	0.9525	0.9683	0.8983	0.925	0.1098	0.9470

In the final ranking, we submitted the combined model of our selected top 3 models. As shown in Table 3 Our team's model fusion strategy secured **3rd** place with specific metrics of **AUROC 0.9525** and **AUPRC 0.9683**, demonstrating robust classification performance. The **Sensitivity 0.8983** and **Specificity**

0.925 indicate a balanced ability to identify both positive and negative samples. Although the model's computation time was longer at **0.1098** due to multiple inference times, our model fusion strategy successfully combined the strengths of lightweight and medium-sized models, enhancing computational efficiency while extracting complex features. Ultimately, the fusion significantly improved the model's generalization, ensuring high classification performance across different scenarios.

4 Conclusion

In conclusion, we introduced **Many-MobileNet** – an architecture consisting of multiple nnMobileNet for retinal image quality classification. By combining lightweight and medium-sized models, each trained with different data augmentation techniques, our approach effectively mitigates overfitting and improves model robustness. The fusion strategy leverages the computational efficiency of smaller models and the feature extraction power of more complex models, resulting in a balanced system that excels in accuracy and generalization. The final ranking of this method in the MICCAI UWF4DR 2024 challenge demonstrates its potential for broader applications in medical image analysis and its potential to generalize well in data-limited challenges.

References

1. Color fundus photography and deep learning applications in Alzheimer's disease. Mayo Clinic Proceedings: Digital Health (2024)
2. Ahmad, A., Mansoor, A.B., Mumtaz, R., Khan, M., Mirza, S.: Image processing and classification in diabetic retinopathy: a review. In: 2014 5th European Workshop on Visual Information Processing (EUVIP), pp. 1–6. IEEE (2014)
3. Arega, T.W., Legrand, F., Bricq, S., Meriaudeau, F.: Using MRI-specific data augmentation to enhance the segmentation of right ventricle in multi-disease, multi-center and multi-view cardiac MRI. In: International Workshop on Statistical Atlases and Computational Models of the Heart, pp. 250–258. Springer (2021)
4. Che, H., Jin, H., Chen, H.: Learning robust representation for joint grading of ophthalmic diseases via adaptive curriculum and feature disentanglement. In: MICCAI, pp. 523–533 (2022)
5. Dai, L., et al.: A deep learning system for detecting diabetic retinopathy across the disease spectrum. Nat. Commun. **12**(1), 3242 (2021)
6. Dumitrascu, O.M., Zhu, W., Qiu, P., Nandakumar, K., Wang, Y.: Automated retinal imaging analysis for Alzheimer's disease screening. In: IEEE International Symposium on Biomedical Imaging: From Nano to Macro (ISBI) (2022)
7. Han, D., Yun, S., Heo, B., Yoo, Y.: Rethinking channel dimensions for efficient model design. In: Proceedings of the IEEE/CVF Conference on Computer Vision and Pattern Recognition, pp. 732–741 (2021)
8. Heo, B., et al.: Adamp: slowing down the slowdown for momentum optimizers on scale-invariant weights. arXiv preprint arXiv:2006.08217 (2020)
9. Holden, B.A., et al.: Global prevalence of myopia and high myopia and temporal trends from 2000 through 2050. Ophthalmology **123**(5), 1036–1042 (2016)

10. Hu, J., Shen, L., Sun, G.: Squeeze-and-excitation networks. In: Proceedings of the IEEE Conference on Computer Vision and Pattern Recognition, pp. 7132–7141 (2018)
11. Jiang, Y., et al.: SatFormer: saliency-guided abnormality-aware transformer for retinal disease classification in fundus image. In: Proceedings of the Thirty-First International Joint Conference on Artificial Intelligence, IJCAI, pp. 987–994 (2022)
12. Khan, S., Naseer, M., Hayat, M., Zamir, S.W., Khan, F.S., Shah, M.: Transformers in vision: a survey. ACM Comput. Surv. (CSUR) **54**(10s), 1–41 (2022)
13. Li, X., Hu, X., Yu, L., Zhu, L., Fu, C.W., Heng, P.A.: CANet: cross-disease attention network for joint diabetic retinopathy and diabetic macular edema grading. IEEE Trans. Med. Imaging 1483–1493 (2020)
14. Likassa, H.T., Chen, D.G., Chen, K., Wang, Y., Zhu, W.: Robust PCA with Lw, and L2, 1 norms: a novel method for low-quality retinal image enhancement. J. Imaging **10**(7), 151 (2024)
15. Lin, Z., et al.: A framework for identifying diabetic retinopathy based on anti-noise detection and attention-based fusion. In: MICCAI, pp. 74–82. Springer, Cham (2018)
16. Liu, R., et al.: DeepDRiD: diabetic retinopathy-grading and image quality estimation challenge. Patterns **3**(6) (2022)
17. Liu, S., Gong, L., Ma, K., Zheng, Y.: GREEN: a graph residual re-ranking network for grading diabetic retinopathy. In: MICCAI, pp. 585–594. Springer, Cham (2020)
18. Liu, Z., Mao, H., Wu, C.Y., Feichtenhofer, C., Darrell, T., Xie, S.: A convnet for the 2020s. In: Proceedings IEEE Computing Society Conference Computer Vision Pattern Recognition, pp. 11976–11986 (2022)
19. Rakhlin, A.: Diabetic retinopathy detection through integration of deep learning classification framework. BioRxiv, p. 225508 (2017)
20. Sánchez, C.I., et al.: Evaluation of a computer-aided diagnosis system for diabetic retinopathy screening on public data. Investig. Ophthalmol. Vis. Sci. **52**(7), 4866–4871 (2011)
21. Sandler, M., Howard, A., Zhu, M., Zhmoginov, A., Chen, L.C.: MobileNetv2: inverted residuals and linear bottlenecks. In: Proceedings IEEE Computer Society Conference Computer Vision Pattern Recognition, pp. 4510–4520 (2018)
22. Sun, R., Li, Y., Zhang, T., Mao, Z., Wu, F., Zhang, Y.: Lesion-aware transformers for diabetic retinopathy grading. In: Proceedings IEEE Computer Society Conference Computer Vision Pattern Recognition, pp. 10938–10947 (2021)
23. Tompson, J., Goroshin, R., Jain, A., LeCun, Y., Bregler, C.: Efficient object localization using convolutional networks. In: Proceedings of the IEEE Conference on Computer Vision and Pattern Recognition, pp. 648–656 (2015)
24. Uysal, E.S., Bilici, M.Ş., Zaza, B.S., Özgenç, M.Y., Boyar, O.: Exploring the limits of data augmentation for retinal vessel segmentation. arXiv preprint arXiv:2105.09365 (2021)
25. Vasa, V.K., Qiu, P., Zhu, W., Xiong, Y., Dumitrascu, O., Wang, Y.: Context-aware optimal transport learning for retinal fundus image enhancement. arXiv preprint arXiv:2409.07862 (2024)
26. Vo, H.H., Verma, A.: New deep neural nets for fine-grained diabetic retinopathy recognition on hybrid color space. In: 2016 IEEE International Symposium on Multimedia (ISM), pp. 209–215 (2016)
27. Wang, H., et al.: RBAD: a dataset and benchmark for retinal vessels branching angle detection. arXiv preprint arXiv:2407.12271 (2024)
28. Wang, Z., Yin, Y., Shi, J., Fang, W., Li, H., Wang, X.: Zoom-in-net: deep mining lesions for diabetic retinopathy detection. In: MICCAI, pp. 267–275 (2017)

29. Woo, S., Park, J., Lee, J.Y., Kweon, I.S.: CBAM: convolutional block attention module. In: Proceedings of the European Conference on Computer Vision (ECCV), pp. 3–19 (2018)
30. Yorston, D.: Retinal diseases and vision 2020. Commun. Eye Health **16**(46), 19–20 (2003)
31. Yu, S., et al.: MIL-VT: multiple instance learning enhanced vision transformer for fundus image classification. In: MICCAI, pp. 45–54. Springer (2021)
32. Zhou, Y., et al.: Collaborative learning of semi-supervised segmentation and classification for medical images. In: Proceedings IEEE Computer Society Conference Computer Vision Pattern Recognition (2019)
33. Zhu, W., et al.: Self-supervised equivariant regularization reconciles multiple instance learning: joint referable diabetic retinopathy classification and lesion segmentation. In: 18th International Symposium on Medical Information Processing and Analysis (SIPAIM) (2022)
34. Zhu, W., et al.: Beyond MobileNet: an improved MobileNet for retinal diseases. In: International Conference on Medical Image Computing and Computer-Assisted Intervention, pp. 56–65. Springer (2023)
35. Zhu, W., et al.: nnMobileNet: rethinking CNN for retinopathy research. In: Proceedings of the IEEE/CVF Conference on Computer Vision and Pattern Recognition (CVPR) Workshops, pp. 2285–2294 (2024)
36. Zhu, W., et al.: OTRE: where optimal transport guided unpaired image-to-image translation meets regularization by enhancing. In: International Conference on Information Processing in Medical Imaging, pp. 415–427. Springer (2023)
37. Zhu, W., Qiu, P., Farazi, M., Nandakumar, K., Dumitrascu, O.M., Wang, Y.: Optimal transport guided unsupervised learning for enhancing low-quality retinal images. arXiv preprint arXiv:2302.02991 (2023)

DME-MobileNet: Fine-Tuning nnMobileNet for Diabetic Macular Edema Classification

Xuanzhao Dong[1](✉)[ID], Yalin Wang[1], Yanxi Chen[1], Xin Li[1], Hao Wang[2], Peijie Qiu[3], Xiwen Chen[2], Abolfazl Razi[2], Yujian Xiong[1], Oana M. Dumitrascu[4], and Wenhui Zhu[1][ID]

[1] School of Computing and Augmented Intelligence, Arizona State University, Tempe, USA
{xdong64,ylwang,ychen855,xinli38,wzhu59}@asu.edu
[2] School of Computing, Clemson University, Clemson, USA
{hao9,xiwenc}@g.clemson.edu, arazi@clemson.edu
[3] McKelvey School of Engineering, Washington University in St. Louis, St. Louis, USA
peijie.qiu@wustl.edu
[4] Department of Neurology, Mayo Clinic, Rochester, USA
Dumitrascu.Oana@mayo.edu

Abstract. Diabetic retinopathy (DR) is a leading cause of vision loss in diabetic patients. Early identification of DR relies highly on standard color fundus photography (CFP), which faces limitations due to a restricted field of view and suboptimal image quality. Ultra-widefield (UWF) fundus images, offering broader retinal coverage, have emerged as a promising alternative. However, diagnosing DR based on UWF images is often time-consuming and laborious, highlighting the need for a unified, automated solution. In this work, we present a highly optimized lightweight Convolutional Neural Networks (CNNs) training pipeline based on MobileNet for the automated classification of diabetic macular edema (DME), a significant complication of DR. Our model significantly accelerates the analysis of UWF images compared to manual methods, enabling faster DR diagnosis and improved patient management. Notably, our approach achieved third place in the MICCAI UWF4DR 2024 Challenge for the Classification of Diabetic Macular Edema. The pipeline is publicly available at https://github.com/Retinal-Research/NN-MOBILENET.

Keywords: Retinal Diseases · Diabetic Retinopathy · Classification

1 Introduction

Diabetic retinopathy (DR) is a leading cause of vision loss in diabetic patients [9]. Early identification of DR primarily relies on Standard color fundus photography (CFP) [16]. However, CFP captures only a limited portion of the retina, resulting in insufficient detection of peripheral lesions, which are important in DR diagnosis [10]. Additionally, CFP frequently results in a higher proportion of ungradable images due to human or equipment-related factors [24] (e.g., poor patient positioning and media opacities). As a result, more effort is required to obtain usable photographs.

Ultra-widefield (UWF) fundus images, which provide a broader field of view and improved coverage of retinal lesions, present a promising alternative for DR diagnosis. Despite its advantages, classifying based on UWF images can be challenging, since it requires significant effort from human graders to identify patient-specific lesions, artifacts, and low-resolution regions [29]. Thus, developing a unified, automated, and robust technique for UWF image classification is essential.

In the past decade, deep learning (DL) models [6, 7, 44, 46–48], particularly convolutional neural networks (CNNs), have achieved state-of-the-art performance across various retinal fundus imaging tasks due to their strong learning capabilities. This success has motivated several applications of DL-based methods to ultra-widefield (UWF) imaging, including ophthalmic disease detection [35, 36], and image quality enhancement [15]. However, compared to standard CFP, the use of DL algorithms for UWF analysis remains relatively limited. A key task in this context is the identification of diabetic macular edema (DME), a major cause of vision loss in diabetic patients due to fluid accumulation in the macula [8]. Inspired by the state-of-the-art performance of nnMobileNet [45] in retinal classification tasks, we conducted a series of experiments across different architectures to optimize DME classification performance. This work aims to advance automated approaches for UWF image analysis further and contribute to more efficient DR diagnosis and patient care.

We proposed a fine-tuned MobileNet architecture for UWF-based DME classification based on our experiments. Our contributions are twofold: first, we mitigated overfitting issues by incorporating a variety of data augmentation techniques alongside channel-wise dropout modules. Second, we optimized several configurations within nnMobileNet [45], resulting in notable improvements in DME classification performance. These advancements earned our approach third place in the MICCAI UWF4DR 2024 Challenge, task 3. In the following sections, we will discuss our methodology, experiment setup, and detailed results, emphasizing the advantages of our approach in terms of both classification performance and computational cost.

2 Related Work

2.1 Ultra-widefield (UWF) Fundus Images

The first fundus camera was developed by the Carl Zeiss Company in 1926, capable of capturing images with a 20° field of view (FOV) of the posterior pole [4]. With advancements in digital imaging technologies, the FOV limitations of earlier systems have been addressed through the stitching of multiple smaller FOV images to create a composite wide-field view. Additionally, the resolution of digital fundus images has significantly improved, now reaching up to 4,069 × 2,736 pixels. This resolution is comparable to that of film-based images and is more than adequate for accurate diabetic retinopathy (DR) diagnosis [23].

Before 2019, the definition of ultra-widefield (UWF) images lacked uniformity across studies. However, a consensus was reached in 2019, establishing an anatomical definition of UWF images as those that display retinal features anterior to the vortex vein ampullae in all four quadrants [3]. Today, several UWF imaging systems are available, including the Optos, Heidelberg wide-angle system, Clarus, Staurenghi lens system, and RetCam [26].

2.2 AI-Based Methods for DR Diagnosis

Convolutional neural networks (CNNs) are the most popular architecture in RD-related diagnosis [2,17,19,31,37,42,43]. Early studies utilizing CNN approaches often integrated lesion features and additional clinical information into their models, such as Zoon-in-Net [37], attention fusion network [19], CANet [17] and DETACH [2]. With the emergence of more advanced architectures, end-to-end approaches that use only fundus images as inputs have also demonstrated impressive performance. For example, Jian et al. proposed Triple-DRNet, a triple-cascade network model for grading DR across five categories (No DR, Mild-, Moderate-, SevereNPDR and PDR) [12]. Triple-DRNet achieved a classification accuracy of 92.08% on the APTOS 2019 dataset. Earlier this year, Shamrat et al. proposed DRNet13, a robust CNN architecture specifically designed for DR diagnosis, and achieved 97% accuracy on the Kaggle's Diabetic Retinopathy 224 × 224 Gaussian Filtered dataset [32]. While these models have shown promising results, their complexity challenges scalability and generalizability. More recently, Wen et al. fine-tuned a series of models based on MobileNetV2, a well-established architecture, achieving state-of-the-art (SOTA) performance on multiple retinal disease datasets [45].

With the rising popularity of Vision Transformers (ViTs) in the field of computer vision, new approaches leveraging attention mechanisms, such as MIL-VT [38], lesion-aware transformer (LAT) [34] and SatFormer [13]. While these methods continue to push the boundaries of state-of-the-art performance, the data-intensive nature of ViTs poses a challenge for training and applying them on larger-scale datasets. Additionally, the localized nature of retinal disease (RD) features raises questions about the necessity of attention-based operations for extracting long-range dependencies, which may not be essential for such tasks [20,27].

2.3 AI-Based Methods for DME Diagnosis

Diabetic macular edema (DME), one of the most common complications of diabetic retinopathy (DR), specifically affects the macula—the region of the retina responsible for sharp, central vision. While DME exhibits distinct underlying features, methodologies developed for DR diagnosis can be effectively adapted

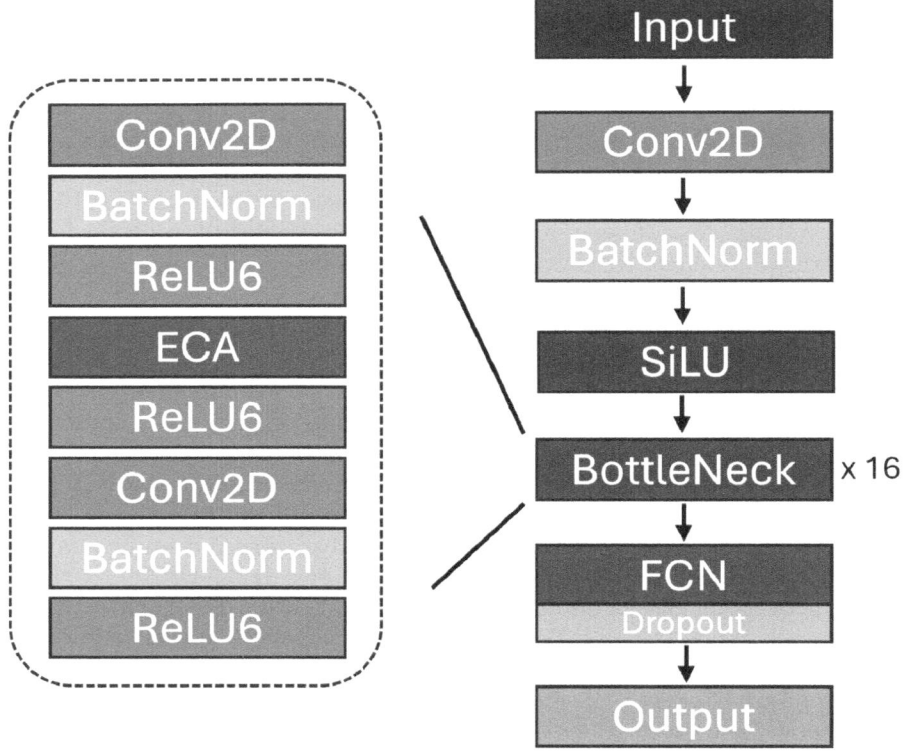

Fig. 1. DME-MobileNet Structure.

for DME detection. For example, Singh et al. introduced DMENet, an ensemble comprising two clusters of convolutional neural networks (CNNs) designed for disease classification and severity grading in a two-stage process [33]. Li et al. proposed a joint network based on Transformer architecture capable of simultaneously classifying both DR and DME [18]. Furthermore, several models leveraging Vision Transformers (ViTs) have been explored for these tasks [1,25].

In summary, most classification models originally developed for DR diagnosis and severity grading can be adapted for DME detection with minor adjustments to model parameters, underscoring their versatility in addressing related retinal pathologies.

3 Methods

Compared to Vision Transformers (ViTs), convolutional neural networks (CNNs) are better suited for capturing fine details in images, making them particularly effective for processing complex medical images [11,21]. Furthermore, medical imaging datasets are often small, with limited availability of labeled data. While

ViTs generally require large amounts of training data and heavily rely on pre-trained models, CNNs are inherently more efficient in scenarios with limited data. As a result, CNNs typically demonstrate superior performance in medical imaging tasks when the dataset size is constrained.

Upon reviewing our training dataset, we observed that it is not only small in size but also comprises non-traditional color fundus images. To mitigate overfitting and enhance generalization capability, we adopted a lightweight model framework. Lightweight models, characterized by fewer parameters and reduced complexity, are less prone to memorizing intricate details of the training data. Instead, they tend to focus on capturing overall patterns and essential features [30]. Consequently, these models are more effective in preventing overfitting, particularly when the training data contains noise or anomalies.

Based on this rationale, we selected nnMobileNet [45], a lightweight convolutional neural network (CNN) architecture derived from MobileNet, specifically designed for medical image classification tasks. To further mitigate the risk of overfitting, we also employed a variety of data augmentation techniques [45]. Our next objective is to fine-tune nnMobileNet for our specific dataset to optimize classification performance. The structure of the proposed DME-MobileNet is illustrated in Fig. 1.

3.1 Fine Tuning Strategies

Dropout Rate (DR). The selection of the dropout rate plays a crucial role in balancing the trade-off between feature disruption and overfitting, especially when dealing with limited training data. In our experiments, we systematically explored a range of dropout rates, from 0.06 to 0.5, with intervals of 0.02. We observed that both extremely low and high dropout rates resulted in a significant reduction in classification performance. The optimal dropout rate was found to be 0.1, which provided the best balance between regularization and feature retention, leading to superior classification results.

Data Augmentation (DA). To address the challenge of limited data volume for the DME classification task, we applied extensive data augmentation techniques. Specifically, we employed Mixup [40], CutMix [39], Color Jitter, Random Erase [41], Random Crop, and AutoAugment [5] with a randomly selected augmentation policy. These augmentations helped increase the diversity of the training data and improved the model's generalization ability by simulating a wide range of variations.

Optimizer. The choice of optimizer significantly influences both the convergence speed and the generalization ability of the model [14,22,28]. We conducted a thorough investigation into the impact of various optimizers, including SGD, Adam, AdamW, NAdam, RAdam, and AdamP, on the DME classification task. Our results indicated that RAdam with default β yielded the best overall performance, achieving faster convergence and superior classification performance compared to other optimizers.

Table 1. Best model weights performed on official validation set.

DME-MobileNet	AUROC	AUPRC	Sensitivity	Specificity	CPU time
Weight1	0.9940	0.9948	1.0	0.9524	0.1290
Weight2	0.9921	0.9929	1.0	0.9524	0.1253
Weight3	0.9921	0.9932	0.9583	0.9523	0.1247
Ensemble with max	0.9921	0.9929	1.0	0.9524	0.2290
Ensemble with average	0.9921	0.9932	0.9583	0.9523	0.2205

Table 2. Final challenge rank based on official testing set.

Team	AUROC	AUPRC	Sensitivity	Specificity	Time
Rank 1st	0.9975	0.9960	0.95	1	0.0584
Rank 2nd	0.9785	0.9683	0.95	0.9718	0.0416
Ours (Rank 3rd)	0.9863	0.9801	0.975	0.9155	0.2060

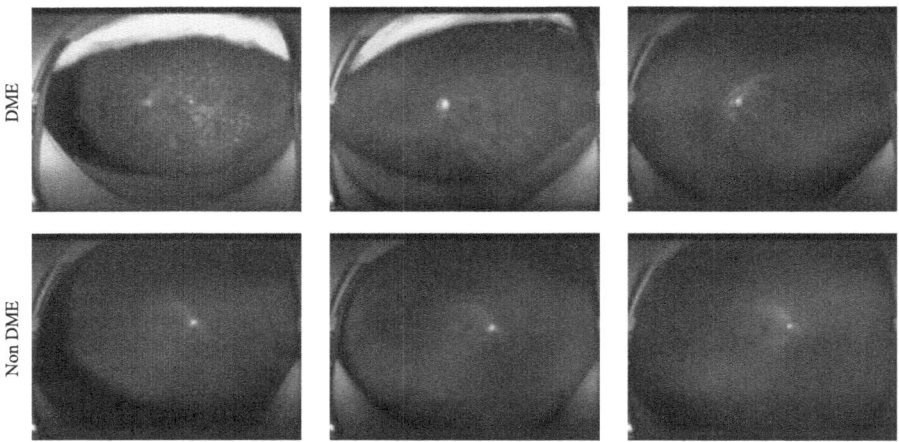

Fig. 2. UWF image illustration.

Learning Rate (LR). Although adaptive learning rates can mitigate the effects of suboptimal LR selection, careful tuning is still essential to ensure a balance between convergence speed and training stability. In our experiments, we explored learning rates ranging from 5×10^{-4} to 1×10^{-3}, with an interval of 5×10^{-5}. The optimal learning rate was determined to be 1×10^{-4}, which provided the best classification performance. Additionally, we employed a cosine learning rate scheduler with a 20-epoch warm-up phase to refine the learning rate adjustments throughout training.

Given the limited availability of UWF training data, we leveraged pre-trained weights from [45] to initialize our model, thus benefiting from the knowledge acquired through training on a larger dataset. Further details on the training configuration for DME-MobileNet are presented in Table 3.

Table 3. Training configurations for DME-MobileNet

Training configuration	DME-MobileNet
DA	AutoAugmentaion-Random (ResizedCrop, AutoContrast, Equalize, Invert Rotate, Posterize, Solarize Color, Sharpness, Shear Brightness, HorizontalFlip), RandomErase, Mixup, Cutmix
Optimizer	RAdam
Batch size	32
LR	1×10^{-4}
Weight decay	5×10^{-3}
scheduler	Cosine scheduler with 20 warm-up epochs
DR	0.1
Mixup Alpha	0.4
Cutmix Alpha	0.75
Color jitter	0.3
Epoch	200
Loss Function	SoftTargetCrossEntropy

4 DMEC - Diabetic Macular Edema Classification

4.1 Dataset and Evaluation Metrics

The DME classification challenge presents a significant limitation in terms of training data, comprising only 167 ultra-widefield (UWF) images, divided into two classes. Among these, 90 images are labeled as class 0, indicating no DME complications, while 77 images are labeled as class 1, representing patients diagnosed with DME. Figure 2 shows UWF images with different labels.

We use the below several metrics for evaluation, including Quadratic weighted Kappa (kappa), F1 score, Specificity, Sensitivity, Area Under the Curve (AUC), Negative Predictive Value (NPV), and Positive Predictive Value (PPV). The optimal model weights were selected based on the average performance across these seven metrics. For image preprocessing, all images were resized to 224 × 224 for both the training and evaluation phases, followed by appropriate normalization.

4.2 Experimental Results

For the DME classification task, we submitted the best-trained model weights to the evaluation platform. As shown in Table 1, the top three performing model weights for DME-MobileNet were selected. We then applied ensemble operations based on these top three weights for the final submission. Specifically, the max ensemble operation selected the maximal output value for each class, while the average ensemble calculated the mean of the outputs as the final prediction score. However, these ensemble operations did not result in improved performance. Consequently, we selected Weight1 for the final submission. As illustrated in Table 2, this model secured third place in the challenge.

5 Conclusion

In this paper, we fine tuned a novel, lightweight, and efficient CNN-based architecture for DME diagnosis. Our results demonstrate that carefully optimized CNNs, even without complex built-in modules, can achieve competitive performance in DME classification. This suggests that simpler models can be highly effective when appropriately optimized, offering a promising direction for developing scalable and efficient diagnostic tools. Future work may explore further refinement of the architecture and its applicability to other retinal diseases.

References

1. Cai, L., et al.: Classification of diabetic maculopathy based on optical coherence tomography images using a vision transformer model. BMJ Open Ophthalmol. **8**(1), e001423 (2023)
2. Che, H., Jin, H., Chen, H.: Learning robust representation for joint grading of ophthalmic diseases via adaptive curriculum and feature disentanglement. In: MICCAI, pp. 523–533 (2022)
3. Choudhry, N., et al.: Classification and guidelines for widefield imaging: recommendations from the international widefield imaging study group. Ophthalmol. Retina **3**(10), 843–849 (2019)
4. Ciardella, A., Brown, D.: Wide field imaging. In: Fundus Fluorescein and Indocyanine Green Angiography: A Textbook and Atlas, pp. 79–83. Slack Inc., New York (2007)
5. Cubuk, E.D., Zoph, B., Mane, D., Vasudevan, V., Le, Q.V.: AutoAugment: learning augmentation policies from data. arXiv preprint arXiv:1805.09501 (2018)
6. Dumitrascu, O.M., et al.: Color fundus photography and deep learning applications in Alzheimer's disease. In: Mayo Clinic Proceedings: Digital Health (2024). https://doi.org/10.1016/j.mcpdig.2024.08.005, https://www.sciencedirect.com/science/article/pii/S2949761224000804
7. Dumitrascu, O.M., Zhu, W., Qiu, P., Nandakumar, K., Wang, Y.: Automated retinal imaging analysis for Alzheimer's disease screening. In: IEEE International Symposium on Biomedical Imaging: From Nano to Macro (ISBI) (2022)
8. Elyasi, N., Hemmati, H.: Diabetic macular edema: diagnosis and management. Am. Acad. Opthalmol. EyeNet Mag. **66**, 35–7 (2021)
9. Fong, D.S., Aiello, L.P., Ferris III, F.L., Klein, R.: Diabetic retinopathy. Diabetes Care **27**(10) (2004)
10. Group, E.T.D.R.S.R., et al.: Grading diabetic retinopathy from stereoscopic color fundus photographs-an extension of the modified Airlie house classification: ETDRS report number 10. Ophthalmology **98**(5), 786–806 (1991)
11. Han, D., Yun, S., Heo, B., Yoo, Y.: Rethinking channel dimensions for efficient model design. In: Proceedings of the IEEE/CVF Conference on Computer Vision and Pattern Recognition, pp. 732–741 (2021)
12. Jian, M., Chen, H., Tao, C., Li, X., Wang, G.: Triple-DRNet: a triple-cascade convolution neural network for diabetic retinopathy grading using fundus images. Comput. Biol. Med. **155**, 106631 (2023)
13. Jiang, Y., et al.: SatFormer: saliency-guided abnormality-aware transformer for retinal disease classification in fundus image. In: Proceedings of the Thirty-First International Joint Conference on Artificial Intelligence, IJCAI, pp. 987–994 (2022)

14. Keskar, N.S., Socher, R.: Improving generalization performance by switching from Adam to SGD. arXiv preprint arXiv:1712.07628 (2017)
15. Lee, K.G., Song, S.J., Lee, S., Kim, B.H., Kong, M., Lee, K.M.: FQ-UWF: unpaired generative image enhancement for fundus quality ultra-widefield retinal images. Bioengineering **11**(6), 568 (2024)
16. Li, F., Liu, Z., Chen, H., Jiang, M., Zhang, X., Wu, Z.: Automatic detection of diabetic retinopathy in retinal fundus photographs based on deep learning algorithm. Transl. Vis. Sci. Technol. **8**(6), 4 (2019)
17. Li, X., Hu, X., Yu, L., Zhu, L., Fu, C.W., Heng, P.A.: CANet: cross-disease attention network for joint diabetic retinopathy and diabetic macular edema grading. IEEE Trans. Med. Imaging 1483–1493 (2020)
18. Li, Z., Wang, Y., Wang, L.: Transformer-based joint classification network for diabetic retinopathy and diabetic macular edema. In: 2024 7th International Conference on Advanced Algorithms and Control Engineering (ICAACE), pp. 488–492. IEEE (2024)
19. Lin, Z., et al.: A framework for identifying diabetic retinopathy based on anti-noise detection and attention-based fusion. In: MICCAI, pp. 74–82. Springer, Cham (2018)
20. Liu, Z., et al.: Swin transformer: hierarchical vision transformer using shifted windows. In: Proceedings of the IEEE International Conference on Computer Vision (ICCV), pp. 10012–10022 (2021)
21. Liu, Z., Mao, H., Wu, C.Y., Feichtenhofer, C., Darrell, T., Xie, S.: A convnet for the 2020s. In: Proceedings of the IEEE Computer Society Conference on Computer Vision Pattern Recognition, pp. 11976–11986 (2022)
22. Loshchilov, I.: Decoupled weight decay regularization. arXiv preprint arXiv:1711.05101 (2017)
23. Mead, A., Burnett, S., Davey, C.: Diabetic retinal screening in the UK. J. R. Soc. Med. **94**(3), 127–129 (2001)
24. Munk, M.R., Kurmann, T., Marquez-Neila, P., Zinkernagel, M.S., Wolf, S., Sznitman, R.: Assessment of patient specific information in the wild on fundus photography and optical coherence tomography. Sci. Rep. **11**(1), 8621 (2021)
25. Nazih, W., Aseeri, A.O., Atallah, O.Y., El-Sappagh, S.: Vision transformer model for predicting the severity of diabetic retinopathy in fundus photography-based retina images. IEEE Access **11**, 117546–117561 (2023)
26. Patel, S.N., Shi, A., Wibbelsman, T.D., Klufas, M.A.: Ultra-widefield retinal imaging: an update on recent advances. Ther. Adv. Ophthalmol. **12**, 2515841419899495 (2020)
27. Ramachandran, P., Parmar, N., Vaswani, A., Bello, I., Levskaya, A., Shlens, J.: Stand-alone self-attention in vision models. Adv. Neural Inf. Process. Syst. **32** (2019)
28. Reddi, S.J., Kale, S., Kumar, S.: On the convergence of Adam and beyond. arXiv preprint arXiv:1904.09237 (2019)
29. Sagong, M., van Hemert, J., de Koo, L., Barnett, C., Sadda, S.R.: Assessment of accuracy and precision of quantification of ultra-widefield images. Ophthalmology **122**(4), 864–866 (2015)
30. Salman, S., Liu, X.: Overfitting mechanism and avoidance in deep neural networks. arXiv preprint arXiv:1901.06566 (2019)
31. Sánchez, C.I., et al.: Evaluation of a computer-aided diagnosis system for diabetic retinopathy screening on public data. Invest. Ophthalmol. Vis. Sci. **52**(7), 4866–4871 (2011)

32. Shamrat, F., et al.: An advanced deep neural network for fundus image analysis and enhancing diabetic retinopathy detection. Healthc. Anal. **5**, 100303 (2024)
33. Singh, R.K., Gorantla, R.: DMENet: diabetic macular edema diagnosis using hierarchical ensemble of CNNs. PLoS ONE **15**(2), e0220677 (2020)
34. Sun, R., Li, Y., Zhang, T., Mao, Z., Wu, F., Zhang, Y.: Lesion-aware transformers for diabetic retinopathy grading. In: Proceedings of the IEEE Computer Society Conference on Computer Vision Pattern Recognition, pp. 10938–10947 (2021)
35. Tang, Q.Q., Yang, X.G., Wang, H.Q., Wu, D.W., Zhang, M.X.: Applications of deep learning for detecting ophthalmic diseases with ultrawide-field fundus images. Int. J. Ophthalmol. **17**(1), 188 (2024)
36. Wang, Y., et al.: Automated early detection of acute retinal necrosis from ultra-widefield color fundus photography using deep learning. Eye Vis. **11**(1), 27 (2024)
37. Wang, Z., Yin, Y., Shi, J., Fang, W., Li, H., Wang, X.: Zoom-in-net: deep mining lesions for diabetic retinopathy detection. In: MICCAI, pp. 267–275 (2017)
38. Yu, S., et al.: MIL-VT: multiple instance learning enhanced vision transformer for fundus image classification. In: MICCAI, pp. 45–54. Springer (2021)
39. Yun, S., Han, D., Oh, S.J., Chun, S., Choe, J., Yoo, Y.: CutMix: regularization strategy to train strong classifiers with localizable features. In: Proceedings of the IEEE International Conference on Computer Vision(ICCV), pp. 6023–6032 (2019)
40. Zhang, H., Cisse, M., Dauphin, Y.N., Lopez-Paz, D.: Mixup: beyond empirical risk minimization. In: International Conference on Learning Representations (2018)
41. Zhong, Z., Zheng, L., Kang, G., Li, S., Yang, Y.: Random erasing data augmentation. In: Proceedings of the AAAI Conference on Artificial Intelligence, vol. 34, pp. 13001–13008 (2020)
42. Zhou, Y., et al.: Collaborative learning of semi-supervised segmentation and classification for medical images. In: Proceedings of the IEEE Computing Society Conference on Computer Vision Pattern Recognition (2019)
43. Zhu, W., et al.: Self-supervised equivariant regularization reconciles multiple instance learning: joint referable diabetic retinopathy classification and lesion segmentation. In: 18th International Symposium on Medical Information Processing and Analysis (SIPAIM) (2022)
44. Zhu, W., et al.: Beyond MobileNet: an improved MobileNet for retinal diseases. In: International Conference on Medical Image Computing and Computer-Assisted Intervention, pp. 56–65. Springer (2023)
45. Zhu, W., et al.: nnMobileNet: rethinking CNN for retinopathy research. In: Proceedings of the IEEE/CVF Conference on Computer Vision and Pattern Recognition, pp. 2285–2294 (2024)
46. Zhu, W., et al.: OTRE: where optimal transport guided unpaired image-to-image translation meets regularization by enhancing. In: International Conference on Information Processing in Medical Imaging, pp. 415–427. Springer (2023)
47. Zhu, W., Qiu, P., Farazi, M., Nandakumar, K., Dumitrascu, O.M., Wang, Y.: Optimal transport guided unsupervised learning for enhancing low-quality retinal images. arXiv preprint arXiv:2302.02991 (2023)
48. Zhu, W., Qiu, P., Lepore, N., Dumitrascu, O.M., Wang, Y.: Self-supervised equivariant regularization reconciles multiple-instance learning: joint referable diabetic retinopathy classification and lesion segmentation. In: 18th International Symposium on Medical Information Processing and Analysis, vol. 12567, pp. 100–107. SPIE (2023)

Automatic Identification Method for Diabetic Macular Edema in Ultra-widefield Fundus Images

Heyou Chang[1,2]($\boxtimes$), Zhikang Ge[1], Jian Zhang[1], Heng Zhang[1], and Hao Zheng[2]

[1] School of Computer Engineering, Jiangsu Ocean University,
Lianyungang, Jiangsu, China
[2] School of Information Engineering, Nanjing XiaoZhuang University,
Nanjing, Jiangsu, China
hychang@njxzc.edu.cn

Abstract. In this paper, we present a comprehensive summary of our proposed methodology and experimental results for Task3 in the Ultra-Widefield Fundus (UWF) Imaging for Diabetic Retinopathy Challenge 2024, which focuses on the precise identification of Diabetic Macular Edema (DME). The primary challenges of Task3 lie in two aspects: firstly, the limited availability of training samples poses a risk of overfitting deep learning-based model; secondly, the UWF images encompass a wider retinal area, thereby augmenting complexity associated with image interpretation. To address these challenges, we have devised specialized training strategies and developed a novel model based on Swin-Transformer v2 to achieve accurate DME identification. Our approach has demonstrated exceptional performance with an AUROC value of 0.9835 during the testing phase. The code is available at: https://github.com/yourfla/UWF-DME-AutoID.

Keywords: Ultra-Widefield Fundus Imaging · Diabetic Macular Edema · Swin Transformer · Image Classification

1 Introduction

Diabetic Retinopathy (DR) is a prevalent microvascular complication among individuals with diabetes [6], and diabetic macular edema (DME) falls within the spectrum of moderate Non-Proliferative Diabetic Retinopathy (NPDR) or more severe forms [17]. Therefore, identifying DME plays a pivotal role in facilitating timely referral and early treatment [1,7,10]. Ultra-Widefield (UWF) imaging technology offers an extensive view of the retina, capturing an area exceeding 200° [15]. This comprehensive field of view enables physicians to effectively assess peripheral regions of the retina that may contain crucial pathological information for various retinal diseases [8]. However, manual classification of UWF fundus images is both time-consuming and labor-intensive [16]. Human graders must meticulously analyze each image to identify specific features and abnormalities associated with DME. This process demands substantial effort from trained professionals who must dedicate considerable time and attention to accurately interpret these complex images [5]. With the development of artificial intelligence, especially deep learning-based methods, leveraging artificial intelligence capabilities can streamline diagnostic process while reducing human error and variability [2,3]. However, limited research has been done on automated identification for DME in UFW images.

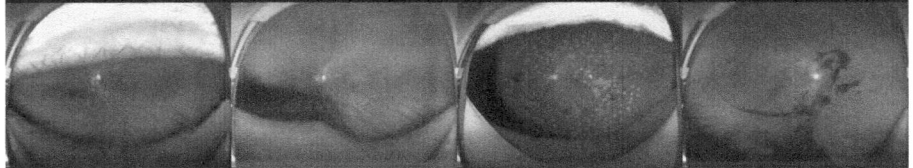

Fig. 1. Some UFW images provided by the Diabetic Retinopathy Challenge 2024.

Automated identification of Diabetic Macular Edema (DME) in ultra-widefield (UWF) images is a challenging task, as illustraged in Fig. 1. Firstly, the limited availability of samples poses a significant challenge to deep learning models, often leading to overfitting and reduced generalization performance [19]. This issue is further exacerbated by the complexity and variability in DME manifestations, ranging from early-stage microaneurysms or minor edema to late-stage extensive leakage and vascular abnormalities [14]. Secondly, UWF images exhibits inherent imaging limitations such as blurriness, insufficient contrast or overexposure, particularly in the peripheral regions of the retina due to equipment constraints, leading to potential distortions or reduced clarity [10]. Moreover, the intricate distribution pattern of DME lesions on the retina further complicates the task, necessitating the model to effectively capture the intricate interplay between local details and global context for accurate identification [4,18].

To tackle the aforementioned challenges, we propose an automatic identification method based on Swin-Transformer v2 [11], with the following innovative contributions:

- We meticulously devised a preprocessing and data augmentation approach specifically tailored for the task, aiming to mitigate the limitations in training dataset and addressing the issues related to inconsistent image quality.
- We constructed a novel model by integrating the Swin Transformer V2 as the backbone network, modifying the classification head, and freezing parameters to accommodate DME identification task. To our knowledge, this is the first application of Swin Transformer to such a task.
- Extensive experimentation was conducted on the UWF4DR dataset, resulting in our remarkable achievement of a Top 5 position in Task3 during the MICCAI UWF4DR Challenge 2024.

The remaining sections of this paper are organized as follows: Sect. 2 provides a detailed description about the proposed method, encompassing data preprocessing and augmentation, as well as the DME automatic identification model. Section 3 delves into the experimental setup and results, and the final section concludes the paper.

2 Methodology

2.1 Data Preprocessing and Augmentation

For Task 3, we exclusively utilized the UWF4DR Training Set provided by the official competition, which consists of 167 meticulously prepared training samples and 45 validation samples. The images have dimensions of 1016×800 pixels. Further details regarding the UWF4DR dataset can be found on the official website of MICCAI UWF4DR 2024 Challenge[1].

Due to the large dimension of the UWF image, we initially perform random cropping on a region of the training sample and resize this region to dimensions of 512 × 512 pixels. Subsequently, each channel of the resized region is normalized to have a mean value of [0.485, 0.456, 0.406] and a standard deviation of [0.229, 0.224, 0.225]. To address the challenges such as irregular lesion distribution, insufficient contrast, or overexposure in the training samples, we subject each training sample to twenty different data augmentation operations, including: horizontal and vertical flipping, random rotation, color jittering as well as affine transformations and perspective transformations. The procedure of data preprocessing and augmentation is shown in Fig. 2. These techniques facilitate the model in learning representative and discriminative features from diverse viewpoints and deformations under varying lighting conditions while enhancing its adaptability towards three-dimensional spatial variations, thereby leading to improved accuracy and robustness in classification.

2.2 DME Automatic Identification Model

When dealing with high-resolution images like UWF, Swin Transformer V2 [11] offers several advantages over traditional deep learning models for image classification. Firstly, it employs a top-down hierarchical structure that progressively reduces the spatial resolution of the image layers (similar to pooling operations in convolutional neural networks), effectively capturing features at different scales [12]. Secondly, it incorporates Window Multi-head Self-Attention (W-MSA) and Sliding Window Multi-Scale Attention(SW-MSA), facilitating the construction of hierarchical feature maps with computational complexity linearly dependent on the image size. The shift window segmentation strategy is illustrated in Fig. 3.

The overall architecture of the proposed model is illustrated in Fig. 4. Here, we adopt the Swin Transformer V2 as the backbone of our proposed model. It comprises an input layer, a patch embedding layer, a positional dropout layer,

---

[1] https://codalab.lisn.upsaclay.fr/competitions/18605.

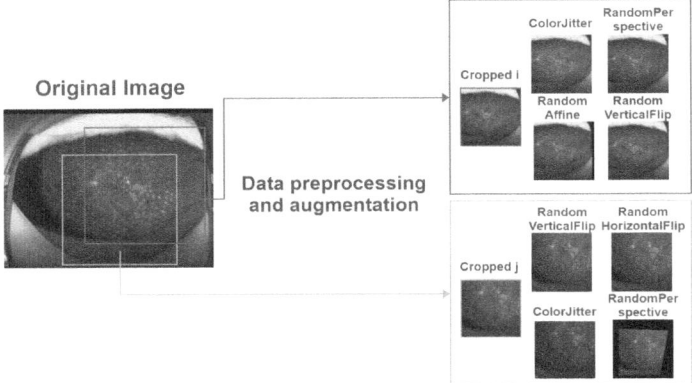

Fig. 2. The procedure of data preprocessing and augmentation.

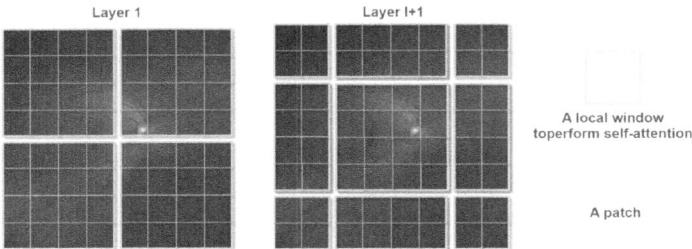

Fig. 3. The illustration of shift window segmentation strategy. Left: In layer l, a regular window partitioning scheme is adopted, and self-attention is computed within each window. Right: In layer $l + 1$, the window partitioning is shifted, resulting in new windows. The self-attention computation in the new windows crosses the boundaries of the previous windows in layer l, providing connections among them.

Swin Transformer layers (consisting of four stages), a normalization layer, a global pooling layer, and a fully connected layer. The modules within the Swin Transformer layers encompass window-based multi-head self-attention mechanism, shifted windows, patch merging, and an MLP (multi-layer perceptron) feedforward network. W-MSA emphasizes local details while SW-MSA enhances the capture of global features. By effectively combining both local and global features, this mechanism maximizes the information advantages offered by UWF high-resolution images while maintaining linear computational complexity to improve training speed. It should be noted that since our task is a binary classification problem, we modify the output layer's dimensionality of Swin Transformer V2 to 2. During training process, all layers' weights are frozen except for the classification heads [13], which are updated to facilitate faster convergence and enhancing overall model performance.

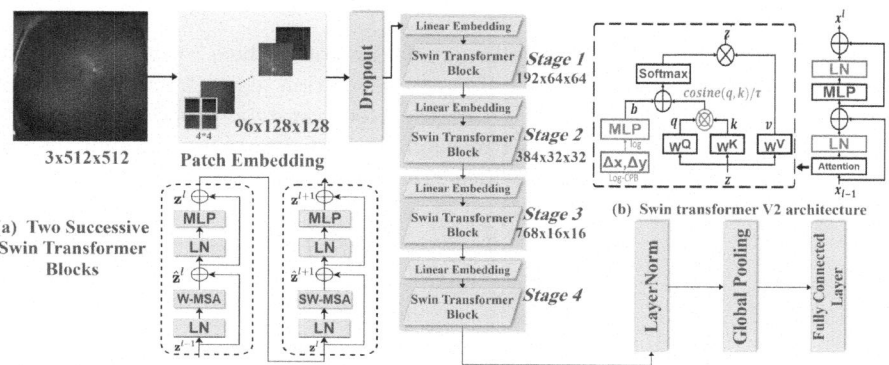

Fig. 4. The architecture of the proposed model. (a) two successive Swin Transformer Blocks, W-MSA and SW-MSA are multi-head self attention modules with regular and shifted windowing configurations, respectively. (b) res-post-norm and scaled cosine attention.

The input image $\mathbf{I} \in \mathcal{R}^{3 \times 512 \times 512}$ is initially divided into small patches $\mathbf{P}_i \in \mathcal{R}^{3 \times 4 \times 4}$, resulting in a total of patches 128×128 ($i = 1, \cdots, 128 \times 128$). Subsequently, each patch $\mathbf{P}_i$ undergoes linear mapping and position embedding operations, leading to a dimension of 96. The hyper-parameter values of the proposed model are as follows: the processing depth at different scales is set to [2, 2, 6, 2], and the number of heads in the multi-head self-attention mechanisms at each stage is [3, 6, 12, 24]. The window size of local attention mechanism is set to 16. The hidden dimension of the MLP is four times that of the input dimension. Bias terms are incorporated into the Query, Key, and Value matrices. A DropPath ratio of 0.2 is applied along with normalization for each patch. Additionally, absolute position encoding, gradient checkpointing and window resizing are not activated in the experiment. The model operates fully automatically where training samples undergo DME characteristics learning based on their labels.

3 Experimental Setup and Results

3.1 Experimental Setup

The experiment was conducted utilizing an automated pipeline on an NVIDIA RTX 4080 GPU, implementing the PyTorch framework. The training procedure incorporated specific configurations, including a total of 10 training epochs and a batch size of 8. For optimization algorithm, AdamW with a learning rate of 1×10^{-4} and weight decay factor of 5×10^{-5} were employed. The model parameters were initialized with pre-trained weights available from the official Swin Transformer repository[2].

---

[2] https://github.com/microsoft/Swin-Transformer.

3.2 Results

The MICCAI UWF4DR 2024 challenge offers a comprehensive set of quantitative metrics for the rigorous evaluation of registration algorithms. The primary metrics include AUROC (Area Under the Receiver Operating Characteristic Curve), AUPRC (Area Under the Precision-Recall Curve) [9], Sensitivity, Specificity, Time, and Ranking Score, which are defined as follows:

$$AUROC = \int_0^1 TPR(FPR)dFPR \qquad (1)$$

$$AUPRC = \int_0^1 Precision(Recall)dRecall \qquad (2)$$

$$Sensitivity = \frac{TP}{TP + FN} \qquad (3)$$

$$Specificity = \frac{TN}{TN + FP} \qquad (4)$$

where TP (True Positives) refers to the count of instances accurately classified as positive, while FP (False Positives) denotes the count of instances mistakenly classified as positive. FN (False Negatives) indicates the count of instances inaccurately classified as negative, and TN (True Negatives) signifies the count of instances correctly classified as negative. True Positive Rate (TPR), also known as Recall and Sensitivity, represents the proportion of correctly predicted positive instances, while False Positive Rate (FPR), also known as Specificity, represents the proportion of incorrectly predicted positive instances. Precision is defined as the ratio of true positive predictions (correctly classified instances) and the total number of positive predictions (both correctly and incorrectly classified instances): $Precision = \frac{TP}{TP+FP}$.

Table 1. The performance of the proposed method on the validation and testing set

Phase	AUROC	AUPRC	Sensitivity	Specificity	CPU Time
Validation Phase	0.9583	0.9667	0.9167	0.8571	0.5142
Test Phase	0.9834	0.9759	0.925	0.9577	0.2537

The performance of the proposed method on the DME classification task is presented in Table 1. It can be seen that the performance of our method in test phase surpasses that in the validation phase. Specifically, in the validation phase, our method achieves an AUROC value and AUPRC value of 0.9583 and 0.9667 respectively, which are slightly lower by 0.0251 and 0.0092 compared to those in the test phase. However, there is a noticeable difference between the specificity values of our method in the validation phase (0.8571) and test phase (0.9577), with a gap of 0.1 between them indicating improved performance during testing. Similarly, CPU Time required during testing is approximately half that needed during validation. The evaluation metrics employed in the experiment demonstrate the effectiveness of our proposed method.

The training loss and validation accuracy of the proposed method are illustrated in Fig. 5. It can be observed that the training loss exhibits a rapid decline from the first epoch, plummeting from approximately 0.14 to below 0.06. This signifies the model's swift acquisition of features during the initial phase of training. Furthermore, starting from the second epoch, the validation accuracy swiftly converges to near-perfect performance at around 1.0 and remains consistently throughout all subsequent epochs. This indicates that the proposed model excels on the validation set by accurately predicting all samples with high confidence. To mitigate potential risks associated with over-fitting, we have determined an optimal number of training epochs based on empirical knowledge.

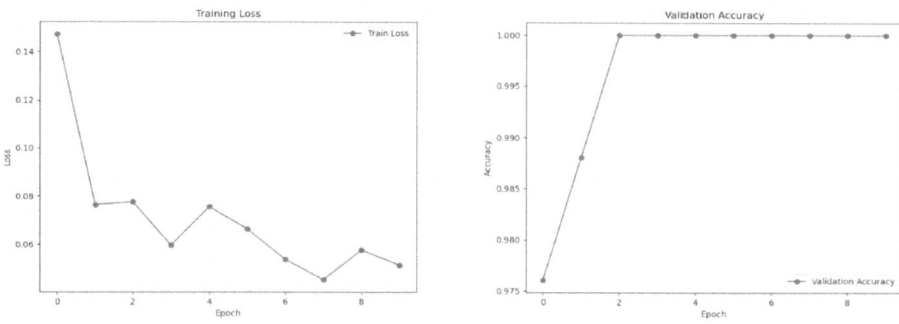

Fig. 5. Training loss and validation accuracy of the proposed method.

4 Conclusion

In this paper, we presented a comprehensive presentation of the proposed method for the identification of DME in the UWF Imaging for Diabetic Retinopathy Challenge 2024. To address the limitation of training images, we employed a series of data augmentation techniques to generate additional training samples. Moreover, we tailor the Swin Transformer v2 specifically for this task by modifying its classification heads to accommodate ultra-wide images and freezing parameters other than classification heads to enhance training efficiency.

Although good performance has been reported, it is important to note that the proposed method may exhibit limited sensitivity towards small and complex lesions observed in UWF images. In future work, we will explore more efficient attention mechanisms and multi-modal data fusion methods to further improve DME diagnosis performance in UWF imaging.

References

1. Bhambra, N., Antaki, F., Malt, F.E., Xu, A., Duval, R.: Deep learning for ultra-widefield imaging: a scoping review. Graefes Arch. Clin. Exp. Ophthalmol. **260**(12), 3737–3778 (2022)
2. Chang, H., Gao, G., Chen, Y., Zheng, H.: Multi-task contexture learning network for automated vertebrae segmentation and tumor diagnosis from MRI. Comput. Electr. Eng. **113**, 109032 (2024)
3. Chang, H., Zhao, S., Zheng, H., Chen, Y., Li, S.: Multi-vertebrae segmentation from arbitrary spine MR images under global view. In: Martel, A.L., et al. (eds.) MICCAI 2020, Part VI. LNCS, vol. 12266, pp. 702–711. Springer, Cham (2020). https://doi.org/10.1007/978-3-030-59725-2_68
4. Cui, T.: Deep learning performance of ultra-widefield fundus imaging for screening retinal lesions in rural locales. JAMA Ophthalmol. **141**(11), 1045–1051 (2023)
5. Deng, X.Y.: Retinal vascular morphological characteristics in diabetic retinopathy: an artificial intelligence study using a transfer learning system to analyze ultra-wide field images. Int. J. Ophthalmol. **17**(6), 1001 (2024)
6. Fong, D.S., Aiello, L.P., Ferris III, F.L., Klein, R.: Diabetic retinopathy. Diab. Care **27**(10) (2004)
7. Fountoukidou, T., Sznitman, R.: A reinforcement learning approach for VQA validation: an application to diabetic macular edema grading. Med. Image Anal. **87**, 102822 (2023)
8. Kumar, V., et al.: Ultra-wide field retinal imaging: a wider clinical perspective. Indian J. Ophthalmol. **69**(4), 824–835 (2021)
9. Lee, P.K., Ra, H., Baek, J.: Automated segmentation of ultra-widefield fluorescein angiography of diabetic retinopathy using deep learning. Br. J. Ophthalmol. **107**(12), 1859–1863 (2023)
10. Li, Z., et al.: Automated detection of retinal exudates and drusen in ultra-widefield fundus images based on deep learning. Eye **36**(8), 1681–1686 (2022)
11. Liu, Z., et al.: Swin transformer v2: scaling up capacity and resolution. In: Proceedings of the IEEE/CVF Conference on Computer Vision and Pattern Recognition, pp. 12009–12019 (2022). https://github.com/microsoft/Swin-Transformer
12. Liu, Z., et al.: Swin transformer: hierarchical vision transformer using shifted windows. In: Proceedings of the IEEE/CVF International Conference on Computer Vision, pp. 10012–10022 (2021)
13. Liu, Z., et al.: Video swin transformer. In: Proceedings of the IEEE/CVF Conference on Computer Vision and Pattern Recognition, pp. 3202–3211 (2022)
14. Sun, G., et al.: Deep learning for the detection of multiple fundus diseases using ultra-widefield images. Ophthalmol. Ther. **12**(2), 895–907 (2023)
15. Wang, H., et al.: Advancing UWF-SLO vessel segmentation with source-free active domain adaptation and a novel multi-center dataset. arXiv preprint arXiv:2406.13645 (2024)
16. Wang, M.H., et al.: Deep learning for macular fovea detection based on ultra-widefield fundus images. In: Second International Conference on Electrical, Electronics, and Information Engineering (EEIE 2023), vol. 12983, pp. 510–521. SPIE (2024)
17. Wilkinson, C.P., et al.: Proposed international clinical diabetic retinopathy and diabetic macular edema disease severity scales. Ophthalmology **110**(9), 1677–1682 (2003)

18. Xiao, Y., et al.: Assessment of early diabetic retinopathy severity using ultra-widefield clarus versus conventional five-field and ultra-widefield optos fundus imaging. Sci. Rep. **13**(1), 17131 (2023)
19. Yang, J., et al.: Artificial intelligence in ophthalmopathy and ultra-wide field image: a survey. Expert Syst. Appl. **182**, 115068 (2021)

Author Index

A
Abdulwahab, Saddam 63, 75

B
Bakshi, Monalisa 135

C
Chang, Heyou 165
Chen, Xiwen 144, 155
Chen, Yanxi 144, 155
Cho, Yunnie 55
Cochener, Béatrice 88
Conze, Pierre-Henri 88

D
Dong, Xuanzhao 144, 155
Dumitrascu, Oana M. 144, 155

E
El Habib Daho, Mostafa 88
Engelmann, Justin 110, 118

G
Gago, Lucas 110, 118
Ge, Zhikang 165
Gu, Yunchao 47

H
Haderer, Moritz 18

K
Kim, Hyeonmin 55
Kim, Siwon 125
Kwon, Ohhyun 55

L
Lamard, Mathieu 88
Lee, Dongha 55
Lee, Soomok 125
Li, Qicheng 1, 10

Li, Xin 144, 155
Liu, Di 1, 10

M
Marinschek, Martin 18
Mazher, Moona 36
Menzatiuk, Oleksandra 18
Musluh, Saif Khalid 63, 75

N
Niederer, Steven A. 36

O
Oh, Jeongbin 125
Okran, Ammar M. 63, 75

P
Park, Yeon Su 101
Pils, Vera 18
Puig, Domenec 63, 75

Q
Qayyum, Abdul 36
Qiu, Peijie 144, 155
Quellec, Gwenolé 88

R
Rashwan, Hatem A. 63, 75
Razi, Abolfazl 144, 155

S
Scheuringer, Berthold 18
Seelamantula, Chandra Sekhar 135
Sun, Junfeng 47

V
Vasa, Vamsi Krishna 144

W
Wang, Hao 144, 155
Wang, Xinliang 47
Wang, Yalin 144, 155
Won, Ji Hye 101

X
Xiong, Yujian 144, 155

Y
Yan, Yangyang 1, 10
Yang, Bo 1, 10
Yun, Wooyung 125

Z
Zhang, Heng 165
Zhang, Jian 165
Zhang, Philippe 88
Zhang, Yue 1, 10
Zheng, Hao 165
Zhu, Wenhui 144, 155